MALLOCH'S SPITFIRE

The story and restoration of PK350

NICK MEIKLE

CASEMATE

Philadelphia & Oxford

Published in the United States of America and Great Britain in 2014 by
CASEMATE PUBLISHERS
908 Darby Road, Havertown, PA 19083
and
10 Hythe Bridge Street, Oxford, OX1 2EW

First published in 2013 by 30° South Publishers

ISBN 978-1-61200-252-1
Digital Edition: ISBN 978-1-61200-253-8

Cataloging-in-publication data is available from the Library of Congress and
the British Library.

10 9 8 7 6 5 4 3 2 1

Printed and bound in the United States of America.

For a complete list of Casemate titles please contact:

CASEMATE PUBLISHERS (US)
Telephone (610) 853-9131, Fax (610) 853-9146
E-mail: casemate@casematepublishing.com

CASEMATE PUBLISHERS (UK)
Telephone (01865) 241249, Fax (01865) 794449
E-mail: casemate-uk@casematepublishing.co.uk

Dedicated to the memory of
Captain Jack Malloch,
who made it happen,
and to his loyal Affretair engineers,
especially the late Bob Dodds
and the very much alive Dave Hann

CONTENTS

ACKNOWLEDGEMENTS

There are numerous people who have given so much of their time and advice in this journey to tell the story of rebuilding PK350. I am deeply grateful to everyone. In acknowledging first, my ex-Air Force colleagues, I list them all according to their rank at retirement from Squadron Leader and above and, hopefully, in the correct seniority:

Air Marshals Mick McLaren and Frank Mussell; Air Vice-Marshal Chris Dams; Air Commodore Keith Kemsley; Brigadier Peter Ngulu; Group Captains Ossie Penton, John Mussell, Peter Peter-Bowyer, Ken Burmeister, Steve Kesby and Bill Sykes; Colonel Tony Smit (South African Air Force [SAAF] and ex Royal Rhodesian Air Force [RRAF]); Wing Commanders Wally Hinrichs, Roy Morris, Rex Taylor, Peter Knobel, Prop Geldenhuys, Chris Dixon, Alf Wild, Ben Cowan and Chris Dickinson; Squadron Leaders Mike Saunders, Pete Woolcock, Terry Bennett, Steve Baldwin, Clive Ward, Geoff Oborne and Dave Haynes. The rest—Des Anderson, Chris Hudson, Bob Garrett, John Reid-Rowland, Bud Cockcroft, Mike Kruger, Dave Shirley, Ian Wallis, Chuck Osborne, Neville Weir, Fidor Scholvinck, Robin Thurman, Pete Besant, Stu Robertson, Rob Sweeting, Clive Dutton, Pat King, John Bulpit, Jeff Hagemann and Steve Nobes.

From the Old Rhodesian Air Force Sods (ORAFs), Eddy Norris, the overseer of our Air Force network and facilitator extraordinaire.

Within the wider Rhodesian ex-military and civilian community: Richard and Chris Bradshaw (Dickie Bradshaw's sons), Auv Raath, John Desfountain, Hugh Bomford, Sean Carson, Brian Carson, Paul Maher, Garth Reynolds (Ossie Penton's grandson), Jackie Stone (Spike Owens' daughter by his first marriage), Debbie Addison (née Carmody), Errol and Gaye Bennett, Leon Keyter, Angela Buckland, Dave Mullany, Alan Brough, Derek Pratt, Phil Nobes, Nigel Launder and Peter Miller.

Air Trans Africa/Affretair personnel: Dave Hann, Colin and Vicky Miller, Jim Townsend, Ian Hunt, Ernie Dagovia, George Paterson, Rich Sandercock, Carlos Martins, Andy Wood, Ian Buckle, Bob Lane, Ross Malloch, Tony Norton, Willy Light, Grant Domoney, Piet Bezuidenhout, Tony Smith, Russel Clements and lastly Nicky Pearce (née Elphinstone), a late find in my research but an invaluable facilitator and help.

Help from overseas: Lauren Woodard and Guy Revell at the RAF Museum, Daniel

Scott Davies (one-time curator of Alex Henshaw's papers and logbooks), and Dr Alfred Price.

A big thank you to Dave Dodds for his colour photographs of Spitfire PK350 taken in April 1980.

Thank you to Mike Bradrocke for the cutaway drawing of a Spitfire F Mk 21.

My very special thanks go to Alyson Dawson (*née* Malloch) and Ross and Greg Malloch for your special support and help along the way, and also to Dave Hann, Spitfire Project Manager and structural aircraft engineer extraordinaire—your memory is simply outstanding, matching the reputation you gained from managing this project; Phil Wright, for your wonderful drawings and help with research and photos; Air Marshal Mick McLaren, Air Vice-Marshal Chris Dams and Air Commodore Keith Kemsley, for generous and invaluable support and all-important encouragement. Getting to know you gentlemen once again, all these years later, made me appreciate why you attained command positions in our superb little Air Force.

Special thanks are due also to Bill Sykes for your exceptional contribution, support, advice and resources; John Reid-Rowland for your unstinting help, in particular with the index, as well as your knowledge and wise words; Peter Arnold for your knowledge of Spitfires; Wing Commander Peter Ayerst, it has been a privilege getting to know you albeit sadly only over the phone; Chris Faber, for your unstinting interest, help and generous hospitality; Joan Cameron for your patience and diligence in editing this story and Chris and Kerrin Cocks for embracing this tale.

Finally, to my wife Audrey and my family, I give my gratitude for their quiet but vital support.

Nick Meikle

FOREWORD

This foreword should have been penned by the man whose passion, belief and dedication made it possible for this story to be told. Jack Malloch has rightly been described as a legendary charismatic character, who was widely respected throughout every level of the aviation world. This fascinating story is marred only by his sad and untimely death. To have been asked by the author to write this foreword has made me feel especially privileged and humbled, but at the same time proud to have been part of that incredible journey—'Spitfire–The Pursuit of a Dream'.

To have joined that special band of aviators who have actually flown a Spitfire means more to me as a pilot than anything else that matters in my career—other than the honour to have served Rhodesia and Ian Smith in the company of the finest and bravest group of men who made up our uniformed forces.

Read and enjoy this saga, which has been compiled and made possible through the unbelievable efforts of so many hardworking and dedicated personnel.

Thank you Nick—*Alae Praesidio Patriae* [Our wings are the fortress of the country]

Air Marshal M.J. McLaren OLM (Retired)

PREFACE

Thirty-one years have gone by since the death of our Dad, Jack Malloch. At the time we couldn't believe that he could cease to exist. He was spiritual, but in a private way, and he had an uncanny sixth sense that seemed to protect him in innumerable dangerous situations. How, on that fateful day in March 1982, could that sixth sense have failed him?

Our Mom, Zoe, was a wonderful woman and the perfect partner for our dad. What we took to be an ordinary relationship, as that was all we knew, gave us very high expectations for what a marriage should be. Ours was a peaceful and open home. Our parents were fair, never hypocritical, and stressed the importance of hard work and doing just a bit more than was expected of you. We arrived late in their marriage and we always felt that we were adored.

The rebuilding of the Spitfire is an important story in the saga of Jack Malloch's life and in telling it, Nick seems to have captured the essence of who he was: humble and unassuming, but an adventurous daredevil who, at the same time, did what he did because he believed in it.

Knowing Nick over the past 15 years and spending long hours together in the cockpit, we've found him to be a man of absolute integrity, thorough and calm, with characteristics not unlike those of our Dad himself. We feel that through his research and a wealth of historical knowledge, he is the perfect person to tell this story.

We, as a family, are extremely grateful to Nick for documenting this great chapter in Rhodesian aviation and giving us, and our children, this record.

Alyson Dawson (*née* Malloch), Ross and Greg Malloch

AUTHOR'S NOTE

I was drawn to this story principally because it was about a Spitfire—a Spitfire about which I knew something. It was February 1982, during the efforts to produce a film commemorating the restoration of PK350, that I was tasked to fly a two seat de Havilland Vampire with the man behind the film project, Wing Commander (later Group Captain) Bill Sykes. The purpose was to record by means of cine film, yes *cine* film, as much air-to-air footage of the Spitfire in flight as could be made on 20 minutes of film. I carried out two memorable flights with Bill, and I will never forget the sight of the Spitfire, with the legendary Jack Malloch at the controls wearing his period flying helmet, and the unforgettable growl of the Griffon engine, as Bill formated on Jack. Bill did most of the flying; he knew what shots he needed and he was very experienced, if not current on type.

If my memory serves me correctly, I have a feeling we pushed the boundaries of airmanship on the second flight, led of course by Jack Malloch. After all, it is not every day that one would have a Vampire formating on a Spitfire—and there was always an attentive audience at Salisbury Airport in those days.

So it was that I was introduced to the great Jack Malloch and a real Spitfire, which I had witnessed making its very first flight as a restored aircraft on 29 March 1980.

Much later, in 1995, after a certain 'Spike' Owens passed away and with whom I had had regular contact until that point, I became the most fortunate recipient of some of his Spitfire memorabilia. Inside a large On Government Service envelope were a great many photographs of Spitfire PK350/SR64, whilst in the service of the Southern Rhodesian Air Force (SRAF) and during her rebuild, and correspondence confirming Spike Owen's early efforts to have a Spitfire restored. I stored them away and occasionally wondered what to do with these records.

In August 2009 it suddenly dawned on me that I knew a number of the people involved in the rebuild project, and that this was possibly a story worth telling before some of the older key personalities passed away. Even though the two most important men in the story, Spike Owens and Jack Malloch were no longer alive, I was in the fortunate position of working with both of Jack Malloch's sons, Ross and Greg. Ross, in particular, could recall many of the engineers and pointed me in the right direction to make contact.

That soon put me in touch with Dave Hann, manager of the Spitfire PK350 project, who was then living in Johannesburg. Thanks to the mobility of my job with MK Airlines at the time I had great access to him. Once I had met Dave Hann, in November 2009, and listened to some of his extraordinary recollections, I knew I had to tell this story.

In the process I have been re-acquainted with a number of old Air Force colleagues and have become newly acquainted with many other people. This has been a particularly rewarding aspect of this project. One of the very first personalities I met was Air Marshal Mick McLaren, at about the time that my eagerness to tell the story received the blessing of the Malloch siblings, Alyson Dawson, Ross and Greg Malloch. Mick McLaren was immediately very supportive, as is apparent in the Foreword he has kindly written for this book. Others have included Air Vice-Marshal Chris Dams and Air Commodore Keith Kemsley, both key personalities in the story; numerous original SRAF Spitfire pilots; Bill Sykes; and so it continues ... The official acknowledgements convey my eternal gratitude for all the help I have received, name by name.

The journey also revealed the identity of and put me in contact with PK350's original test pilot, all of 92 years of age and a Battle of Britain pilot. Further, it has provided great clarity about the original agreement between the Air Force and Jack Malloch, the former which owned the aircraft, as well as the Air Force's intentions about the future of the aircraft. Of course, that decision was ruled null and void by the tragic events on 26 March 1982, when Jack Malloch crashed and died in PK350.

An important quest within the story was the establishment of the exact co-ordinates of the accident site. This eventually led to the brief reunion of a small group of four ex-Air Force of Zimbabwe (AFZ) colleagues, led by Brigadier Peter Ngulu and Group Captain Ken Burmeister, and a trip to revisit the actual site. The successful excursion provided the subject matter for the postcript to this story, keenly told by the erudite Bill Sykes, and led to a heart-warming encounter with the only witness to the tragedy, Joseph Manjonjo, and his family. At the time Joseph was a herd-boy to his father's cattle. His kraal is positioned today as though he remains the custodian to the crash site and thus to the memory of Jack Malloch and PK350.

Finally, this story contains much technical as well as historical information. I have made every effort to check both areas for accuracy, including accessing a world authority on the Spitfire, Peter Arnold; utilising the best authority on PK350, Dave Hann himself; as well as checking the historical accuracy with old hands within the SRAF, such as Chris Dams and Keith Kemsley. I believe these efforts have ensured that the most critical information or statements are accurate. However, as with all human endeavours there will always be scope for error; if there are any errors in this story then these are mine alone, as are certain conclusions that are reasonably based on the information to hand.

Nick Meikle
September 2013

GLOSSARY OF TERMS

Performance Measurement

The Spitfire's original performance was measured in miles per hour, and being a British aircraft, it was built using Imperial measures. However, the Royal Air Force (RAF) decided in the early post-war years to change the Air Speed Indicators (ASIs) on all their aircraft to measure their air speed in knots. This was accomplished overnight to minimise confusion. The Southern Rhodesian Spitfires thus had ASIs that showed the aircraft speed in knots. A nautical mile (6,080 feet) is 1.16 longer than a statute mile (5,280 feet); thus 300 mph is 258.6 knots. Today of course, most country's measures are metric. However, aircraft speed is generally measured in knots, altitude is measured in feet and weights are measured in kilograms. Listed below are some useful conversions:

1 statute mile = 1.61 kilometres e.g. 300mph = 483kmh
1 nautical mile = 1.85 kilometres e.g. 300kts = 555.6kmh
1 metre = 3.28 feet
1 yard = 3 feet
1 inch = approximately 25 millimetres
1 kilogram = 2.2045 lbs

Country and Place Names

Much political change has occurred in Africa since the early 1950s when this story begins. As a result both country names and place names have changed. However, for the purposes of this story original names have been used, appropriate to that time. Below is a list of the countries and place names with their modern equivalent:

Northern Rhodesia – Zambia
Nyasaland – Malawi
Southern Rhodesia and Rhodesia – Zimbabwe
Tanganyika – Tanzania

Fort Victoria – Masvingo
Gatooma – Kadoma
Gwelo – Gweru

Kumalo – Khumalo (a suburb of Bulawayo, Zimbabwe's second city)

Marandellas – Marondera

Salisbury – Harare (the name only changed in 1982)

Umtali – Mutare

Affretair

During the 1970s, Jack Malloch's principal operating company in Rhodesia was Air Trans Africa (ATA). Affretair was the name of an associate company based in Gabon, to facilitate ATA flights within and from Africa into Europe and back to Africa. The name Affretair was chosen as the official company name after Zimbabwe became independent, and this is how most people remember ATA. For historical accuracy, ATA is the name that will be used up until April 1980.

ABBREVIATIONS

A&AEE	Aeroplane & Armament Experimental Establishment, at RAF Boscombe Down
AF	Air Force: meaning any one of the Southern Rhodesian Air Force (SRAF), Royal Rhodesian Air Force (RRAF), Rhodesian Air Force (RhAF) or Air Force of Zimbabwe (AFZ)
AFC	Air Force Cross: RAF medal awarded to a commissioned rank or warrant officer for an act or acts of valour, courage or devotion to duty whilst flying (though not on active operations against the enemy in the context of this story)
AFZ	Air Force of Zimbabwe
agl	above ground level
Air Cdre	Air Commodore: senior staff-ranked officer in the RRAF, RhAF and AFZ
Air HQ	Air Force Headquarters
Air Lt	Air Lieutenant: a unique RhAF and AFZ rank, equivalent to an RAF Flying Officer and the Army rank of Lieutenant
Air Mshl	Air Marshal: most senior ranked officer in the RRAF, RhAF and AFZ, usually referred to as the Commander
amsl	above mean sea level
AP	Air Force Publication
ASI	Air Speed Indicator
ASF	Aircraft Servicing Flight
ATA	Air Trans Africa
ATC	Air Traffic Control
AVM	Air Vice-Marshal: second-most senior ranked staff officer in the RRAF, RhAF and AFZ; immediate subordinate to the Air Marshal and acted as Chief of Staff
B Dn	Boscombe Down
BFM	Belt-Feed Mechanism
Bf 109	Messerschmitt Bf 109, a German World War II fighter aircraft
BoI	Board of Inquiry
Boss	common term used in the AF referring to one's Squadron Commander

C	Centigrade
CAA	Central African Airways, in the context of this story; not to be confused with the Civil Aviation Authority
CAF	Central African Federation; also known as the Federation of Rhodesia and Nyasaland
CLM	Commander of the Legion of Merit: Rhodesian Armed Services Award
C/n	Construction umber
C of G	Centre of Gravity
C Sgt	Colour Sergeant: an army non-commissioned rank used in the Southern Rhodesian Auxiliary Air Force (SRAAF) and SRAF before RAF ranks were reintroduced to the RRAF
DCA	Department of Civil Aviation: in this case in Rhodesia
DFC	Distinguished Flying Cross: RAF Medal awarded to a commissioned rank or warrant officers for an act or acts of valour, courage or devotion to duty whilst flying in active operations against the enemy (in this context in World War Two)
DGSS	Director General Support Services (DGSS)
DH	de Havilland
DSO	Distinguished Service Order: British Armed Services Medal
E & I	Electrical and Instrument
EFTS	Elementary Flying Training School
ERS	Engine Repair Shop
F	Fighter: the role of a military aircraft.
F700	The technical or maintenance log of an in-service aircraft
FAF	Forward Airfield: set up as operational bases for the Fire Forces and light strike units during the Rhodesian Bush War
FE	Flight Engineer
F/FR	Fighter/Fighter reconnaissance: the role of a military aircraft
FGA	Fighter/Ground Attack
Fire Force	The term used to describe the airborne battle formations used by Rhodesians to combat the nationalist insurgent guerrillas.
Flt Cdr	Flight Commander: immediate subordinate to a Squadron Commander, usually a Flight Lieutenant in the SRAF, RRAF, RhAF and AFZ

Flt Lt	Flight Lieutenant: Air Force commissioned rank
Flt Sgt	Flight Sergeant: Air Force non-commissioned rank
FO	Flying Officer
FR	Fighter reconnaissance: the role of a military aircraft
ft	foot/feet
Fundi/s	Rhodesian slang for a knowledgeable person, based on the Ndebele word *mfundisi* which means teacher
Fw190	Focke-Wulf 190, a German World War II fighter aircraft
FW Adj	Flying Wing Adjutant: administrative assistant to Officer Commanding Flying Wing (OCFW)
FWHQ	Flying Wing Headquarters at an Air Force base
FWTO	Flying Wing Technical Officer: immediate subordinate to Officer Commanding Technical Wing (OCTW)
g	measure of load factor in increments of 1g positive and negative acceleration at 32 ft/sec or 9.1 m/s
GA	Ground Attack: the role of a military aircraft
gal	gallon: Imperial, in this context, equivalent to 4.45 litres
GF	General Flying
Gp Capt	Group Captain: senior commissioned rank in the RRAF, RhAF and AFZ, usually a station commander or staff officer
HA	High Altitude: in the context of the SRAF Spitfire colour scheme high altitude blue
HQ	Headquarters
IAS	Indicated Air Speed: the speed of an aircraft indicated by the ASI to the pilot
ins	inches
Instr	Instructor
ITCZ	Inter-Tropical Convergence Zone
JSPIS	Joint Services Photographic Interpretation Service
km/h	kilometres per hour
kts	knots: nautical miles per hour
lbs	pounds
LRT	Long-Range Tank
Lt	Lieutenant: in this context, an Army rank as used by the SRAAF and SRAF before RAF ranks were introduced to the RRAF

Lt Col	Lieutenant Colonel
m	metres
MAP	Ministry of Aircraft Production
ME	Middle East
Mk	Mark: used with a number to indicate a new development of an aircraft or system
mm	millimetres
mph	miles per hour: statute miles per hour
MU	Maintenance Unit: RAF Unit
NATO	North Atlantic Treaty Organisation
NCO	Non-Commissioned Officer in the military
NDT	Non-Destructive Testing: describes different techniques used to closely examine and assess the condition of aircraft structures and components
NFC	Netherlands Flying Cross: Netherlands Air Force Medal for a distinguished act of valour or devotion to duty during active operations
NS	New Sarum
OC	Officer Commanding
OCFW	Officer Commanding Flying Wing: normally a Wing Commander
OCTW	Officer Commanding Technical Wing
OCU	Operational Conversion Unit: Air Force unit whose role is to train pilots in the operational utilisation of military aircraft including the use of weapons
OLM	Order of the Legion of Merit: Rhodesian Armed Services Award
Op Order	Operations Order
ORAFs	Old Rhodesian Air Force Sods
PAI	Pilot Attack Instructor
PR	Photo Reconnaissance: the role of a military aircraft
psi	pounds per square inch: a measure of pressure
PTC	Pilot Training Course: RRAF, RhAF and AFZ
QFI	Qualified Flying Instructor
Radar	Radio detection and ranging
RAF	Royal Air Force
RAAF	Royal Australian Air Force

RAE	Royal Aircraft Establishment at Farnborough
RATG	Rhodesian Air Training Group: part of the Empire Training scheme to train aircrew in WW2
RCAF	Royal Canadian Air Force
Ret	Retired
RAuxAF	Royal Auxiliary Air Force
RhAF	Rhodesian Air Force
RRAF	Royal Rhodesian Air Force
R/w	Runway
SAAF	South African Air Force
Sgt	Sergeant: an Air Force non-commissioned rank
'Skin Basher'	A slang term for a panel beater
Sqn	Squadron
Sqn Ldr	Squadron Leader: an Air Force commissioned rank
SRAAF	Southern Rhodesian Auxiliary Air Force: this designation applied to No. 1 Squadron only, until August 1953
SRAF	Southern Rhodesian Air Force
SR	Southern Rhodesia
SU	Skinners Union injection carburettor
SSU	Short Service Unit: SRAF and RRAF pilot training course
TAS	True Air Speed: the true speed of an aircraft; for a given IAS the TAS increases with altitude
TLC	Tender Loving Care
UK	United Kingdom
unk.	unknown
UN	United Nations
USAF	United States Air Force
Wg Cdr	Wing Commander: an Air Force commissioned rank
WO1	Warrant Officer Class One: an Air Force senior non-commissioned rank
WW2	World War Two
yds	yards

LIST OF ILLUSTRATIONS

SECTION 1

OC No. 1 Squadron SRAAF. *SRAF/Dave Barbour*

Dakota SR25 en route to RAF Abingdon 9–14 November 1951 with second Spitfire ferry team. *John Campbell*

Second Spitfire ferry pilots at RAF Abingdon. Standing from left: Rhodesian Air Attaché Ted Cunnison, Bill Smith, Charles Paxton, John Campbell, Owen Love, Bob Blair, Alan O'Hara. Kneeling from left: Dave Richards, Ray Wood, Peter Pascoe, Ossie Penton. *Dave Barbour*

Second Spitfire ferry team in Khartoum, 12 December 1951. On engine: all unknown. On stairs: Jimmy Pringle. Standing from left: Ray Wood, John Campbell, Peter Pascoe, Bob Blair, Harold Hawkins and Dave Richards. *SRAF/John Campbell*

Second Spitfire ferry members relaxing in Khartoum. Light reading in the shade! Ted Cunnison looks on; others unknown. *SRAF/John Campbell*

Second Spitfire ferry arrival at Belvedere Airport, 19 December 1951. *Rhodesia Herald/ John Campbell*

Ted Cunnison's PK401 being recovered after tail wheel failed to extend on arrival at Belvedere. *Rhodesia Herald/John Campbell*

Belvedere Airport in the SRAF Spitfire era. When the Spitfires were based at Cranborne, Belvedere was used for its greater runway length. *Bill Sykes*

Mess Night at Cranborne. From left: Alan Douglas, Basil Hone, Ray Wood (in suit), Doug Whyte, Ben Bellingan, John Konschel (kneeling), Hardwicke Holderness and Dave Barbour. *SRAF/Dave Barbour*

Mess Night at Cranborne. From left: Dickie Bradshaw, Ossie Penton, Don McGibbon, Nev Brooks, Harold Hawkins, unk., John Campbell and Dave Richards (sitting). *SRAF/Dave Barbour*

No. 1 Squadron SRAAF 1951. Standing from left: Lt O. Penton, Lt D. Richards, Lt D. Bagnall, Lt B. McKenzie, Lt A. O'Hara, Lt. D. Bradshaw, Lt J. Konschel, Lt J. Campbell, Lt B. Hone, Lt D. Bellingan, Lt. P. Potter, Lt G. Forder DFC, Lt R. Wood. Seated from left: Lt. A. Douglas, Capt J. Deall DSO DFC NFC, Major H. Holdeness DSO DFC AFC, Capt N. Brooks, Capt D. McGibbon DFC. Absent: Lt C. Baillie, Lt J. Malloch, Lt D. Barbour. *SRAF/Dave Barbour*

A striking shot of one of the SRAF Spitfires in her new colour scheme, still sporting a high-gloss finish, which suggests this photo was taken in 1951 or early 1952, soon after she was painted. *SRAF*

Spitfires at Cranborne with Rolls-Royce's Harry Marshal and SRAF member Dixie Dean in SR63. *SRAF/Bill Sykes*

SR64, after being grounded, stands as an exhibit at a RRAF Open Day at New Sarum. *RRAF/Dave Hann*

SR65 parked outside at New Sarum. Her RRAF markings are clearly visible with the triple assegais and the 'Flying Assegai' emblem. *RRAF/Robin Thurman*

No. 1 Squadron SRAAF in front of New Sarum HQ, including No. 2 SRAAF Auxiliary and No. 1 SSU Courses. Standing from left: Des Anderson, Don Macaskill, Nigel Bridges, Arthur Hodgson, John Mussell, Dave Harvey, Ken Edwards, Bob d'Hotman, Keith Kemsley, Brian Horney, Peter Piggott, Basil Myburgh. Seated from left: John Cameron, John Rogers, 'Noompie' Phillips, John Deall, Charles Paxton, Ossie Penton and Mick McLaren. *SRAF Photographic Section.*

No. 3 SSU Course. Standing from left: Dick Purnell, J.C. Allen, Chris Hudson, Dave Broughton, Chris Dams, Mike Saunders, Solly Ferreira. Seated from left: Tommy Robinson, Ted Cunnison (Instructor), Dickie Dickenson (RAF/Instructor) and Barry Raffle. *SRAF Photographic Section/Chris Hudson*

No. 2 SSU Course. Back from left: Frank Mussell, Ray Maritz, Charlie Jameson, Barry Stevens, Wally Hinrichs, Vic Paxton. Middle from left: Marshall Robinson, Rex Taylor, Keith Taute. Front from left: Vince King, Roy Morris and Bernard du Plessis. *SRAF Photographic Section/Roy Morris*

The Rebuild Phase 1977–80

SR64 being lifted off the plinth at New Sarum on 26 January 1977. In attendance are Bob Garrett and Stu Robertson behind the tail, as well as 6 Sqn technicians around the front, including John Bulpit, Clive Dutton, Howell Bowker and Les Booth. The crane operator is Jimmy Gordon-Brander. *RhAF Photographic Section, New Sarum*

SR64 back on *terra firma* for the first time in 23 years. In attendance are Stu Robertson and Mike Rochat from 6 Sqn. *RhAF Photographic Section, New Sarum*

SR64 is transported to Thornhill in a Bedford truck. *RhAF Photographic Section, New Sarum*

SR64 reassembled at Thornhill outside 6 Sqn. WO1 Spike Owens briefing Flight Lieutenant Dave Thorne, Acting OC 6 Sqn. *RhAF Photographic Section, Thornhill/ Jeff Hagemann*

SR64 being examined by 6 Sqn crew. From left: Flight Lieutenants Rob McGregor, Steve Caldwell, Roger Watt and Pete Simmonds, WO1 Spike Owens and Dave

Final preparation of PK350 before her first flight. The Cessna 172 belonged to Alyson Malloch. *The Herald/Paddy Gray*

COLOUR SECTION

The Spitfire ferry routes in March and December 1951. *Map by Phil Wright*

Gate Guard, 1964–77

SR64 on the plinth at New Sarum in her initial RRAF Federal colours. *RRAF/Bill Sykes*

SR64 on the plinth at New Sarum now in her RRAF post-Federal colours. *RRAF/ Steve Kesby*

SR64 at New Sarum in RhAF colours prior to her removal from the plinth and renumbered '64'. *RhAF/Nick Meikle*

Rebuild Phase, 1977–80

SR64, in May 1977, being pushed into the 6 Sqn hangar at Thornill by 31 PTC cadet pilots. *Michel Seegmuller*

SR64 in pieces in the ATA hangar after her arrival in mid-1977. From left: unk., Pete Massimiani, Piet Bezuidenhout. *Dave Hann*

Chris Dixon and Jack Malloch outside ATA after the 'Green Leader' raid over Lusaka in October 1978. *Dave Hann*

Final reassembly phase with panels off, exposing the engine bearing beams and a 5-gal leading-edge fuel tank on the wing. The flying controls and pneumatics were still being worked on at this stage. *Peter Knobel*

Final reassembly phase 6–8 weeks before the ground runs. *Peter Knobel*

Final reassembly. Note the 'lower profile, less full' canopy made by Peter Knobel. *Peter Knobel*

Jack Malloch's most recognisable DC-8, A4O-PA, at Dusseldorf in 1977, which played a key part in importing spares such as the propeller and canopy. *By kind permission of AirTeamImages*

Jack Malloch's DC-7F that transported the Griffon engine to South Africa and back, in her post-independence Affretair colours. *Dave Hann*

A nervous Bob Dodds carries out PK350's first engine ground run, still in her primer. *Dave Hann*

Flypast, 3 May 1980

Flypast along runway 06 at Salisbury International Airport on 3 May 1980. Jack
Malloch returning from a local flight and flypast over the home of young Paul
Maher in the suburbs of Salisbury. *Rich Sandercock*

Taxiing into its usual position at Affretair on 3 May 1980. *Rich Sandercock*

Parking after the same flight on 3 May 1980. *Rich Sandercock*

A good crowd greets the Spitfire while the engineers get on with the after-flight on
3 May 1980. *Rich Sandercock*

Cockpit with good detail and Jack Malloch's period leather flying helmet on 3 May
1980. *Rich Sandercock*

PK350 receiving her after-flight service with Rich Sandercock, a pilot with Affretair
in the foreground. *Rich Sandercock*

PK350 quietly parked and cooling down, on 3 May 1980. *Rich Sandercock*

Visit to Thornhill, 22 May 1980

About to taxi for the flight to Thornhill on 22 May 1980. Morgan Maitland-Smith
at the left wing. *Greg Malloch*

Thornhill visit of 22 May 1980. Jack Malloch was met by two of No. 1 Squadron's
Hawker Hunters flown by Tony Oakley (in 1286) just in view, and Alf Wild (in
1258) over the Ngezi dam area. *Alf Wild*

Thornhill visit. Tony Oakley comes into formation with Jack Malloch at 250 knots.
At relatively low speed the Hunter has a marked nose-up flying attitude compared
with the Spitfire. *Alf Wild*

Thornhill visit. Chris Faber stands in front of his Dove VP-YKF on a breezy day at
Thornhill. *Chris Faber*

Thornhill visit. PK350 is flanked by the Silver Provost 'Omega' and Chris Faber's
DH Dove, prior to start-up for the Spitfire/Provost flypast. *Chris Faber*

Thornhill visit. PK350 taxies out behind the Provost flown by Steve Baldwin and
accompanied by Bill Sykes. Morgan Maitland-Smith is in his usual position, riding
on the port wing. *Alf Wild*

Thornhill visit. Jack Malloch and PK350 in a farewell formation flypast with the
Provost before returning to Salisbury. *Alf Wild*

Visit to Charles Prince, September 1980

PK350's visit to Charles Prince Airport. The Spitfire was on display for the public

The painting, *The Last Moments Together*, of the Spitfire and the Vampire, on 26 February 1982. *Painting by William Sykes (son of Bill Sykes)*

Air-to-Air Photography, September 1980 to February 1982

Jack Malloch wearing his period flying helmet on his first photographic sortie with a Bell 205. The tail wheel is still locked down. *Phil Scott/Nick Meikle*

A rare shot of the port side of the Spitfire, taken from the Bell 205. As opposed to the Dakota, the helicopter affords the cameraman a choice of angle. September 1980. *Phil Scott/Nick Meikle*

Jack Malloch, taken from a Dakota flown by Squadron Leader Clive Ward with Mark Vernon, on 23 October 1981, the day before the Air Force '81 air show. This iconic photograph was used extensively by the media for many years. *AFZ photographer*

Taken by Peter Knobel from a Dakota flown by Clive Ward and Norman Ingledew, on 3 February 1982. *AFZ photographer*

Peter Knobel joined the Air Force specifically to fly Spitfires, only to be denied at the last moment, in 1954, when the squadron was taken off line. *AFZ photographer*

... and this is why it is so unique that Peter was given the chance to fly one of those same Spitfires nearly thirty years later, and so fulfil his life's dream. *AFZ photographer*

The following three photographs—the most evocative and beautiful of all the photos—show Wing Commander Steve Kesby flying PK350 on 11 January 1982. They were taken from a Dakota flown by Clive Ward and Sid Buxton. *AFZ photographer*

The Air Force '81 Air Show

PK350 taxies across to the New Sarum side in preparation for the Air Force '81 air show on 25 October 1980. The person riding on the wing is undoubtedly Morgan Maitland-Smith, who regularly assumed this role for his Boss. *Unknown*

PK350 parks close to the intersection of runways 06/24 and 14/32 in readiness for the Air Force '81 air show. *Unknown*

The Air Force '81 air show on 25 October 1981. For the Spitfire, the air show was the culmination of all the hard work and dedication that had been put into the rebuild of PK350. Poignantly, this was its one and only full public display. *AFZ photographer/Steve Harvey.*

To have caught Jack as he sped past at over 300 mph is a masterpiece of photographic timing. *AFZ photographer/Steve Harvey*

SECTION 3

On a cool, fresh morning loaded with anticipation, Bob Dodds helps guide PK350 from the ATA hangar on the day of the first flight, 29 March 1980. *The Herald/ Paddy Gray*

PK350 is pushed onto the ATA ramp for her first flight. Her inboard cannons are missing their streamlined fairings due to a last-minute hitch, the only flight on which they were absent. *The Herald/Paddy Gray*

PK350 being positioned on the ramp outside the ATA hangar. *The Herald/Paddy Gray*

... parked ... *The Herald/Paddy Gray*

... refuelled ... *The Herald/Paddy Gray*

... and pre-flighted ... *The Herald/Paddy Gray*

... oxygen topped up, VHF comms okay ... *The Herald/Paddy Gray*

... the external power unit standing by ... *The Herald/Paddy Gray*

... and ready to go. *The Herald/Paddy Gray*

A final pose for the photographer. *The Herald/Paddy Gray*

An historic line-up—past and present commanders of the Air Force along with ex-SRAF/RRAF Spitfire pilots. From left: Group Captain Charles Paxton, Air Vice-Marshal Chris Dams, Group Captain Johnny Deall, Captain Dave Harvey, Squadron Leader Ian Shand, Air Marshal Frank Mussell, Captain Jack Malloch, Air Marshal Archie Wilson, Air Marshal Mick McLaren, Flying Officer Des Anderson and Group Captains Ozzie Penton and John Mussell. *The Herald/Paddy Gray*

Jack Malloch with Bob Dodds, carrying out his pre-flight inspection. *The Herald/ Paddy Gray*

Parachute on, and with concealed trepidation Jack Malloch climbs into the cockpit. *The Herald/Paddy Gray*

... with the ever-present Bob Dodds to help him strap in. *The Herald/Paddy Gray*

Paddy Gray runs to the starboard wing to get a final close-up of Jack. *The Herald/ Paddy Gray*

Last-minute conference between Jack, Bob and John Fairey. *The Herald/Paddy Gray*

Ready for taxi. Morgan Maitland-Smith (left) and Carlos Martins remove the chocks. *The Herald/Paddy Gray*

The RR Griffon powers PK350 on her way to runway 06. *The Herald/Paddy Gray*

Jack Malloch yields for an Air Rhodesia Viscount ZS-JPU, RH 839 on its way to Bulawayo, Rhodesia's second city. *The Herald/Paddy Gray*

Thornhill/Jeff Hagemann

Jack Malloch taxies in at Thornhill. *AFZ Photographic Section, Thornhill/Jeff Hagemann*

… and parks in front of Flying Wing Headquarters. *AFZ Photographic Section, Thornhill/Jeff Hagemann*

Full circle—Spike Owens welcomes the Spitfire to Thornhill some six years after he initiated the restoration project. A proud moment indeed. *AFZ Photographic Section, Thornhill/Jeff Hagemann*

Visit to Charles Prince Airport, 20 September 1980

The view from the 'Connie' clubhouse at Charles Prince. The Spitfire seems to revel in the attention given it by the crowd. *Brian Carson*

PK350 flies low along the runway, in salute, before setting course for home. Tail wheel is still fixed down. *Brian Carson*

A fine study of PK350's cockpit during the Charles Prince visit. *Brian Carson*

September 1980 to March 1982

An iconic image of Jack Malloch in PK350, with the canopy open, taken from the right-hand-side door of the Bell 205, probably in September 1980. *AFZ Photographic Section, New Sarum*

Jack Malloch receiving the Pat Judson Trophy, flanked on his right by Geoff Pullan, Vice-President, Zimbabwe Division of the RAeS, and on his left by Mr A.G. Newton, Engineering Director, Rolls-Royce. *The Herald*

Steve Kesby after his first solo in PK350/SR64, on 23 November 1981. *Steve Kesby*

The RAeS Zimbabwe Division programme, on the occasion of its recognition of the contribution to aviation by Jack Malloch and his engineers, for their restoration of PK350, on 20 November 1980. *Dave Hann*

Steve Kesby after his first solo on 23 November 1981. His partially concealed grin says it all. *Steve Kesby*

Some evidence of the rough ride and damage experienced by the Vampire whilst pursuing the Spitfire, just prior to the tragic loss of Jack Malloch and the Spitfire. *AFZ Photographic Section, New Sarum/Guy Cunningham/Steve Nobes*

The large crater at the accident site, clearly indicating a high-speed impact. Ken Burmeister is on the left. *AFZ Photographic Section, New Sarum/Guy Cunningham/ Steve Nobes*

An excellent aerial perspective of the impact crater. This confirms Charlie Cordy-

Hedge's recollection of how difficult it was to see the crater from the air. *AFZ Photographic Section, New Sarum/Guy Cunningham/Steve Nobes*

The remains of the Griffon Rolls-Royce engine in the impact crater. *AFZ Photographic Section, New Sarum/Guy Cunningham/Steve Nobes*

The Griffon engine—with only eight of the original twelve cylinders—rests on the hangar floor with a few other recognisable pieces of the wreckage, after recovery by Chuck Osborne and his team from ASF New Sarum. *AFZ Photographic Section, New Sarum/Guy Cunningham/Steve Nobes*

APPENDIX A

Spitfire F Mk 21 cutaway drawing. *By kind permission of Mike Bradrocke*

INTRODUCTION

Today there are approximately 40 restored Spitfires still flying around the world. Unsurprisingly, most of them are located in Great Britain, the home of the Spitfire. They are nearly representative of the whole Spitfire family from the Mark (Mk) I to the PR XIXs which are part of the famous Battle of Britain Memorial Flight. With operational records and wartime service some of these aircraft are literally priceless heirlooms.

It was the 1969 Battle of Britain movie that led to an upsurge in the restoration of Spitfires and the establishment of a significant industry in support of that activity. However, the restoration of a World War Two (WW2) aircraft or a 'warbird', as they have generally been called, is an expensive business. Consequently many restored Spitfires have been financed and are thus owned by wealthy individuals, mostly men. Just like the young boys who witnessed the frenetic contrails of Spitfires and Hurricanes in mortal combat above their homes in southern England during the Battle of Britain, and who were then inspired to become Spitfire pilots, so these latter day multi-millionaires were no doubt inspired by strong childhood memories of one of the most famous names in aviation history—the Spitfire. They wished to be associated with a Spitfire and to do one better, to own one. Aviation today is in a strange way indebted to these wealthy individuals, which reminds us of another, far more substantial debt, owed by the free world to the 'Few' fighter pilots who beat back the Luftwaffe hordes in 1940.

Together with the Battle of Britain Memorial Flight, it is the enthusiasm of these former pilots and their love of the Spitfire, which keeps the aircraft alive in our memories. If one is lucky enough it is still possible to see them fly on the Air Show circuit.

With the exception of a restored Seafire Fighter/Fighter reconnaissance (F/FR) Mk 47 (a Spitfire customised for use by the navy), owned and flown by a wealthy American, there are no late Mark (Mk 21, 22 and 24) Spitfires flying today. There are only a handful of them in museums around the world and one of four Mk 22s can be found in the Military Museum in Gweru, Zimbabwe. This Spitfire, PK355 or SR65, which is one of 22 exported to Southern Rhodesia in 1951, is the sister ship to one PK350 or SR64. To date, this is the *only* other late Mark Spitfire (as opposed to a Seafire) ever to be restored to full flying condition, thus making it a very unique aircraft.

This very successful undertaking, completed in 1980, was the inspiration of two men, Warrant Officer Class 1 (WO1) Bill 'Spike' Owens of the Rhodesian Air Force and Captain Jack Malloch, a successful entrepreneur and owner of an airline in Rhodesia. It was Spike Owens, backed up by Air Commodore Keith Kemsley, who agitated long and hard to restore the Spitfire. Spike Owens even managed to persuade the Air Force to release one of two Spitfires on gate guard duties to allow him to determine the completeness of the airframe. Although Spike Owens was a senior non-commissioned officer he had excellent access to the command structure of the Rhodesian Air Force (RhAF), proof of its being more egalitarian in nature than the structure it had inherited from the Royal Air Force (RAF). However, any dream that Spike Owens may have had of overseeing an actual restoration was snuffed out by the political and military realities prevailing at the time. In stepped Jack Malloch, a man with a legendary reputation and a wartime record of flying Spitfires in the latter part of WW2. With a dream to fulfil, it was Jack Malloch who persuaded the RhAF to release the aircraft into private hands and who directed the restoration of PK350.

The principal thread in the story that follows is the complete history of Spitfire PK350, its rebuild and its sad demise in 1982, barely two years after its successful restoration. However, the story is also very much about Jack Malloch, whose leadership and charisma made it all happen. The account is also a part history of the Southern Rhodesian Air Force (SRAF) and the Royal Rhodesian Air Force (RRAF), in particular the phase during which the Spitfire Mk 22 was its principal fighter and advanced trainer aircraft.

Whilst Jack Malloch was the driving force in the project to restore PK350, he could never have pursued his dream without an outstanding team of engineers and two men in particular—Bob Dodds and Dave Hann—and his extensive personal and business network.

Finally, his quest was undeniably made easier with the help and support of the RhAF and its resources and access to the South African Air Force (SAAF).

Despite this particular Spitfire not having a wartime record, it did serve on the only regular RAF Squadron (Sqn) to be briefly equipped with Mk 22s, and it did serve with distinction throughout the period that the SRAF operated the Spitfire. In the process it was probably flown by most of the SRAF/RRAF Spitfire pilots.

Notwithstanding all these achievements, which even Rolls-Royce was determined to recognise, the story has a bittersweet flavour. In the end Jack Malloch was to perish at the controls of PK350, the aircraft he had laboured so hard to restore, leaving us with only our recollections of their shared journey, their triumph and ultimate tragedy.

This record, hopefully, will ensure that most of this very substantial achievement is not forgotten, which otherwise may have been the case. It is hoped that the richness of the story will once again be savoured by those of us who love a good Spitfire story, as well as those who knew and remember Jack Malloch, in particular his staff at Affretair, and of course, old RhAF members and the wider aviation community.

For all the time PK350/SR64 was in Jack Malloch's care she was indeed and will always be remembered as 'Malloch's Spitfire'.

Chapter 1
29 MARCH 1980

29 March 1980 was the last Saturday of the month. The rainy season was drawing to a close and evidence of an overnight rainstorm lay in pools on the edge of the taxiways at Salisbury International Airport, which serviced the majority of civil and military aviation needs of what was then still Rhodesia. Apart from high level cirrus cloud, a clear day had dawned after the overnight rain. A sense of expectancy mingled with the fresh early morning smells that usually prevail after an African rainstorm, in the still-moist air. The reason for that expectancy was known only to persons within aviation circles. However, *The Herald* newspaper reporter, Colin Blair, had announced to a wider audience a much anticipated event; his article in *The Herald* of the day was headed 'Achtung! Spitfire Comeback'. For those with recall of WW2, during which Britain stood alone against the might of Germany between July and October 1940, the name Spitfire epitomised everything about that resolute and defiant stand which ultimately saw Britain successfully repel the German Luftwaffe in the Battle of Britain. This time a Spitfire was about to take to the air again, not for aggressive, but very peaceful reasons.

The text of Colin Blair's article follows:

> Veteran Rhodesian pilot Captain Jack Malloch hopes to renew an old World War acquaintance in the skies over Salisbury today. If the reunion does come off, it will create local and international aviation history.
>
> The former Second World War Spitfire pilot, now managing director of Air Trans Africa (ATA), will be making the first test flight in a faithfully and painstakingly restored Mark (Mk) 22 Spitfire which last flew on December 18, 1952. Its last pilot was Air Force Chief of Staff, Air Vice-Marshal Chris Dams.
>
> If the flight is successful, the Spitfire, No. PK350, will be the only airworthy Mk 22 in existence.
>
> Captain Malloch, who logged 500 hours in Spitfires over North Africa, Corsica, Italy and the south of France, was full of praise for his ATA engineers and technicians, led by quality controller Mr Bob Dodds and structural engineer Mr Dave Hann, who joined a small band of dedicated enthusiasts to restore the Spitfire to almost its original condition when it left the factory at Castle Bromwich, England, in 1945.
>
> But the original idea for restoring the Spitfire, which was stripped of its

vital parts and cemented to a plinth at Salisbury's New Sarum airbase after it was pensioned off from the air force in 1954, came from WO1 Bill Owens at Thornhill two and half years ago.

For two years, the ATA staff, working in their spare time, faithfully restored the Spitfire. Aircraft radio and electrics man, Mr Phil Mason, recalled that the electrical instruments proved one of the toughest problems to solve. Parts were collected from 'everywhere', especially from Britain.

Asked if he was nervous about flying the Spitfire for the first time in 35 years, Captain Malloch said: "When I did the taxiing tests I was totally unprepared for its power and responsiveness but the old feeling soon came rushing back."

He added: "If everything is not right tomorrow, I shall not attempt to fly the aircraft." Which is understandable—it could fetch more than $1,000,000 in America.

The public announcement had thus been made and some of the key names and facts in the restoration project were now known. While a knowledgeable reader would have noticed a couple of inaccuracies in the text, the excitement buzzing amongst the gathering would have glossed over these. A relatively small crowd had gathered on that late summer morning to witness the long awaited event, including all participants in the restoration project. About two hundred and fifty people were assembled, most of whom were gathered on the western side of one of the longest runways in the world at the ATA premises. Captain Jack Malloch's impressive hangar, in which PK350 had been so painstakingly restored, dominated the skyline west of the main runway at Salisbury International Airport. A smaller group of Air Force personnel and families had gathered on the eastern side of the runway, which was home to the Air Force base New Sarum, the last military home of PK350 when it was known as SR64.

The group gathered on the ATA hangar side included senior Air Force personnel, from previous Commanders of the Air Force to the present Commander, Air Marshal Frank Mussell CLM, OLM, who had flown Spitfires himself including PK350 as SR64; Air Vice-Marshal Chris Dams OLM, who had overseen the contract to restore the aircraft; ex-Spitfire pilots; and most importantly, the men who had worked on the aircraft at ATA under the leadership of Captain Jack Malloch. The smaller group of Air Force personnel on the New Sarum side included WO1 Spike Owens, the man who started the project, and me (Nick Meikle). Family and loved ones of the participants also were present, notably a small boy whose profile was later that morning captured for posterity by the photographer with *The Herald*; the child was standing next to the runway as Jack Malloch roared past at low altitude and high speed. The Spitfire legend was thus guaranteed another faithful disciple to ensure that tales of this awesome fighter from a by-gone era will endure.

Professional observers included the air traffic controllers. On duty were the tower controller and his assistant; they would control the airspace in the immediate vicinity of the airport, affording Jack Malloch the freedom to test and display PK350 in the best possible manner, performing high speed passes with the associated growl of the Rolls-Royce Griffon engine. These controllers had already managed unusual military activity over the previous few months, controlling the arrival of the Monitoring Force to supervise a ceasefire between the protagonists of the recent Rhodesian civil war.

For the first time in history, at the beginning of 1980 Rhodesia had been placed under direct rule by Great Britain. Lord Soames, the last colonial Governor in Rhodesia, was to preside over the transition to independence on 18 April 1980, in accordance with the Lancaster House Agreement. The Monitoring Force had arrived in a bevy of heavy military transporters never before seen on Rhodesian soil, including the United States Air Force (USAF) C5A Galaxies, C141 Starlifters, and the RAF C130 Hercules. PK350's first flight in her restored condition would thus prolong an exciting trend.

Other professional but incidental observers would have included Air Rhodesia technicians and flight crew, who were readying their Viscounts and Boeing 720s for the day's flights. *The Herald*'s photographer again captured a very evocative image of a Viscount ZS-JPU,[1] flight number RH 839 for Bulawayo, taxiing past the idling Spitfire. Its Captain, Dave 'Polly' Postance, accompanied by his First Officer, Peter Miller,[2] would surely have drawn the attention of the starboard side passengers to the spectacle on their right, temporarily boosting the number of spectators at the event.

Adding to the spectacle, the starboard Rolls-Royce Dart driven propeller blades were condensing the moist air into visible spirals that flowed back over the wing as if in some kind of aerodynamic salute—one pair of Rolls-Royce turbo prop engines acknowledging one very famous Rolls-Royce Griffon. The Griffon was the last of an era of mighty piston engines produced by Rolls-Royce, an icon in the aviation industry. Even though the high pitched sound of the Darts would have drowned out briefly the Griffon as the Viscount taxied past, the Griffon's characteristic throaty growl soon confirmed its presence as it powered this ultimate Spitfire back into the air at 0744 local (0544Z) that morning, off Runway (R/w) 06.

The successful flight was to last 35 minutes as recorded in Jack Malloch's logbook. Although Jack Malloch had to contend with a couple of challenges neither of these would have been detected by the vast majority of the spectators. John Fairey, son of the late Sir Richard Fairey of Fairey aviation from Great Britain, in liaison with Bob Dodds and Dave Hann, had been on the radio at ATA assisting Jack Malloch deal with those problems. Nothing had been left to chance in the planning of this flight. The only clue to an informed eye would have been the fact that Jack did not land with the familiar selection of 75 degrees of flap to help reduce the landing speed. Runway 06/24, at 4,725 metres, was more than long enough to deal with this.

And thus it was that The *Sunday Mail* ran an article the following day proclaiming the success of the flight. The reporter, name unknown, used the headline 'Spitfire Takes Off Again—26 Years Later' and had the following to say:

> Former Second World War fighter pilot Captain Jack Malloch lifted off from Salisbury airport yesterday and turned the clock back 26 years.
>
> His 'time machine' was a Supermarine Spitfire Mk 22, built in 1945 and last flown in December 1954.
>
> Mechanics who put three years' painstaking work into restoring the machine after it stood for years on a plinth at New Sarum airbase, watched proudly as the fighter, in full wartime camouflage, rose steeply into the early morning sun.
>
> Thirty minutes later the aircraft roared in to make a last low pass over the crowd of about 200 lining the runway before turning to make a perfect landing. Stepping down from the cockpit, Captain Malloch, who regularly flew the machine—PK350—as an Air Force Auxiliary pilot before it was finally grounded, told the crowd between gulps of champagne: "It was the first five minutes that bothered me—it took time for it all to come back to me—but after that I really enjoyed myself."
>
> It was an emotional occasion for many of the onlookers, including the Commander of the Rhodesian Air Force, Air Marshal Mick McLaren, who also flew the machine regularly in the 1950s.
>
> One of his predecessors, Air Marshal Archie Wilson, said: "I tried my darndest to talk Jack into letting me take her up, but no chance…he wasn't having any."
>
> A notable absentee was former Prime Minister Mr Ian Smith, another former Spitfire pilot, although his wife Janet was present.
>
> "Ian has a meeting in the Midlands and is as mad as a snake he couldn't be here," she said.

When the Spitfire was first removed from its plinth engineers were amazed to find much of the equipment in working order, including the hydraulics.

The only real casualty from years of exposure was the propeller. Ironically, only a German firm could be found to make a replacement.

Again some key facts were revealed in the article above and in effect corrections were made to previous inaccuracies—PK350 had last flown in December 1954 and not 1952; she was discovered to be in a remarkably good technical state after her removal from the plinth at New Sarum and had not been stripped of components as previously suggested; and lastly, Air Marshal Mick McLaren was not the current Commander, but had been the previous Commander, under whom the decision to rebuild PK350 had been taken, in early 1977.

Bottom line though, it was a fantastic achievement and everyone involved had every reason to be very satisfied with a job well done, and none more so than Jack Malloch himself. He had handled the aircraft with great skill in spite of his age and the technical challenges he faced in the air. Jack Malloch and his two engineering stalwarts, Bob Dodds and Dave Hann, would have experienced a huge drop in adrenalin after the aircraft was returned safely to the ATA ramp. The latter two men had declared the aircraft fit to fly and Jack Malloch's faith in them had been completely vindicated. Thus it was that PK350 now joined the elite ranks of close on 20 restored Spitfires around the world. As a Mk 22 she was especially unique—there were no other airworthy Fighter (F) Mk 22s or late Mark Spitfires anywhere in the world, at that time.

Chapter 2
THE ULTIMATE SPITFIRE

The Vickers Supermarine Spitfire F Mk 22 was the penultimate Spitfire going by the numbering of all the marks of Spitfires. The Mk 24, which followed the Mk 22, was to all intents and purposes the same aircraft, but for a few minor differences. Thus the Mk 22s and 24s became the 'Ultimate Spitfires', representing the final development of this amazing family of fighters. They embodied all the features and improvements that the hard lessons of war had impressed upon their design team and test pilots, encouraging enhancements to the original blueprints. While broadly and superficially similar to the original Spitfire that first flew in March 1936, the Spitfire now was a vastly different machine. In fact to some, like the famous Spitfire test pilot and pre-WW2 sport pilot, Alex Henshaw, she was a "powerful, almost ugly fighting machine…with forceful[1] lines that were no longer those of a Spitfire". To others, like Jeffrey Quill AFC, Supermarine's chief test pilot, she was a "little overpowered perhaps, but a magnificent aeroplane"[2] which, after all, is what she was designed to be.

By March 1945, when the Mk 22s first started to come off the production line, WW2 was just about over and the demand for fighters had substantially diminished; consequently the Mk 22s and 24s did not see service under war-time conditions. In fact, the jet age had entered the world of military aviation and piston powered fighters would in future steadily be replaced by jet fighters. In 1955 the Spitfire was declared obsolete to the requirements of the RAF.

Powered by the Rolls-Royce 37 litre V12 Griffon 61 engine producing 2,035 horsepower, the Mk 22 represented one half of the famous Spitfire family. The Griffon had also powered the Mk XII, XIV, XVIII, PR XIX and Mk 21.[3] All the earlier operational marks, including the well-known Marks I, II, V, VIII, IX, PRX1 and XVI had been powered by the Rolls-Royce 27 litre Merlin engine, which also powered the Hurricane, Lancaster and Mosquito. See the table below which presents the evolution of the Spitfire family.

THE SPITFIRE FAMILY

Merlin-Powered	Year in Service	Griffon-powered
Mk I	1938	
Mk II	1940	
Mk III (became Mk IV)	1940	
Mk V, PR IV	1941	Mk IV/XX (DP845)
Mk VI	1942	Mk IV/20 (DP851)
Mk VII	1942	
Mk VIII	1943	Mk XII
Mk IX	1942	
PR X	1944	MK XIV & PR XIX (19)
PR XI	1943	
PR XIII	1943	
Mk XVI (Packard Merlin)	1944	
	1945	Mk XVIII (18)
	1945	Mk 21
	1945	Mk 22
	1948	Mk 24[3]

However, it was not only the engine that differentiated this late mark Spitfire from the earlier marks; the wing was more tapered than elliptical but substantially stronger; and its wide chord Spiteful tail-plane really set the Mk 22 apart from the rest of Spitfire family. The wing's torsion box was substantially strengthened to enable fitting of a longer and wider undercarriage, to accommodate an even greater diameter 5-bladed propeller than the propellers fitted to the Mk XIVs and XVIIIs. Whilst these latter marks shared features such as the cutback rear fuselage that facilitated the teardrop canopy; increased internal fuel capacity with fuel tanks in the leading edges of the wings; and a retractable tail wheel, it was the permanent fit of the four 20mm Hispano cannons which gave the Mk 22 a very potent profile, distinguishing it from these earlier Griffon stable-mates. These changes showed again that the Spitfire's design displayed an amazing capacity for growth and development.

The Spitfire family also incorporated the Seafires, a version designed explicitly for the navy. The Griffon-powered Seafire F/FR Mk 46 was the direct equivalent of the Mk 22 and 24. The F/FR Mk 47 was the final development of the Seafire and thus of the whole Spitfire family. At the end of the production run in 1948, 22,759 Spitfires and Seafires had been manufactured, in 52 variants. Thus the Spitfire became the most prolific aircraft ever produced in Britain and of course the most famous.

The key parameters by which fighter performance is compared and judged are top speed, time to altitude/rate of climb, ceiling and range. Other very important attributes are handling and agility, the pilot's visibility from the cockpit and firepower. It seems self-defeating if, having reached a good position from which to shoot down an enemy aircraft, one's firepower is weak. Similarly, if the pilot's view to the rear of his aircraft is impeded, he is unable to see an enemy on his tail early enough to take evasive action.

The F Mk 22 scored very well in terms of the above parameters. Its top speed was 449 mph at 26,000 feet with an initial rate of climb of 4,500 feet/min and a ceiling of 43,000 feet. It had a good rate of roll, good visibility, and excellent firepower with the four 20mm cannons. By comparison, the Seafire 47, with an extra two years' worth of development, a more powerful Griffon engine and its 6-bladed contra-rotating propeller was 5 mph faster, had an initial rate of climb of 5,100 feet/min and at 12,500 lbs was the heaviest of the Spitfire/Seafire family. Compare these figures to the Mk I Spitfire—capable of 365 mph, an initial rate of climb of 2,100 feet/min, a ceiling of just on 35,000 feet and a weight of 5,900 lbs—and one can easily see the progress made during WW2.

The best starting point from which to track the Mk 22's evolution is the Battle of Britain, which took place between 10 July and 31 October 1940. Even though the Spitfire first flew in March 1936 and entered squadron service with the RAF in mid-1938, it was the Battle of Britain that sealed the Spitfire's place in history as a great air defence fighter, highlighting both its strengths and weaknesses.

However, before taking a closer look at the Spitfire's strengths and weaknesses and the evolution of the Mk 22, we need to remind ourselves of some of the key personalities in the Spitfire story.

PERSONALITIES

It was Air Chief Marshal Sir Hugh Dowding who placed the Spitfire at the centre of the Home Defence system that he and Robert Watson-Watt designed, between 1938 and 1940. (Watson-Watt was the inventor of radar.) Together with the Hawker Hurricane, these two great fighters would bear the brunt of the Luftwaffe's non-stop aerial assault on Great Britain during the critical months of the Battle of Britain.

Dowding had foreseen the aerial battle that would materialise between the RAF

Left: John 'Jack' McVicar Malloch in the early 1960s. *Greg Malloch*

Above: Wing Commander Peter Ayerst DFC (RAF), the original test pilot of PK350, in his 73 Sqn Hurricane in February 1940 at Rouvres, France. *Gemma Baggot/Peter Ayerst*

No. 237 (Rhodesia) Squadron at Calvi Air Base, Corsica, posing in front of a Spitfire Mk IX, August 1944. Jack Malloch is second from the right in the back row. *Greg Malloch*

No. 1 Squadron SRAAF in 1950 before the Spitfires arrived. Jack Malloch, now an auxiliary, is seated front right with his characteristically cocked cap.
SRAF/Dave Barbour

Left: ATA in the early 1970s with the DC-7s and Lockheed Constellation of Afro Continental Airways *Greg Malloch*

Below: The first production Spitfire F Mk 22 PK312 in 1945 with the original Mk XIV type tail-plane. This is how PK350 probably appeared when she came off the production line in July 1945.
By kind permission of Flypast magazine

Most of the first ferry pilots at Rolls-Royce Derby. Standing from left: unk., unk., Harold Hawkins, Jack Malloch, Bob Bair, John Moss, Dave Barbour, Jock Barber, Dickie Bradshaw, Unk. Kneeling from left: Unk., Ossie Penton, Peter Pascoe, Johnny Deall and Charles Paxton. *SRAF/Dave Barbour*

Left: PK672 flown by Ted Jacklin before departure on 12 March 1951 from the RAF Chivenor. Mike Schuman's PK330 is parked behind PK672. *SRAF/Robin Thurman*

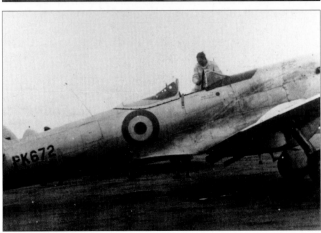

Left: The first SRAF Spitfire ferry arrival, 22 March 1951. Ted Jacklin is disembarking from PK672, which shows the signs of a long journey. Note the 90-gallon LRT under the belly. *SRAF /Dave Barbour*

Above: The first Spitfire ferry arrival at Cranborne. Ted Jacklin being greeted by (from left) Keith Taute, Prime Minister Sir Godfrey Huggins, unk. and Major General Garlake. *SRAF/Dave Barbour*

Below: Dakota SR25 en route to RAF Abingdon, 9–14 November 1951 with second Spitfire ferry team. *John Campbell*

The first Spitfire ferry arrival. Dave Barbour being greeted by Hardwicke Holderness, OC No. 1 Squadron SRAAF. *SRAF/Dave Barbour*

Second Spitfire ferry pilots at RAF Abingdon. Standing from left: Rhodesian Air Attaché Ted Cunnison, Bill Smith, Charles Paxton, John Campbell, Owen Love, Bob Blair, Alan O'Hara. Kneeling from left: Dave Richards, Ray Wood, Peter Pascoe, Ossie Penton. *Dave Barbour*

Second Spitfire ferry team in Khartoum, 12 December 1951. On engine: all unknown. On stairs: Jimmy Pringle. Standing from left: Ray Wood, John Campbell, Peter Pascoe, Bob Blair, Harold Hawkins and Dave Richards. *SRAF/John Campbell*

Second Spitfire ferry arrival at Belvedere Airport, 19 December 1951. *Rhodesia Herald/John Campbell*

Second Spitfire ferry members relaxing in Khartoum. Light reading in the shade! Ted Cunnison looks on; others unknown. *SRAF/John Campbell*

Ted Cunnison's PK401 being recovered after the tail wheel failed to extend on arrival at Belvedere. *Rhodesia Herald/John Campbell*

Belvedere Airport in the SRAF Spitfire era. When the Spitfires were based at Cranborne, Belvedere was used for its greater runway length. *Bill Sykes*

Mess Night at Cranborne. From left: Alan Douglas, Basil Hone, Ray Wood (in suit), Doug Whyte, Ben Bellingan, John Konschel (kneeling), Hardwicke Holderness and Dave Barbour. *SRAF/Dave Barbour*

Mess Night at Cranborne. From left: Dickie Bradshaw, Ossie Penton, Don McGibbon, Nev Brooks, Harold Hawkins, John Campbell and Dave Richards (sitting). *SRAF/Dave Barbour*

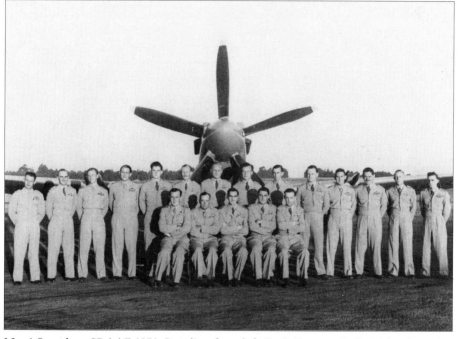

No. 1 Squadron SRAAF 1951. Standing from left: Lt O. Penton, Lt D. Richards, Lt D. Bagnall, Lt B. McKenzie, Lt A. O'Hara, Lt. D. Bradshaw, Lt J. Konschel, Lt J. Campbell, Lt B. Hone, Lt D. Bellingan, Lt. P. Potter, Lt G. Forder DFC, Lt R. Wood. Seated from left: Lt. A. Douglas, Capt J. Deall DSO DFC NFC, Maj H. Holdeness DSO DFC AFC, Capt N. Brooks, Capt D. McGibbon DFC. Absent: Lt C. Baillie, Lt J. Malloch, Lt D. Barbour. *SRAF/Dave Barbour*

A striking shot of one of the SRAF Spitfires in her new colour scheme, still sporting a high-gloss finish, which suggests this photo was taken in 1951 or early 1952, soon after she was painted. *SRAF*

Spitfires at Cranborne with Rolls-Royce's Harry Marshal and SRAF member Dixie Dean in SR63. *SRAF/Bill Sykes*

Aerial shot of New Sarum *circa* 1953 with Spitfires, Harvards and Tiger Moths visible.
By kind permission of Dave Millam, RRAF Photographic Section, New Sarum

The aftermath of John Mussell's wheels-up landing in SR60 in September 1952 on runway 14 at New Sarum. Jimmy Pringle is standing on the wing.
SRAF/Bill Sykes

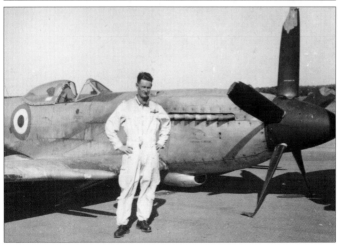

Brian Horney next to PK326 (SR80) after her wheels-up in September 1952. Note the wooden propeller which helped reduce collateral damage to the engine in particular.
SRAF/John Mussell

No. 1 Squadron flypast for No. 2 SSU's Wings Parade on 27 February 1953. SR64, flown by Keith Kemsley, is the first in line astern. *SRAF/Bill Sykes*

Above: Arthur Hodgson's tyre failure in SR85. Jack Malloch suffered a similar failure at Salisbury in PK350 and managed to prevent the nose-over. *SRAF/Bill Sykes*

Right: A demonstration bombing strike at New Sarum on the occasion of the Rhodes Centenary Display, 13–14 June 1953. *SRAF/John Mussell*

Spitfire (possibly SR88) on the line at New Sarum with 60lb concrete-head practice rockets. The spinner would shortly have been repainted red. *SRAF/Bill Sykes*

Ossie Penton giving quarter attack gunnery lessons to John Cameron from No. 1 SSU. *SRAF/Bill Sykes*

Some of the Spitfire technicians. Sitting on the wing from left: unk., unk., Dave Whittingham, unk. Standing: Spike Owens (later WO1) and Gus Simmons. Kneeling: unk., Taff Evans. *SRAF/Bill Sykes*

Arthur Hodgson from No. 1 SSU. *SRAF/Bill Sykes*

Spitfire SR62 from the logbook of Vince King, No. 2 SSU. *Pat King, son of Vince King*

Spitfire SR60 starting up for a rocket sortie on 17 June 1954, with Chris Hudson at the controls. *Chris Hudson*

SR64, with its red spinner, starting up at New Sarum. *SRAF/Bill Sykes*

The last squadron flight of the RRAF Spitfires, now in RRAF colours but without the three assegais in the visible roundels. Spike Owens is standing between the two closer Spitfires, SR65 and another. *SRAF/Bill Sykes*

SR65 (foreground) and SR64 parked outside at New Sarum after they were grounded in December 1954. *RRAF/Robin Thurman*

Chris Dams, the last pilot to fly SR64, here in SR81, April/May 1954, during his Spitfire Operational Conversion Unit (OCU). *SRAF/Spike Owens*

Keith Kemsley in SR64 on his last flight in a Spitfire on 20 September 1954, and the last photo of SR64 in service taken by Sandy Mutch. Note the 'Flying Assegai' insignia. *Keith Kemsley*

SR64, after being grounded, stands as an exhibit at a RRAF open day at New Sarum. *RRAF/Dave Hann*

SR65 parked outside at New Sarum. Her RRAF markings are clearly visible with the triple assegais and the 'Flying Assegai' emblem. *RRAF/Robin Thurman*

No. 1 Squadron SRAAF in front of New Sarum HQ, including No. 2 SRAAF Auxiliary and No. 1 SSU courses. Standing from left: Des Anderson, Don Macaskill, Nigel Bridges, Arthur Hodgson, John Mussell, Dave Harvey, Ken Edwards, Bob d'Hotman, Keith Kemsley, Brian Horney, Peter Piggott, Basil Myburgh. Seated from left: John Cameron, John Rogers, 'Noompie' Phillips, John Deall, Charles Paxton, Ossie Penton and Mick McLaren. *SRAF Photographic Section.*

No. 3 SSU Course. Standing from left: Dick Purnell, J.C. Allen, Chris Hudson, Dave Broughton, Chris Dams, Mike Saunders, Solly Ferreira. Seated from left: Tommy Robinson, Ted Cunnison (Instructor), Dickie Dickenson (RAF/Instructor) and Barry Raffle. *SRAF Photographic Section/Chris Hudson*

No. 2 SSU Course. Back from left: Frank Mussell, Ray Maritz, Charlie Jameson, Barry Stevens, Wally Hinrichs, Vic Paxton. Middle from left: Marshall Robinson, Rex Taylor, Keith Taute. Front from left: Vince King, Roy Morris and Bernard du Plessis.
SRAF Photographic Section/Roy Morris

SR64 being lifted off the plinth at New Sarum on 26 January 1977. In attendance are Bob Garrett and Stu Robertson behind the tail, as well as 6 Sqn technicians around the front, including John Bulpit, Clive Dutton, Howell Bowker and Les Booth. The crane operator is Jimmy Gordon-Brander. *RhAF Photographic Section, New Sarum*

SR64 back on *terra firma* for the first time in 23 years. In attendance are Stu Robertson and Mike Rochat from 6 Sqn. *RhAF Photographic Section, New Sarum*

SR64 is transported to Thornhill in a Bedford truck.
RhAF Photographic Section, New Sarum

SR64 reassembled at Thornhill outside 6 Sqn. WO1 Spike Owens briefing Flight Lieutenant Dave Thorne, Acting OC 6 Sqn.
RhAF Photographic Section, Thornhill/Jeff Hagemann

SR64 being examined by 6 Sqn crew. From left: Flight Lieutenants Rob McGregor, Steve Caldwell, Roger Watt and Pete Simmonds, WO1 Spike Owens and Dave Thorne.
RhAF Photographic Section, Thornhill/Jeff Hagemann

SR64 undergoing successful undercarriage tests outside 6 Sqn at Thornhill.
RhAF Photographic Section, Thornhill/Jeff Hagemann

SR64 parked with 1 Sqn Hunters—one thoroughbred next to another. *RhAF Photographic Section, Thornhill/ Jeff Hagemann*

SR64 being stripped in the 6 Sqn hangar at Thornhill. Spike Owens is discussing the propeller with an engine fitter, identity unknown. *RhAF Photographic Section, Thornhill/Jeff Hagemann*

SR64 being separated from her Griffon engine.
RhAF Photographic Section, Thornhill/Jeff Hagemann

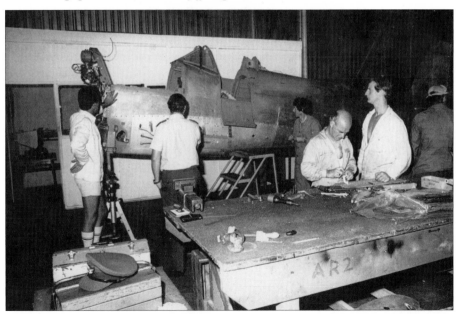

Initial reassembly. From left: Dave Hann, Chris Dixon, Johnny Norman, George Graham, Piet Bezuidenhout, unk. *RhAF Photographic Section, New Sarum*

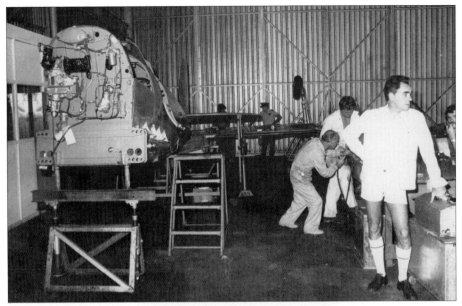

Above: Initial reassembly and a good view of the components on the engine side of the firewall and the carry-through beam. From left: George Graham, Piet Bezuidenhout, Dave Hann, unk. *RhAF Photographic Section, New Sarum*

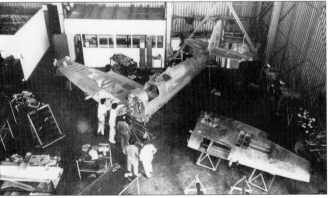

Middle: Initial reassembly. From left: Al Binding, Dave Hann, Johnny Norman, Piet Bezuidenhout, unk., Morgan Maitland-Smith, unk., Tommy Minks, unk. *RhAF Photographic Section, New Sarum*

Above: Aerial view during initial reassembly. *RhAF Photographic Section, New Sarum*

View of some of the internal structure of the wings during initial reassembly.
RhAF Photographic Section, New Sarum

Like new in her 'fledgling state'. *RhAF Photographic Section, New Sarum*

An aerial view of PK350 in her fledgling state in the ATA hangar.
RhAF Photographic Section, New Sarum

Group of engineers after the initial reassembly. From left: George Graham, Ken
Smith, Andy Wood, Unk., unk., Bob Dodds, unk., unk., Piet Bezuidenhout, Dave
Hann, Ian Fraser, Morgan Maitland-Smith, Carlos Martins, Ben Darck, unk.
RhAF Photographic Section, New Sarum

The instrument panel before it was installed in the cockpit by Phil Mason and his ATA team. *RhAF Photographic Section, New Sarum*

The engine rebuild team from the SAAF, late 1979 or early 1980. From left: R. den Boestert, P.S. Weyers, and A. Moffs who headed the rebuild team. *SAAF/Dave Hann*

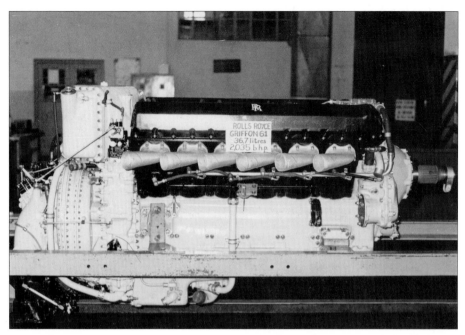

The Rolls-Royce Griffon 61 just before it was returned to Rhodesia from the SAAF for final fitting in late 1979 or early 1980. *SAAF/Dave Hann*

Final preparation of PK350 before her first flight. The Cessna 172 belonged to Alyson Malloch. *The Herald/Paddy Gray*

and the Luftwaffe. He had also long been aware of the Spitfire's potential and was determined to exploit its qualities as an air defence fighter and interceptor. Exploiting the unique capabilities of Watson-Watt's radar and a superb command and control system, Dowding and his fighter squadrons were able to repel the Luftwaffe's aerial assault. This dissuaded Germany from invading Britain and earned huge political capital for Great Britain at a very critical juncture in the war. It also prompted the famous morale-boosting speech by Prime Minister Winston Churchill, acknowledging the enormous debt owed to the famous "few" RAF fighter pilots. It was the Spitfire that best symbolised this extraordinary act of defiance.

Dowding himself had his thumbprint on the RAF specifications that led to the design of the Spitfire in the early 1930s. However, it was the legendary designer Reginald J. Mitchell who penned the graceful lines of the Spitfire and chose the unique elliptical shape of its wings. Mitchell, or 'RJ' as he was known at Supermarine, had been the chief designer there since 1920. He supervised the design of a number of very successful seaplanes including the Walrus, which saw sterling service rescuing many a downed airman from the English Channel during hostilities. He sealed his reputation as a great designer with his famous Schneider Trophy[4] seaplane racers, in particular the Supermarine S6B which not only won the Schneider Trophy for Great Britain in 1931, but also set a world speed record of 407.5 mph after the event. This was a staggering achievement when the RAF's fighter squadrons were still flying 200 mph biplanes. The S6B was powered by a Rolls-Royce 37 litre V12 R engine producing 2,700 horsepower. It was the result of the close relationship that Mitchell and Supermarine had developed with Rolls-Royce in their quest for speed. Not only was this relationship absolutely critical to the successful development of the Spitfire, this specific R engine became the direct forebear of the Rolls-Royce Griffon, which powered the Mk 22 Spitfire.

Regrettably, Mitchell did not see his beloved Spitfire enter squadron service before he passed away in mid-1937, ravaged by cancer. However, his status as a legendary designer endures to this day, by virtue of the Spitfire.

His role as chief designer at Supermarine was filled by Joe Smith. A very practical engineer, Smith is credited with the further development of the Spitfire. Test pilot Jeffrey Quill regarded Smith as the best person for this undertaking: in his opinion Smith had a very good feel for the strengths and weaknesses of the aircraft and later displayed great inspiration at critical junctures in its evolution.

As chief test pilot, Jeffrey Quill was another key personality in the Spitfire's story.

Although it was Mutt Summers, the chief test pilot at Vickers Aviation (the parent company to Supermarine since 1928) who carried out the first few test flights on the 'Fighter', as it was known in March 1936, it was Jeffrey Quill who directed the developmental test flying of the Spitfire. He was only 23 when he took on these onerous duties and was able to do so thanks to his exceptional abilities as an airman. Quill had been trained in the RAF as a fighter pilot, had honed his skills on demanding meteorological observation flights and in late 1935 was persuaded to become a test pilot at Vickers. He flew non-stop in this capacity until 1947 when he was grounded due to ill health. In the process he flew every single variant of Spitfire. His contribution to the evolvement of the Spitfire matches all the other superlatives in the Spitfire story.

It was Jeffrey Quill who persuaded another aviation legend, Alex Henshaw, to join Supermarine. Henshaw had developed his reputation as a sport pilot in the pre-war years, specifically during an epic non-stop flight from London to Cape Town and back in 1939. He had joined Vickers Aviation as a test pilot early in the war but when Quill met him he was frustrated and felt he was being under-utilised by Vickers.[5] Their chance meeting led to Henshaw assuming responsibility for production test flights at the famous Castle Bromwich factory outside Birmingham. In the process he flew more than 2,000 new Spitfires and developed a fabled reputation for his magical aerobatic displays, which even Winston Churchill came to see. Henshaw left the factory in January 1946, having directed production test flying of most of the Mk 22s.

The above-mentioned men are very much the primary characters in the Spitfire story. However, there is one additional Supermarine personality who deserves special mention—Len Gooch, the Works Engineer. Working closely with Lord Beaverbrook, Gooch organised the dispersal of the Supermarine works in late 1940, following the devastating Luftwaffe attacks on the Southampton factory. This masterstroke of management instilled within Supermarine's structure an adaptability and versatility that proved most useful when modifications and changes were made to the Spitfire at short notice during the height of the war. Jeffrey Quill identified these qualities as having played a key part in the successful development of the aircraft without creating large disruptions on the production lines. Examples of these efforts included refitting operational Spitfires with metal covered ailerons and the introduction of bob-weights into the elevator control system when longitudinal stability problems were exposed.

The political establishment also contained some key personalities, such as Viscount Swinton, the Air Secretary, who committed the Air Ministry to the Spitfire with an initial order for 310 units in 1936, after its successful test flight by the RAF. He had also pressed for the development of the Merlin engine. However, it was Lord Beaverbrook, as the newly appointed Minister of Aircraft Production, who in May 1940 broke the back of the production problems that had blighted the early years of the Spitfire. He persuaded Lord Nuffield to step down and allow Vickers Aviation to take full control of the massive Castle Bromwich factory. This single act ensured that Spitfire production exceeded 100 aircraft a month, just as the Battle of Britain commenced. This was double the production rate of the previous three months.

Even at this juncture, in mid-1940, the Ministry of Air Production (MAP) planned to replace or supplement the Spitfire with the Bristol Beaufighter, Hawker Tornado and Westland Whirlwind. Production problems had virtually blinded the political establishment to the qualities of the Spitfire, another reason for the Battle of Britain being such a critical moment in the Spitfire story. Time alone has revealed the true vision and leadership qualities of men such as Dowding, who was backed up by his very able lieutenant, Air Vice-Marshal (AVM) Sir Keith Park. It was the latter who commanded 11 Group during the Battle of Britain and 11 Group which bore the brunt of the attacks. Park displayed an extraordinary ability to marshal his limited forces in response to the Luftwaffe onslaught. The Luftwaffe pilots had been persuaded to believe there was only a handful of Spitfires left in the RAF but were confronted, instead, by squadrons of Spitfires and Hurricanes. It was Dowding and Park who manipulated their reserves and supplies of aircraft to achieve this state of affairs.

STRENGTHS AND WEAKNESSES

The Spitfire was now the darling of the moment. Her fighting qualities were confirmed by the fact that Spitfires shot down more enemy aircraft *pro rata* than the Hurricane, even though the latter, by virtue of her superior numbers, shot down more aircraft in total.[6] There was no doubt as to the Spitfire's attributes: her performance; her ease of handling, especially close to the stall; and her nimbleness and ability to out-manoeuvre her nemesis, the Messerschmitt Bf 109. In fact, Jeffery Quill believed it was the Spitfire's ease of handling close to the stall that saved many a pilot's life. This was due to her elliptical wing and design washout, which ensured the root of the wing stalled first providing the pilot with full aileron authority at the stall. In short, she had no vices—and this explains why pilots simply loved the aircraft from the moment they first flew her. Balanced by the similarly elliptical shape of the tail-plane, 'RJ' Mitchell once again proved correct the old cliché: 'what looks right is right'.

Additionally, the low thickness/chord ratio of the wing allowed the Spitfire to achieve a good turn of speed in the dive. She was capable of Mach .9 in the dive, while the North American Mustang could manage only Mach .8.

Nevertheless, the Spitfire's lateral control and rate of roll, especially at high speed—above 300 mph—was poor. It required two hands to roll the aircraft at such a speed—not a desirable state of affairs when trying to shoot down an enemy aircraft or evade an aircraft on one's tail. Fortunately, Jeffrey Quill experienced this first-hand. He had served with 65 Sqn for three weeks at the height of the Battle of Britain and was able to report back to Joe Smith about this, and other weaknesses that needed to be rectified, as always, right away.

The other weaknesses included: poor optics of the side panels of the windshield; poor visibility to the rear; the relatively weak firepower of the Spitfire's eight .303 Browning machine guns; and an engine cut-out caused by the effects of negative G when pursuing an enemy aircraft into a dive. Many pilots complained bitterly that, despite having attained a good attacking position, the enemy managed to escape with a damaged aircraft instead of being shot down, able to fight another day. On the other hand, the Bf 109 had cannons and achieved much better results from their encounters. However, it was the Spitfire's poor lateral control that needed immediate attention.

With time always at a premium, it would take great leadership, great inspiration and great teamwork for Supermarine to work its way through the crises as they occurred and produce a more capable Spitfire. Jeffrey Quill credits Joe Smith's leadership and the instinctive awareness of his design staff, at the outset of the war, that they must dedicate their total effort to developing the Spitfire and not be distracted by trying to design a new aircraft. This then was the bedrock of their focus.

FIXES

By November 1940 Supermarine had found a very positive solution to the poor lateral control problem. Realising that the fabric-covered ailerons were ballooning at high speed, several experiments ensued; metal covered ailerons were tried and proved to be the best solution. This led to the immediate requirement to refit all the RAF's aircraft with metal ailerons; introduce metal ailerons onto aircraft on the production line; and design them into future marks such as the Mk V. However, in spite of this breakthrough and Supermarine's response, Jeffrey Quill and Joe Smith were well aware that it would take a newly designed wing to provide the degree of lateral control needed for high speeds, especially above 400 mph. The aileron reversal speed[7] was a moderate 580 mph and when the aircraft was in a dive to 470 mph, it was estimated that at 400 mph the ailerons had lost 60% of their effectiveness. The effects of the twisting movement had to be reduced or removed with a stronger wing.

Being aware of the problem was one thing; being able to remedy it was another. It was only on the Mk 21, which sired the Mk 22, that the problem was overcome—with a 47% stiffer, redesigned wing and ailerons. The ailerons were longer, attached to the wing with a piano hinge and featured a geared balance tab. This design change was started only in 1942 and was first tested on what was effectively the Mk 21 prototype, DP851, in December of the same year. The aileron reversal speed of this wing was 825 mph. The Mk 21 became operational only in early 1945, which meant it took most of the war to deal satisfactorily with the problem. A number of the earlier mark Spitfires operated with clipped wings to improve their lateral control, but this was only really effective at low level.

Improving the optics of the windshield panels was dealt with quite quickly, as was an interim solution to improve the pilot's visibility and comfort by producing a bulged canopy. However, the best long-term solution was to redesign the rear fuselage and fit a single-piece teardrop canopy to provide the pilot with all round visibility. This could be achieved only much later in the war on the later Mark Spitfires (the late production Mk IX, XIV, XVI and XVIII), when time was available to redesign the rear fuselage and technology allowed the production of large-area one-piece Perspex canopies. The Mk 22 incorporated this feature from the outset.

Improvements to the firepower involved the introduction of 20mm Hispano cannons but they proved unreliable, mainly due to freezing conditions at high altitude. Working with very limited space, Supermarine's engineers eventually solved this problem by directing hot air from the back of the radiators to heat the side-mounted cannons. This resulted in the common mix of weapons being two cannons and four machine guns on most Spitfires during the course of the war. Some of the Mk V models were dedicated to a low level role or operations in warmer climates and these had four cannons, but generally this was rare. This configuration required a wing with more space to accommodate the cannons and provide the necessary heating. Wings on the new Mk 21 and later Mk 22 were designed with four cannons from the outset, providing the Mk 22 with a hitting power three times greater than that of the Mk I during the Battle of Britain.

It was only after the Battle of Britain, when Fighter Command took the offensive by flying intruder 'Rhubarb' and 'Circus' raids[8] into German-occupied France, that the relatively short range of the Spitfire was exposed. Having been designed as an air defence fighter, it had a limited fuel capacity of 85 gallons which gave a combat range of 425 miles. In fact most of the subsequent marks achieved a range of no more than 490 miles. The only mark that enjoyed a greater range was the Mk VIII, which had an increased internal fuel capacity and a range of 660 miles. Ironically, despite its increased internal fuel capacity of 120 gallons including wing tanks, due to the greater fuel consumption of the Griffon engine the Mk 22 had only a 390 mile range. Overload tanks behind the pilot became one of the remedies for improving the range and were a feature enjoyed by the Mk 24 but not the Mk 22. The most common solution to increasing the range was a fuselage-mounted drop tank of 30, 45 or 90 gallons capacity.

The problem of the engine cut-out was overcome in stages. Miss Beatrice Shilling of the Royal Aircraft Establishment (RAE) at Farnborough provided the first of a series of interim solutions, by reducing the effects of the fuel starvation caused by the negative G when the aircraft was pushed over or bunted into a dive. This was followed by installation of the Bendix-Stromberg pressure carburettor which maintained a positive fuel pressure under negative G. Finally, the Skinner Union (SU) injection carburettor which injected fuel into the supercharger was fitted to the late mark Merlin engines and the Griffon 61 and 85 engines. Stanley Hooker (later Sir Stanley) of Rolls-Royce believed this was a better solution than pursuing the option of fuel injection, as used by the Daimler Benz engine in the Bf 109. The positive effect of the ram air pressure at the supercharger/carburettor intake provided a measure of increased engine performance that outweighed the benefit of fuel injection.

POWER DEVELOPMENT

For all of the above-mentioned improvements to the Spitfire's capability, it was the power development that led the way[9] in improving its performance. According to Jeffrey Quill everything else flowed from this dynamic, including the other Spitfire variants and especially the successful PR models. In view of the close relationship that Supermarine had developed with Rolls-Royce during the Schneider Trophy races, it was no surprise that this was to continue into the war. Maximising the potential of the Merlin, and the introduction of the Griffon with lessons learned from the Merlin, were the principle threads to this part of the story. These developments created two 'quantum jumps'[10] in performance when the Mk IX and Mk XIV were produced. Central to these achievements were improvements to the supercharger technology.

In 1938 Supermarine launched an attempt on the world speed record with the Speed Spitfire. Even though this proved unsuccessful and the honours went to the Germans, both Supermarine and Rolls-Royce learned a great deal about the power potential of the 27 litre Merlin. The Speed Spitfire's engine produced over 2,000 horsepower with the same special fuel mix as the Schneider Trophy S6B racer. Supermarine and Rolls-Royce concluded that a more powerful engine would be required to take over from the Merlin. As a result, in late 1939, Rolls-Royce started work on developing the Schneider Trophy 37 litre R engine. They called it the Griffon. Simultaneously, Joe Smith began planning for the eventuality when the "good big 'un will eventually beat the good small 'un"[11] as he referred to the engines. Even though the Battle of Britain slowed development of a Griffon-powered Spitfire, Supermarine revived these plans in 1941.

In the early stages of the war the Merlin of course was still undeveloped. Its power development would come from the use of improved fuels and improvements to the supercharger[12] design.

The introduction in late 1939 of 100-octane fuel from the USA and later from Iran increased the boosted power of the Merlin III fitted to the Mk I Spitfire. This 100-octane fuel allowed the engine to run at higher manifold pressures and increased the power with emergency boost from 1,030 horsepower to 1,310 horsepower at 10,000 feet; this in turn increased the speed by 34 mph. The Merlin XII, which powered the Mk II Spitfire, also benefitted from the use of this higher-octane fuel. However, it was the improvements to supercharger design that led to the fuller and more sustained power development of the Merlin. All the early Merlin engines were fitted with a single stage single speed supercharger.

It was Stanley Hooker at Rolls-Royce who supervised improvements to the design of the supercharger. Having already identified inefficiencies in the intake design of the early Merlin III and XII, he redesigned the intake, impellor and diffuser to improve the flow characteristics of the fuel-air mix being drawn into the engine. This led to the Merlin 45 series engines which powered the Mk V Spitfire. Introduced in 1941, the Mk V became the most numerous of all the Spitfires—6,479 were produced—and included the most variants.

The Mk V provided the RAF's Fighter Command with a measure of air superiority when it launched offensive raids into France during 1941 and 1942. These raids were intended to lure the Luftwaffe into combat but they proved costly and became even more so when the Luftwaffe introduced the Focke-Wulf Fw190 in late 1941. Almost immediately the RAF lost its superiority. There was now an urgent need to improve the Spitfire's performance.

Hooker now introduced a two-stage, two-speed supercharger to the Merlin. This not only produced more power at greater altitudes, it also produced a better spread of power over the altitude range of the aircraft. This engine, the Merlin 61 producing 1,565 horsepower, was fitted to an Mk V airframe and the aircraft became the Mk IX. It was capable of 408 mph at 21,000 feet, an initial rate of climb of over 4,000 feet/min and a ceiling of 42,500 feet. This represented the first quantum jump as described by Jeffery Quill. In truth it was an interim type and was introduced into the RAF squadrons in mid-1942 ahead of the equally capable and more thoroughly designed Mk VIII. Nevertheless it became the second most numerous Spitfire in the RAF, with 5,656 aircraft being produced in five variants.

The increased power came at a cost. Stanley Hooker had to introduce an intercooler to cool the fuel-air mix before it entered the second stage of compression, to prevent pre-detonation. This necessitated the introduction of a separate cooling system to the engines, using the same liquid Glycol/water mix. Whereas the MK V had a small cylindrical oil cooler under the port wing, the Mk IX now featured a similar size radiator under its port wing to that fitted under the starboard wing. The aircraft was also extended to accommodate the longer engine. These adaptations represented the first real change to the profile of the Spitfire. Fortunately for the RAF the new contour was not that apparent to the Luftwaffe pilots, which helped conceal the arrival of the Mk IX and the knowledge of its presence in the skies over France. The Mk IX also featured a 4-bladed propeller to absorb the greater power of the Merlin engine.

Further development of the Merlin 60 series engines also continued. The Merlin 63/64 series engines were capable of producing 1,710 horsepower and were fitted to the successful Mk VIII and PR XI Spitfires. In truth this was the end of its potential for the Merlin engine. Logically, if the same supercharger technology were to be applied to the Griffon, this engine would once again take the Spitfire to new levels of performance. Capable of 1,700 horsepower in an undeveloped state, the Griffon was perfectly positioned to take over from the Merlin.

GRIFFON SPITFIRES

As soon as a Griffon was available Joe Smith fitted an RG25M with a two-speed single-stage supercharger to a Mk III airframe. Even though it was a heavier and longer engine, its frontal area was only marginally greater than that of the Merlin. It was fitted and attached without too much difficulty, with stronger more distinctive attachment struts, to the airframe which sported cowlings with distinct aerodynamic concessions to the larger engine profile. This aircraft became the first of two Mk IV prototypes and was known as DP845. Jeffrey Quill first flew her in late 1941 and found that she had tremendous performance but, unsurprisingly, also longitudinal and directional control problems.

Ultimately, confirmation of DP845's efficacy came from an unexpected opportunity to display its spectacular low-level performance and vindicate Joe Smith's inspired decision to pursue a Griffon-powered Spitfire.

Most fortuitously, an Fw190 was captured in June 1942 when its pilot either lost his way or intentionally landed his aircraft in South Wales. Test flying the German aircraft soon revealed that the Mk IX did not, in fact, have the margin of performance that the RAF thought it had. It was particularly between 15,000 and 25,000 feet that the Fw190 outperformed the Mk IX. This eventually led to a change in the philosophy[13] governing air combat: combat had been expected to take place at high altitudes against high altitude intruders; now it was anticipated that contests would be more successful at lower altitudes. Superchargers were tuned to provide more power at lower altitudes and led to the HF Mk IXs (with high altitude rated engines) being replaced by the LF Mk IXs (with low to medium altitude rated engines).

In July 1942 a fly-off was arranged between the captured Fw190, a Hawker Typhoon and a Spitfire. Jeffrey Quill, encouraged by Joe Smith, took along his by now favourite Spitfire, DP845, and proceeded to trounce both the Fw190 and the Typhoon. This was completely contrary to all expectations. Within eight days an order was placed for 100 Mk XII Griffon-powered Spitfires. The change of the Spitfire guard had been set in motion. Griffons were fitted to Mk V airframes and by March 1943 the Mk XII went into service with 41 Sqn at Tangmere. The Mk XIIs served in a specialist low level role and saw limited squadron use but, importantly, they successfully introduced the Griffon into RAF service. With its clipped wings and a broad chord tail similar to the Mk VIII's, the Mk XII cut a very distinctive profile.

A second Mk IV (also known as the Mk 20) prototype, DP851, was then fitted with a Griffon 61 which featured a two-speed two-stage supercharger and produced 2,035 horsepower. Lessons learned from the Merlin 61 were now applied to the Griffon 61 and Joe Smith also incorporated a new interim wing design for DP851. She became known as the Mk 21 prototype and was first flown in August 1942 by Jeffrey Quill.

DP851 was also known as the Supermarine Type 356 and had the full backing of the MAP. However, gestation into a fully operational fighter with its new wing would take time. Now that the Griffon 61 was available and with the knowledge that the Mk IX did not have the margin of performance desired by the RAF, the decision was taken to fit Griffon 61s to six Mk VIII airframes. The first aircraft flew in January 1943 and demonstrated spectacular performance: a speed of 445 mph at 25,000ft; and an initial rate of climb of over 5,000 feet per minute. However, its handling left a lot to be desired. It would require a larger fin and rudder to make it acceptable for squadron service.

In October 1943, following a period of intensive trials which included trying contra-rotating propellers, the MAP placed an order for 120 Mk XIVs. This replaced all outstanding orders for Mk VIIIs. Jeffrey Quill flew the first Mk XIV that same month, demonstrating that once again there had been an amazing collective response to the pressing need to keep the Spitfire ahead of its rivals. Mk XIV was in squadron service by January 1944. According to Jeffrey Quill it was a very fine fighter, even if a bit short on range. With its larger wide chord tail-plane and longer nose accommodating the larger Griffon engine, the Mk XIV's profile was substantially different to its Merlin-powered predecessors. It also featured a 5-bladed propeller. This change continued the trend of increasing the number of blades to absorb the huge increase in power from the Griffon 61. In this instance Jeffrey Quill paid tribute to the efforts of Rotol (Rolls-Royce and Bristol) to produce propellers capable of doing the job.

The entire process of developing the Mk XIV with its excellent performance signified the second quantum jump in the evolution of the Spitfire, according to Jeffrey Quill. Over time 957 of these interim type fighters were eventually produced.

The Mk XIV sired the more thoroughly engineered Mk XVIII, which did not see operational service during the war, as well as the very capable PR XIX,[14] which did see wartime service. The PR XIX was the last Spitfire to be retired from RAF service—from the RAF's Temperature and Humidity Flight in 1957. Nowadays two PR XIXs are part of the famous Battle of Britain Memorial Flight.

LONGITUDINAL STABILITY PROBLEMS

In 1942 Supermarine was seriously challenged by the onset of longitudinal stability problems. This followed the discovery that some RAF squadrons were not following the correct loading instructions. As the Spitfire developed and gained weight so the correct loading of the aircraft became more critical; if the aircraft's centre of gravity (C of G) was at the rear of the plane it would be longitudinally unstable. Supermarine responded rapidly and added elevator control bob-weights to the control lines. Later an aerodynamic solution was found, requiring modification of the elevator itself. This all happened when Spitfires began mysteriously breaking up in flight. The problem affected mostly Mk Vs and altogether 25 were lost in this manner, including a brand new aircraft flown by Jeffrey Quill's good friend and colleague, George Pickering.[15] The problem disappeared once the solutions mentioned above were introduced.

Most importantly, the soundness of the Spitfire design and construction was not found wanting—in fact no Spitfire was ever an outright failure. The longitudinal instability problem was part of a learning process and the right solutions were eventually found, even though its symptoms may not have been correctly understood at the beginning.

MK 21, 22 & 24

In December 1942 the Mk 21 prototype DP851 was lost in a landing accident. By July 1943 a second prototype, PP139, with a stronger and more representative version of the final wing, was airborne. PP139 was soon demonstrating better performance than the Mk XIV, by 10 mph and with excellent lateral control, but with poor longitudinal and directional control. Supermarine recognised that a larger tail-plane would probably solve the problems once and for all, but production pressures meant that it would continue to refine the configuration as it was, with a tail-plane similar to the Mk XIV. In fact the Mk 21 prototype looked very much like the Mk XIV. But in January 1944 the RAF tested the first production Mk 21 and condemned the aircraft. It was even recommended that Spitfire production should cease, which Jeffrey Quill thought was an over-reaction. In spite of this, Supermarine continued to work on the aircraft and improved its handling sufficiently for the RAF to accept the aircraft for squadron service. The Mk 21 went into squadron service in January 1945, just two months before the Mk 22s started coming off the production line.

The handling problems that had hampered development of the Mk 21 highlighted the close margins to which the Spitfire had been designed and built. The increased performance of the Griffon engines had come at a cost, and that cost was primarily the handling of the aircraft. Supermarine continually had to balance the improvements they could manage within the time constraints imposed by the war.

In spite of its new wing and excellent lateral control, the Mk 21 was very much a compromise. With the war effectively at an end in March 1945 when the Mk 22 came off the production line, Supermarine finally had the time to address fully the longitudinal and directional control problems that the Mk 22 had inherited from its predecessor. The Mk 22 still sported the Mk XIV type tail of the Mk 21, as is clearly indicated by pictures of the first production Mk 22 PK312. However, it did feature the cut back rear fuselage and teardrop canopy, so it was quite noticeably different to the Mk 21. Eventually, toward the end of 1945, the larger wide chord tail-plane was fitted[16] and this "handsome"[17] addition transformed the aircraft. Its 27% larger fin and horizontal tail-plane meant that the huge power of the Griffon was effectively harnessed and the stability problems ceased to exist—even though she was a tricky aircraft to handle on the ground. All the 268[18] Mk 22s that were produced were eventually fitted with the larger Spiteful[19] tail-plane, as it became known. Other refinements included a retractable tail wheel and undercarriage doors that covered the wheels when retracted, so providing a small amount of extra performance. The Mk 22 was also the most numerous of the late Mark Spitfires—only 120 Mk 21s and 81 Mk 24s were produced.

The Mk 24 differed from the Mk 22 in three areas: it was fitted with the shorter barrelled Hispano Mk V cannons, which were electrically rather than pneumatically operated; it was fitted with rocket rails;[20] and it had two 33-gallon fuel tanks behind the cockpit, which afforded the Mk 24 a greater range than the Mk 22. Otherwise their performance was identical.

SUNSET YEARS

When the war ended there were 5,864 Spitfires in RAF service. At the time of the Battle of Britain Day in 1946 there were just two Fighter Command squadrons equipped with Spitfires. In 1947 No. 73 Sqn (based in Malta) was equipped with Mk 22s but a year later they were replaced with de Havilland Vampires. In addition, 13 of 20 Royal Auxiliary Air Force (RAuxAF) squadrons were equipped with Spitfires, under the control of Fighter Command. Altogether 172 Mk 22s equipped 12 RAuxAF squadrons on front-line service until 1951, when the Spitfire's 13 years of home defence duties came to an end.

The impressive Mk XVIII Spitfires were the last Spitfires to see operational service, in the Middle East and Far East. Some of these Mk XVIIIs became involved in a bizarre incident during the first Arab-Israeli War in 1948-49, when Israeli Spitfire Mk IXs shot down RAF Spitfires. In another incident Israeli Spitfires attacked RAF Typhoons. The Spitfires were led by one Ezer Weizman, whom we will meet again later in this story.

The final curtain on RAF operational flying came down in the Far East: in July 1950 Seafire Mk 47s flew their last carrier-based missions in the Korean War; and on 1 January 1951 Mk XVIIIs flew their last operational sortie in the Malaysian conflict. The highly regarded Wing Commander Wilfred Duncan Smith, who had seen service right through World War II, led the final sortie.

Many of the surplus Spitfires saw service in foreign air forces after the war, including large numbers of Mk IXs with the South African Air Force, Mk XIVs with the Belgian and Thai Air Forces, Mk XVIIIs with the Indian Air Force and PRXIXs with the Swedish Air Force. Of the ultimate Mk 22 and 24 Spitfires, it was the former that saw the most service with foreign air forces. Fifty-two Mk 22s served in the Southern Rhodesian, Egyptian and Syrian Air Forces.

It is to one of those 22 Mk 22s that served with the Southern Rhodesian Air Force that we now turn.

Chapter 3
ROYAL AIR FORCE (RAF) SERVICE LIFE, 1945–1951

Spitfire F Mk 22 PK350 was part of the first batch of 45 Mk 22s (numbered PK312 to 356) from a total of 268 Mk 22s produced against Contract No. B981687/39 for the RAF. The order was originally for Mk IXs. This first batch was produced between March and July 1945, which means that PK350 probably came off the production line in July at the Castle Bromwich Aeroplane Factory, resplendent in her European day fighter colour scheme (see profiles for the various colour schemes worn by PK350 at different stages of her life) probably fitted with the Mk XIV style tail-plane.

The Castle Bromwich factory was situated on the north-eastern outskirts of Birmingham and was responsible for producing around 12,000 Spitfires and Seafires. It was one of a number of shadow factories that the MAP had set up before the war to address manufacturing requirements for the RAF. By VE day on 7 May 1945, production had fallen markedly from the peak of 300 plus aircraft per month during the war. As from November 1945 the final assembly and test flying of the Mk 22/24 production was conducted at the Supermarine plant at South Marston Aeroplane Factory, a smaller shadow factory near Swindon. The final Mk 24 fuselage came off the production line at Castle Bromwich in March 1946 after which the factory was closed.

PK350 was test flown at Castle Bromwich before being accepted by the RAF. Jeffrey Quill, with the help of George Pickering, had established a standardised test flying procedure in 1937 and this was used throughout the production life of the Spitfire. Alex Henshaw, who was the Chief Test Pilot at Castle Bromwich, describes this format in his own words:

> After a thorough pre-flight check I would take off and, once at circuit height, I would trim the aircraft and try to get her to fly straight and level with hands off the stick. Once the trim was satisfactory I would take the Spitfire up in a full-throttle climb at 2,850 rpm to the rated altitude of one or both supercharger blowers. Then I would make a careful check of the power output from the engine, calibrated for height and temperature. If all appeared satisfactory, I would then put her into a dive at full power and 3,000 rpm, and trim her to fly hands and feet off at 460 mph Indicated Air Speed (IAS). Personally, I never cleared a Spitfire unless I had carried out a few aerobatic tests to determine how good

or bad she was. The production test was usually quite a brisk affair: the initial circuit lasted less than ten minutes and the main flight took between twenty and thirty minutes. Then the aircraft received a final once-over by our ground mechanics; any faults were rectified and the Spitfire was ready for collection.

Henshaw also gives a fascinating insight into how he felt about the Spitfire as it changed over the years, by adding:

> I loved the Spitfire in all of her many versions. But I have to admit that the later marks, although they were faster than the earlier ones, were also much heavier and so did not handle so well. You did not have such positive control over them. One test of manoeuvrability was to throw her into a flick-roll and see how many times she rolled. With the Mk II or the Mk V one got two-and-a-half flick-rolls but the Mk IX was heavier and you got only one-and-a-half. With the later and still heavier versions, one got even less. The essence of aircraft design is compromise, and an improvement at one end of the performance envelope is rarely achieved without deterioration somewhere else.

According to his logbooks, now in the care of the RAF Museum, Alex Henshaw never test flew PK350. It was left to two of his much smaller team of production test pilots to conduct at least two of her acceptance test flights. While Henshaw had managed a team of 25 pilots during the peak production days in the war, in mid-1945, by all accounts, his team consisted of possibly just four pilots, including Alex Henshaw himself. The other three were Wing Commander Peter Ayerst[1] DFC, Squadron Leader Ronald Vernon 'Monty' Ellis DFM and AFC, and Flight Lieutenant Walter James 'Jimmy' Rosser DFC. All three men had seen distinguished service during the war. Peter Ayerst and Monty Ellis had served together flying Hurricanes on 73 Sqn in 1940. Peter Ayerst became a fighter ace and was credited with five confirmed kills, while Monty Ellis had three confirmed kills and four shared kills, before they both became production test pilots with Vickers Supermarine. Alex Henshaw later appointed Monty Ellis as his number one on Spitfires.[2] Jimmy Rosser was credited with two kills and became an 'escape and evasion' specialist, earning his DFC between two tours as a Vickers Supermarine test pilot.

Peter Ayerst, who I am very pleased to report is still alive at the time of writing, has recorded in his logbook that he flew a 20-minute test flight in PK350 on 25 July 1945.[3] He had test flown most of the Mk 22s so he does not recall any specific detail, except that the test flight followed the format recalled by Alex Henshaw above, and that it was carried out in the flying area to the south-east of Castle Bromwich. He also remembers that at this time the Mk 22s were fitted with the larger Spiteful tail.[4]

Peter Ayerst did not pass and sign her off for some reason, so she would have been cleared for RAF service by Monty Ellis or Jimmy Rosser. On 3 August 1945, PK350 was delivered to 33 Maintenance Unit (MU) at RAF Lyneham, and was probably flown by a pilot from the Air Transport Auxiliary. The latter unit had distinguished itself during the war by efficiently delivering thousands of the RAF's aircraft from the factories and repair units to the squadrons, in all sorts of weather and using many female pilots in the process. The purpose of the MUs was to prepare aircraft for service or to store them in the short or long term until the RAF required them.

PK350 would remain at 33 MU until June 1946 when she was flown to Eastleigh, the present day Southampton airport and from where the Spitfire prototype first flew in 1936. Here she underwent modifications but what these were is not clear. If she had been fitted with the smaller Mk XIV type tail when originally delivered to the RAF, it could have been that she had the larger Spiteful tail-plane fitted.[5] PK350 was then returned to 33 MU on 2 September, where she remained until 15 July 1947 when she was flown to RAF Pershore to be prepared for overseas service. On 18 July she was ferried out to the RAF base at Ta Kali (Luqa) on Malta, arriving there on 31 July.

According to one source, *Spitfire Survivors Around the World,* PK350 was thought to have been allocated as a spare aircraft on 73 Sqn based on Malta. However, according to a letter dated 2 March 1977[6] written by WO1 Bill Owens (credited with starting the restoration of PK350), to a Mr Fynn, previously of 73 Sqn, PK350 was not only allocated to the squadron, but he was also able to identify her:

> I have a complete set of the technical or maintenance logs (F700s) from the time of manufacture until the last flight (18 December 1954). The aircraft was manufactured in 1945 and the only squadron service it saw with the Royal Air Force was with No. 73 Squadron. After manufacture it was stored at an MU (33). It was then issued to 73 Squadron and, after service with the squadron, it was returned to another MU (6) where it was kept until it was sold to the Southern Rhodesian Air Force in 1951. The aircraft's number is PK350 and while on 73 Squadron the code letter was 'G'.

This has turned out to be a substantial revelation. It means that PK350 would have been regularly utilised for the next 15 months with 73 Sqn and it explains her relatively high hours by the time she was grounded in the service of the RRAF in 1954.

On 28 October 1948 PK350 was ferried back to 6 MU at RAF Brize Norton, when 73 Sqn was re-equipped with de Havilland Vampires. This was not the last time that PK350 bowed out to the inevitability of progress. She was then (date unknown) flown to Vickers South Marston for modifications and refurbishment and on 29 May 1949 Squadron Leader Guy Morgan[7] DFC flew her back to No. 6 MU at RAF Brize Norton. Guy Morgan was a test pilot at Vickers Supermarine. Here she remained until March 1951, when she was added to the strength of the Southern Rhodesian Air Force.

Chapter 4

SOUTHERN RHODESIAN AIR FORCE (SRAF)
SERVICE LIFE, 1951–1977

The post-war years saw much change as the world once again settled to some semblance of peace. The most significant political dynamic was the onset of the long Cold War between West and East. This was characterised by the arms race between the USA and USSR, and lasted until the fall of the Berlin Wall in 1989. The North Atlantic Treaty Organisation (NATO) was formed as a defence shield in Western Europe to counter the threat to Western Europe of the USSR. NATO provided the USA with a network of bases from which to project its power. Another major political dynamic took place in Africa in the late 1950s when Great Britain and other colonial powers started to divest themselves of their colonial possessions. Africa became the focus of much attention from the superpowers, as well as from China. Communist Russia and China sought to plant the seed of communism by flattering willing and vulnerable leaders with weapons and military advisers. The USA, on the other hand, tried to counter these efforts with less overt activities that exposed its naivety in foreign ventures, particularly in 'darkest' Africa. Britain's penultimate effort to guide her ex-colonies into independence took place in April 1980 when Zimbabwe became independent, after a bitter and bloody civil war in Rhodesia. The de-colonisation process was completed in March 1990 when Namibia became independent after another long, complicated and bloody war, played out mainly in Angola.

The political landscape was in a constant state of change and with it, defence supplies—which naturally included aircraft and weapons systems. These elements would serve as the principal political backdrop for events as they unfolded in Southern Rhodesia and later Rhodesia in the story ahead. Spitfire PK350's destiny was thus to be determined by political decisions from afar and at a very early stage in the Cold War, when the Korean War was underway. Although the Spitfire's days as a front line fighter were fast coming to an end in 1950 in Great Britain, PK350 would enjoy a new lease of life and extended usefulness in the hands of men who were well used to flying Spitfires and single seat fighters in the war.

THE RE-CREATION OF THE SRAF

In 1951 Southern Rhodesia, later Rhodesia, was a self-governing colony and had been since 1923. During the Second World War the country had made a significant contribution to the Allied cause. This contribution came mainly from the white population which, proportionately, made a greater contribution than any other country within the British Empire. In the air war[1] it contributed a total of 977 officers and 1,432 other ranks who served in the Royal Air Force, of whom 498 died in service and 47 were wounded. There were also three Rhodesia Squadrons, Nos. 237, 266 and 44.

In May 1940, No. 1 Squadron of the Southern Rhodesian Air Force became 237 (Rhodesia) Squadron, thus terminating the existence of the pre-war SRAF. Initially equipped with Hawker biplanes, 237 Sqn was used to counter the Italian presence in Abyssinia and Eritrea and was supplemented with Westland Lysanders and Gloster Gladiators to carry out this task. In May 1941, 237 Sqn was relocated to the Western Desert and re-equipped with Hawker Hurricanes for tactical reconnaissance. In 1943, during the latter stages of the North African campaign, it was re-equipped with Spitfire Vs to assume fighter and ground attack duties, and then with Spitfire IXs when the squadron moved into Europe through Italy and Corsica into Southern France. Significantly, as far as this story is concerned, Jack Malloch served on this unit as a Spitfire pilot, together with Ian Smith who much later became Prime Minister of Rhodesia, after the Federation of Rhodesian and Nyasaland separated and during the UDI years.

No. 266 (Rhodesia) was another day fighter squadron—the 'Rhodesia' designation was in recognition of its being a 'gift' squadron from Southern Rhodesia. It was equipped with Spitfires in January 1940 and fought in the Dunkirk and Battle of Britain campaigns. In January 1942 the squadron was re-equipped with Hawker Typhoons and specialised in ground attack duties until the end of the war. It is possible that WO1 Spike Owens, who is credited with starting the project to restore PK350, served on this unit as an aircraft mechanic working on Typhoons. Also, one of the Officers Commanding of 266 Sqn was Wing Commander Johnny Deall, who features later in this story.

Lastly, No. 44 (Rhodesia) Squadron was the first squadron to be equipped, in late 1941, with the four engine Lancaster B1 bomber. Under the leadership of the South African-born Squadron Leader John Nettleton, 44 Sqn quickly established a fine reputation following the famous daylight raid on Augsburg, to bomb the Mann works where the diesel engines for U-boats were being manufactured. A number of Rhodesians were crew members on this raid.

Southern Rhodesia had made another significant contribution to the Allied war effort. In January 1940, as part of the Empire Flying Training Scheme, the Southern Rhodesian Government set up the Rhodesian Air Training Group (RATG) to train aircrew. Altogether there were nine flying training schools at airfields outside Salisbury, Gwelo and Bulawayo, at which over 10,000 pilots and navigators were trained for the RAF during the course of the war. A famous fighter pilot who later entered the world of politics, Ezer Weizman, graduated from 26 Elementary Flying Training School (EFTS) based at Guinea Fowl, outside what was then Gwelo. Weizman became Chief of the Israeli Air Force and then President of Israel. Dave Richards, a member of the Southern Rhodesian Auxiliary Air Force (SRAAF) and a pilot on the second Spitfire ferry, had been a course mate with Weizman.

These contributions ensured that military aviation was to retain a very strong place in the country's psyche, even though the dictates of war meant that the SRAF had ceased to exist. It did not take long for a handful of enthusiastic die-hards to start agitating for an air force to be re-formed after the war. A Government Gazette notice on 28 November 1947 did just that, creating an Air Unit—again named the Southern Rhodesian Air Force (SRAF)—with an Army rank structure under the leadership of Captain Keith Taute DFC and Bar. Captain Taute in turn fell under the command of Colonel Garlake, the General Officer Commanding, Central African Command. At this early juncture, the SRAF had no choice but to utilise the skills and experience of ex-RAF personnel to help man the aircraft and train new pilots. These men formed No. 1 Squadron, Southern Rhodesian Auxiliary Air Force (SRAAF). This unit would retain the 'auxiliary' identity until August 1953, when the services of auxiliaries were terminated.

THE DECISION TO ACQUIRE SPITFIRES

Having already scraped together a handful of aircraft from whatever source could be found, a determined effort to equip the fledgling Air Force soon saw a mix of de Havilland Tiger Moths, North American Harvards and communication aircraft on the inventory. However, with no fighter aircraft, there was no way the Air Force could perform an Empire/Commonwealth defence role. Southern Rhodesia had been assigned this defence role by the British Government, together with an anti-guerrilla role, as part of a NATO commitment to counter the accelerating threat of the USSR and other communist powers in the Far East, such as occurred in Malaya.

With a core of enthusiastic and skilled auxiliaries on No. 1 Squadron, in late 1950 the Southern Rhodesian Government negotiated an Air Agreement to purchase 22

Spitfire Mk 22s from the British Government. The total cost was £20,000 of which £12,000 were for the aircraft and £8,000 were for spare parts. The aircraft, most of which were still new, were to be readied for collection in February 1951. Announcing the agreement, the Prime of Minister of Southern Rhodesia, Sir Godfrey Huggins, stated that the Government was confident of being able to make a useful contribution to Commonwealth defence within two years, with a sufficient number of trained pilots. As time would tell, this very pragmatic decision would be fully vindicated.

The Spitfires represented a substantial increase in performance from the Harvard, the principal trainer at the time; however, the combination was proven and, as time would show, the decision to acquire the Spitfires was a very good one. This experience with the Spitfires enabled the SRAF to forge the skills and discipline that formed the foundation of the operational expertise so proficiently demonstrated in RRAF deployments to Aden and later, during the Unilateral Declaration of Independence (UDI) years, in the war in Rhodesia. In the short term, the SRAF satisfied its commitment to train the required number of pilots for its NATO obligations. In the long term, a number of these pilots would later provide the future leadership of the Rhodesian Air Force.

THE FIRST SPITFIRE FERRY: 14 MARCH TO 22 MARCH 1951

Thus it was that PK350 was destined to continue her service life on the inventory of the SRAF. Now the task was to get her and the other 21 aircraft to Southern Rhodesia. The decision was taken to ferry them, a task not unfamiliar to Rhodesians who already had previous experience of this kind of operation in the build-up to WW2, in 1939, and more recently with the ferry of three Avro Ansons from England. It was a skill the Air Force was to use many times in the future with the Spitfires and all the other piston and jet aircraft she was legally to acquire, as well as some of the sanctions-busting acquisitions in the 1970s. This decision was made despite the RAF and even Rolls-Royce expressing serious misgivings about the ability of the Rhodesians to ferry the Spitfires over such a long distance—some 5,600 nautical miles.

It was decided to bring the aircraft out on two ferry flights. PK350 was to be flown out on the first ferry with ten other aircraft, planned for March 1951. The second ferry for the balance of eleven aircraft was to take place in December 1951.

The Ferry Operation Order No. 2/51[2] was issued on 6 March 1951 by Lieutenant Colonel Ted Jacklin, under the signature of Captain Harold Hawkins (both of whom would become future Commanders of the Air Force). This order, together with the detailed account[3] of the first ferry as it unfolded, by Lieutenant David Barbour, has provided us with all the necessary detail of what was expected to happen and what actually happened. There is another account, from Lieutenant (later Group Captain) John Moss, of the 'Spit Epic'. David Barbour's officially tasked diary was supplemented by a personal account of his time in the auxiliaries, which has proved very useful in getting a feel for Air Force life in the early 1950s.

The Operations Order (Op Order) confirmed the ferry pilots as: Lieutenant Colonel Ted Jacklin, the overall leader of the ferry; Captain Jock Barber, Lieutenants Ben Bellingan, Dickie Bradshaw, Basil Hone, Jack Malloch, and Ossie Penton; and WO1 Bob Blair, Johnny Deall, Charles Paxton and Mike Schuman. Lieutenants Dave Barbour and John Moss, the second pilot on the accompanying Dakota, and WO1 John Hough, were relief pilots.

This was an excellent mix of experience and young blood. WO1 Johnny Deall[4] was the deputy ferry leader. Together with Jock Barber, Jack Malloch and Mike Schuman they all brought with them plenty of experience on high performance aircraft from the war. As Officer Commanding 266 Sqn, Johnny Deall had been one of the RAF's youngest wing commanders and earned himself a chestfull of decorations, including an RAF DSO and DFC and an NFC. Jock Barber had also earned himself a DFC flying PR Mosquitos. Jack Malloch had flown Spitfires on 237 Sqn and Mike Schuman had come from the SAAF with Spitfire experience. During the war he had also served on Martin Marauders (the 'widow maker'), a notoriously difficult aircraft to fly. Dave Barbour was a young inexperienced auxiliary; Bob Blair and Basil Hone lacked experience on high performance fighters, but most of the rest had plenty of flying experience although not on the Spitfire. Dickie Bradshaw, for example, had been instructing with the RATG during the war and had 1,700 flying hours.[5]

These men were the best of the resources the SRAF had, at this stage, for what would be a very challenging undertaking. They had spent the earlier part of January bringing their instrument flying and formation skills up to date on the Harvard to ensure they could handle bad weather along the route and maintain formation integrity.

On 22 January the ferry team left for the UK aboard Dakota SR25 flown by Harold Hawkins and John Moss, backed up by a radio operator, navigator and technician. In addition to the pilots there were five Spitfire technicians under the command of Captain Mick Gibbons. The Dakota flew the proposed ferry route in reverse, which had the benefit of familiarising the ferry team with all the airfields along the route. They arrived at RAF Brize Norton, about 15 miles west of Oxford, on 31 January. This would be their temporary home until 12 March. At the time Brize Norton was also a USAF base, where the Officers Mess provided a great social environment for the ferry pilots. Today, Brize Norton is the RAF's main base for its transport fleet.

Brize Norton was also home to No. 6 MU, where the SRAF Spitfires had been stored and had now been prepared for service. The next three weeks were dedicated to a ground school course presented by the RAF and Rolls-Royce. The ground school was followed by an allocation of six training sorties per pilot on the Spitfire. These sorties included general handling, circuits and landings and some range and endurance flying in preparation for the ferry. In practice most pilots probably flew more than the allocated sorties. Dickie Bradshaw's logbook shows that he flew ten sorties totalling 7:20 hours before leaving for RAF Chivenor on the north-west coast of Devonshire. He had not flown Spitfires before and no doubt would have welcomed the extra sorties. However, even experienced pilots such as Johnny Deall and Jack Malloch would have had to become accustomed to the differences in handling. The propellers of the Griffon-powered Mk 22s rotated in the opposite direction (counter-clockwise as viewed from the cockpit) to the propellers of the Merlin-powered Spitfires. This characteristic caused the nose to swing right on take-off, as opposed to the left. The 2,035 horse power Griffon produced 400 horse power more than the Merlin-powered Spitfires which the older hands had flown. The Mk 22 was a handful on the ground, requiring full left rudder with trim to counter the torque, as well as judicious use of the throttle to get airborne. Jack Malloch ended up flying eight sorties totalling 7:10 hours in preparation for the ferry.

There were a couple of runway excursions amongst the 'early runners' as Dave Barbour calls them; the *fundis* (teachers) who had not anticipated the effect of the huge amount of torque when opening up the throttle more quickly than was necessary. However, it was testimony to their skill and experience that no serious incidents occurred, in spite of the big increment in performance for young bloods like Barbour, and the challenge of the English weather. Dave Barbour's personal records relate how, after take-off on a murky day, the Spitfire's 4,000 feet/min rate of climb meant that he quickly penetrated the low cloud base. He needed plenty of concentration to keep his wits about him and keep control of the aircraft.

Op Order 2/51 confirmed 12 March as the departure date from RAF Chivenor, the official starting point of the ferry. It also stipulated that Dakota SR25 would accompany the Spitfires to provide technical and personnel support. The ferry route was planned to take an ambitious seven days, starting on 14 March and ending on 20 March, with a day off on 17 March for maintenance and a rest. The route (see the map of the Spitfire ferry routes in March and December 1951) was planned through France to Istres, just north-west of Marseilles, on the first day. Istres was a French Armée de l'Air base that had an RAF presence. On the second day they were to fly from Istres to Tunis (El Aouim), and on to RAF Castel Benito (present day Tripoli International Airport). From Castel Benito they were to fly to RAF El Adem just south of Tobruk in eastern Libya, and then RAF Fayid just west of the Great Bitter Lake, east of Cairo, on the third day. After a rest on the fourth day, the route would take the Spitfires to Wadi Halfa in northern Sudan, and then to Khartoum on the fifth day. Plans for the sixth day were to take the aircraft from Khartoum to Juba in southern Sudan (today the new capital of independent South Sudan) and then on to Tabora in then north-western Tanganyika. On the last day the route was from Tabora to Ndola in Northern Rhodesia en route to Cranborne in Salisbury. The longest planned legs were the 668 nm from Chivenor to Istres and the 636 nm from Khartoum to Juba. The latter was the most critical leg, as the only en route alternate was Malakal, an undesirable choice due to unreliable fuel supplies. The French Armée de l'Air base at Dijon would be the en route alternate for Istres.

The planned cruising speed was 200 knots at +2 psi boost[6] and 2,000–2,200 RPM at 10,000 feet above mean sea level. The Spitfires all had a 90 gallon LRT fitted under the belly, giving a total fuel capacity of 210 gallons. In this configuration and at a weight of about 9,100 pounds, the Spitfire would consume about one gallon a minute and thus land with around 20 gallons on completion of the longer three hour legs.

Navigation would be primarily by map reading off prepared strip maps. This required visual conditions and good weather along the way. Each pilot had his own set of maps. Even though the formation leader was responsible for the formation, this did not preclude a formation member from correcting his formation leader, something which certainly happened. There was also a 'fixer' service available over France which, according to Dave Barbour, could be used to assist navigation on the first leg. If the formation encountered cloud, pilots would use time and heading for navigation. The Op Order allocated PK350 to Dickie Bradshaw (later Air Commodore, OLM) and PK355 to Jack Malloch. There would be three formations of four, four and three aircraft called 'Bundu' Red, Yellow and Blue sections respectively. Lieutenant Colonel Jacklin would lead Red Section with Mike Schuman as his No. 2; Jock Barber would lead Yellow section with Charles Paxton as his No. 2; and Johnny Deall would lead Blue Section with Jack Malloch as his No 2. Dickie Bradshaw was designated to be Red Four. It was planned that numbers three and four in each formation would be rotated between the relief pilots, Dave Barbour, John Hough and John Moss.

The accompanying Dakota SR25, would be operated by the same crew that had flown her northbound. She became known affectionately as 'Mother Hen' and carried the six Spitfire technicians, the two relief pilots, a returning Army officer and 3,000 pounds of freight.

There were ten Special Orders in Appendix 'D' of the Op Order. Like any set of military instructions, these directives were born from long, hard experience. Essentially, they reminded the pilots of their numerous tasks and responsibilities, emphasising that the success of the ferry required the pilots to regard each flight as a test flight, requiring close monitoring of their Spitfire's performance, especially engine performance and fuel and oil consumption. Fuel consumption would require special attention in the build-up to the Khartoum–Juba leg and the Op Order laid down a maximum 'cloud cover of 3/8ths or better' (i.e. scattered cloud in modern terminology) along the route to dispatch the aircraft, and that there would be 'no night flying'.

Dave Barbour tells us that by 12 March most of the ferry party were more than ready to go home, with the exception of some of the younger members who were having the time of their lives. The weather that day was cloudy and wintry but the ferry party, dressed in their "gloriously white silk flying overalls", received a warm send-off from Brize Norton for the positioning leg to Chivenor. The formation was led by Mike Schuman in the absence of Lieutenant Colonel Jacklin who, with Mick Gibbons, was busy with last minute arrangements at Rhodesia House in London. The routing went smoothly after a flypast at Brize Norton and tests on the LRTs, but the landings were, according to Dave Barbour, "arrivals". A couple of the pilots had minor excursions from the runway, with one aircraft getting stuck in the mud, luckily with no damage. These incidents were attributed to low experience levels and fortunately were not repeated.

The remainder of that day and all of the next day (13 March) were, in David Barbour's words, dedicated "to diverse activities and… pretty hectic". The ammunition bays in the Spitfires were packed with "gear, emergency rations and spare starter cartridges"[7]; the pilots learned how to open and close cowlings with the use of a screwdriver (Jack Malloch proved very adept at this); strip maps for the whole route were acquired from the Chivenor navigation section which had done an "exceptionally fine" job for the ferry pilots, and had also presented an excellent brief; the pilots were fitted with their safety equipment including Mae Wests, a dinghy and survival equipment transforming them into "veritable giants"; and finally the Dakota was packed and customs cleared.

Bearing in mind the misgivings voiced by both the RAF and Rolls-Royce, about the wisdom of a ferry being undertaken by the SRAF over such a long distance, the Rhodesians departed on Wednesday 14 March 1951 fully aware of the challenge that lay ahead. The Spitfires had all been flying for the past two weeks while the pilots did their conversions, but they had nevertheless been in storage for a few years. It was likely that some of the aircraft would experience technical issues reflecting that inactivity, in spite of the diligent checks carried out by 6 MU—and this indeed proved to be the case.

According to the chronology of the Op Order, the first half of the ferry to RAF Fayid in Egypt went largely according to plan, with a planned break in the ferry on 17 March. However, there had been numerous challenges: the weather played its part on day one and two, but would not seriously challenge the ferry for the rest of the route thereafter; all but two of the Spitfires, Mike Schuman and Ossie Penton in Red Section, had to divert into Dijon before continuing to Istres, mainly due to concerns about insufficient fuel to get to Istres; and it was in Istres that Harold Hawkins started his marathon-long briefings which became a feature of the ferry.

The climb-out over the Mediterranean toward Corsica and Sardinia on the way to Tunis was affected by the weather, which exposed a rough running engine on Jack Malloch's PK355 and radio problems on other aircraft. Mick Gibbons ordered all the fuel filters to be checked in Tunis after PK355's filter showed a lot of dirt, which no doubt had caused the rough running. The intense heat in Tunis caused numerous pilots to struggle with 'hot starts' when using the Coffmann cartridges. This was simply a lack of experience and would dog the ferry during its passage along the North African stops. It caused two aircraft to perform night landings at Castel Benito on day two, where the ground crew attended to snags into the early morning hours.

On day three, after a delayed departure from Castel Benito, hot starts in El Adem caused Blue Section to overnight there and proceed to Fayid the next day, whilst Red and Yellow sections had to carry out night landings at Fayid. Dickie Bradshaw was relieved from Spitfire duties on these legs and according to his log book flew these two legs as co-pilot on the Dakota. This meant that PK350 was probably flown by Bob Blair, as John Moss makes no mention of flying PK350 on these legs in his own account. Dave Barbour makes no mention of this change either, but makes much of the hot starts at El Adem, calling them 'The Duck Shooting Expedition'! Everyone bar John Moss, now flying Ted Jacklin's aircraft according to Dave Barbour, contributed to the pile of empty cartridges left behind at El Adem.

A rest day for most of the pilots on 17 March allowed the technicians to get on top of numerous snags, including a supercharger problem, plug changes, radio and electrical problems. Whilst in Fayid Jack Malloch, who had got a handle on the 'hot starting' technique, gave a briefing to his fellow pilots which would prove very useful in minimising future problems. He had constantly displayed a willingness to get stuck in and assist the technicians during turnarounds. He had also experienced a near mishap when he taxied out at Castel Benito with his pitot tube[8] cover on, showing how easy it was to become complacent when flying the same aircraft all the time.

The second half of the ferry started very well on 18 March, with a trouble-free fifth day between Fayid and Wadi Halfa and then on to Khartoum. The turnaround at Wadi Halfa would be the best of the whole ferry. This was also the last opportunity to check on fuel consumption with the LRTs. Jock Barber's PK408 and Dickie Bradshaw's PK350 had both displayed poor endurance figures on their LRTs, but this was eventually put down to 'inter-feeding'[9] as refuelling indicated that these aircraft did not receive more fuel than the others.

The leg from Khartoum to Juba on the sixth day went smoothly and the entire ferry felt that an important milestone had been passed. However, on departure from Juba, Ossie Penton's PK576 lost all its coolant, necessitating a rapid turn back. He displayed great skill and airmanship in his efforts to safely recover PK576 and received due recognition from Ted Jacklin the next day. This necessitated Blue section remaining behind with the Dakota whilst Red and Yellow sections continued on to Entebbe, in Uganda. It had been a good decision to appoint Johnny Deall leader of the Blue section and deputy ferry leader. Being the most experienced, operationally and as a formation leader, he could be trusted to bring up the rear, as he did out of El Adem and then again in Juba.

Investigation by Mick Gibbons into the loss of coolant from PK576 exposed a perished coolant hose, necessitating a check on all of Blue section's aircraft. It was decided to stay the night in Juba and join up with the rest of the Spitfires at Entebbe the next day. In Uganda all the aircraft were checked for perished hoses and more maintenance was carried out on the aircraft. Ossie Penton would now be a passenger on the Dakota, leaving PK576 in Juba to be recovered later, in April. Also, PK350 received attention for an oil pressure problem, which was followed by a quick 30 minute flight test by Dickie Bradshaw, before the ferry could continue once again. All this meant the ferry would take an extra two days and the schedule was altered to accommodate this major delay.

On day eight the route took the aircraft from Entebbe to Tabora and onward to Ndola. There was a stuttering start to the day when John Moss, probably in PK330 (Mike Schuman's aircraft), had to make a quick return into Entebbe due to high temperatures—the same problem experienced by Ossie Penton at Juba. Fortunately, this time the gauge proved faulty. The pilots could now enjoy what Dave Barbour described as a "wizard morning" for flying. The shorter leg between Entebbe and Tabora meant the aircraft flew at +6 psi boost for a faster cruise. The crews revelled in the conditions they encountered flying along the western edge of the majestic Lake Victoria. They were given a very warm reception at Tabora, which no doubt gave the pilots a huge lift before proceeding to Ndola that afternoon. Navigation was a challenge along this lengthy and featureless leg. That problem, together with the thunderstorms en route, and a narrow runway bounded by long grass at Ndola, meant that the pilots had to maintain their concentration all the way to the landing. Dave Barbour mentions that there were a couple of "baulked approaches" which led to those pilots going around for a second attempt at landing.

Ndola saw the crews cleaning their aircraft with "curses and groans" in preparation for the final leg to Cranborne Airport in Salisbury. Despite growing excitement about nearing home signs of tiredness were evident, but everyone was determined to put on a good show during the arrival on 22 March. Red section included four aircraft led by Ted Jacklin with Mike Schuman, Dickie Bradshaw in PK350 and Ben Bellingan; Yellow included three aircraft led by Jock Barber, with Charles Paxton and Dave Barbour. Blue section led by Johnny Deall included Jack Malloch and Basil Hone.

Having flown at +6 psi boost and at 1,500 to 2,000 feet above ground level, the ferry formation orbited the Inkomo range to the north-west of Salisbury, and formed up in section 'vees' for a close formation flypast over Cranborne. The formation then broke up into sections for an orderly landing sequence. Dave Barbour noted that the pilots were determined not "to prang one of the PM's kites right before his eyes on the first showing". Cranborne's runway was short and clearly a challenge for the pilots. Fortunately no-one let the side down and all ten aircraft were on the ground by 10:10 on 22 March. The Prime Minister, Sir Godfrey Huggins, was quick to recognise and praise the ferry team. An article in the *Rhodesia Herald* of 23 March 1951 called it a flight that confounded the experts and quoted the words of Sir Godfrey Huggins: "I must thank you for putting up such a fine show. The RAF said you would be lucky if you managed to bring six Spitfires to Salisbury and that if you brought eight here it would be a miracle." Huggins also stated that the auxiliary pilots "were particularly deserving of praise".

For all the doom and gloom forecast by the RAF and Rolls-Royce, the first ferry proved to be a very successful undertaking. On 5 April, following an engine change, PK576 was recovered by Johnny Deall, back to Cranborne. The spare engine came from the RAF in the Canal Zone, according to John Moss. It was only then, after this successful recovery, that Rolls-Royce congratulated the Rhodesians on their achievement, lauding the ferry as a "magnificent flight" and starting a tradition of showing an intense interest in aviation happenings in faraway Rhodesia.

Dickie Bradshaw flew PK350 for all but two legs, logging 23:25 hours. Apart from the oil pressure problem at Entebbe which required a 30 minute air test, and the false alarm on her fuel consumption, PK350 performed well and flew at least 28 hours on the ferry.

THE SECOND SPITFIRE FERRY: 7 DECEMBER TO 19 DECEMBER 1951

Reviewing the limited contemporary records, it is clear that the second Spitfire ferry has not been as well remembered as the first, yet it was no less audacious an undertaking. It is possible that it was seen as a less successful undertaking because two aircraft were lost on this ferry (one fatally). However, it was still a substantial achievement and warrants inclusion in this story. Fortunately, we have a very lively and readable account to follow, that of John Campbell. He was an auxiliary and a pilot on the second ferry, who had trained in the RAF and had a fair amount of experience on single seat fighters, including most of the well-known Merlin-powered Spitfires and Mustang IIIs. Written much later, during the 1990s, his account appears below, virtually in its entirety and gives us some insight into events as they unfolded.

From John Campbell's account we know that Lieutenant Colonel Ted Cunnison DFC and AFC, ex-RAF, led the ferry and the rest of the pilots included Bob Blair, Owen Love, Alan O'Hara, Peter Pascoe, Charles Paxton, Ossie Penton, Dave

Richards, Bill Smith, and Ray Wood. There were some familiar names from the first ferry (Blair, Paxton and Penton) and again a strong contingent of six auxiliaries—but no relief pilots as on the first ferry. Harold Hawkins was in charge of the overall operation and was assisted by Bill Dawson, flying the Dakota.

The aircraft numbers were PK326, 344, 370, 401, 432, 482, 494, 548, 572, 594, and 649. As to who flew which aircraft, we know only that Ted Cunnison flew PK401, John Campbell PK649, Owen Love PK344, and Dave Richards PK482. The route would have been largely the same as that on the first ferry, an exception being that this ferry would start from RAF Abingdon in Oxfordshire, and end at Belvedere Airport[10] in Salisbury, having flown in from Lusaka in Northern Rhodesia. The second ferry also stopped for refuelling more frequently, with stops at Malakal in Sudan and Kasama (between Tabora and Lusaka) in Northern Rhodesia. (See colour map.)

John Campbell, who is still alive at the time of writing, picks up the story from when they left Southern Rhodesia in the Dakota:

> Let's begin at the beginning; with the help of my dog-eared log book, I can say we all piled into the Dakota at Belvedere Airport on 9 November. Harold Hawkins and Bill Dawson flew us to RAF Abingdon in five days. I can't remember much about the journey except it was hilarious on occasions and the weather around Lake Victoria was awful.
>
> We travelled the route by which we would return, which made a lot of sense, and this was Kasama (Northern Rhodesia), Kisimu (Kenya), Juba, Khartoum, Wadi Halfa, Fayid, El Adem, Castle Benito, Tunis, Istres, and into Abingdon.
>
> Over two weeks were spent at Cosford testing the Spitfires, which had just been taken from war surplus cocoons.
>
> During this time we went to Hatfield and elsewhere to fly in Vampires and Meteors because the SRAF wanted our opinions for the jet age ahead. Thanks to an old friend of mine, Bill Pegg, Chief Test Pilot for Bristol, I took some of the lads to Filton to see the Bristol Brabazon, which was doing taxi trials. Overtaken by the jet age she never flew commercially.
>
> On 4 December, the Spitfires were declared ready and we flew them to Abingdon, and on 7 December we were off on the long road home. Our first stop at Dijon was a sombre one having lost Owen Love.[11] (Owen Love, who had only recently been trained on the Spitfire, became separated from the formation in the climb over France, lost control and crashed fatally near Paris.)

Onto Istres, which accommodated a French Air Rescue Squadron; a comforting thought for us about to fly over the Mediterranean.

There was a pub on the edge of the airfield vibrating with a wild party which (of course) some of us joined. The barmaids behind the bar kept wriggling and spilling drinks and my inquiring mind made me leap upon the counter and peer behind. A French aviator was on his back having the time of his life!

Ted Cunnison was with me, also Bob Blair who we left propped up outside. We found our way to our billet with difficulty!

Next day Ted and I had starter problems and were left behind. I think the defect must have been invented because neither of us was in any condition to traverse the Mediterranean until later that morning.

From Tunis we flew eastwards to Castle Benito, which meant more sea, over the Gulf of Sirte. Since the start at Cosford my engine in PK649 ran 'rough', but the engineers had found no fault. It was well known that the mighty Griffon engine ran rough by comparison with the earlier, silky Rolls-Royce Merlin motors. It is also well known among pilots flying single engine aircraft over water, that the engines run rough. During the war mine always did over the North Sea and the Channel.

So in consideration of PK649's difficulties, we skirted Sirte so I could have reached the coast if the engine stopped.

We continued eastwards that day from Castle Benito to El Adem, which is a longish run. I should explain that a longish run is two and half hours, say 600 miles, only made possible by the 90 gallon long-range tank slung underneath.

Next day, 10 December, it was onto the RAF station at Fayid where we stayed two days for servicing. During this flight we carried side arms because the Egyptians were being beastly. In fact they yelled obscenities at us over the radio. I can't remember what the trouble was, but it added zest to the occasion.

Something was done to PK649's prop at Fayid, but it did not make life less rough. After Fayid it was south all the way; first, to Wadi Halfa, and then Khartoum. I can't remember who was leading my section, but he missed Wadi Halfa; Campbell, ever eager to get PK649 on terra firma, knew exactly where he was and led the section down.

We spent two nights at Khartoum, mostly it seems in the GB nightclub. Why do I remember this? Oh yes, the dancing girls employed, incongruously, came from Bournemouth and I was tempted to have more starter trouble.

Khartoum was so gracious and cool at that time of the year under the moon and the British Raj, with the great Nile sliding by. It was especially interesting for me because since then I have been there many times on business, and I still go. In fact, by a remarkable coincidence, I am in Khartoum as I write this draft. It is a sad city these days in a country at war with itself.

Next day it was onwards to Malakal, very primitive; and then Juba where we stayed at the (only) Juba Hotel. A great place then in a wild west way, but not so these days. I've been there. It is a town usually under siege.

Juba to Entebbe and this was not nice. The Inter Tropical Convergence Zone (ITCZ) was well developed and we had no radio contact with Entebbe, so we had to let down through the cloud until we could see the waters of Lake Victoria, too close they were, and then fly back to the coast and Entebbe.

Dave Richards hit a bank on landing and wrote off his Spitfire; he was lucky. *And then we were nine.*

Next it was Tabora, and to please Campbell, we flew near the west coast of Lake Victoria keeping an eye on Bukota.

On 18 December we flew onto Kasama and then Lusaka, most of the way between fat, wet cumulus and cumulonimbus storms.

At Lusaka we night-stopped and had a final alcoholic spree. I can remember being very lost and groping my way back to the pub at dawn.

Before you cluck disapproval, remember for us auxiliaries (and indeed the regulars) this had been a great holiday away, like naughty boys, from business and home life.

And, so on the fine morning of 19 December, we landed at Belvedere to be met by the Prime Minister Sir Godfrey Huggins, Keith Taute, Officer Commanding Cranborne, General Garlake and others. It was quite an occasion. I had arrived without my cap, which was embarrassing. I thought I lost it at the GB nightclub. Months later it was found oil covered, at the back end of PK649. I still have it and it fits, but the uniform doesn't!

And, the engineers did find that 649's prop was faulty!

No mention is made of the fact that on landing Ted Cunnison couldn't extend his tail wheel. The *Rhodesia Herald* newspaper documented the latter incident and included a photo of PK401 being lifted by a crane at the tail. A certain young Officer Cadet (later Air Commodore OLM) Keith Kemsley participated in this recovery.

This ferry was unfortunately dogged with bad luck. Both accidents were weather related and the fact that the Spitfire was not an easy aircraft to fly on instruments would not have helped the inexperienced Owen Love when he became separated from his formation. As has been demonstrated so often with the restored war bird accidents in the modern day, these high performance aircraft are as unforgiving now as they were in their heyday. It is also easy to overlook the fact that accidents and loss of life were common events during the war. Even in the above account it is very apparent that after the sad loss of Owen Love (the first SRAF fatal accident since WW2), the ferry continued on its journey the next day without a pause—life carried on. This was a reaction more in line with war time conditions than peace time, but no doubt with its origins in the recent war time experience.

With 20 Spitfires now on its charge, the SRAF was well positioned to carry out its Commonwealth defence commitment whilst training a new generation of pilots.

SERVICE IN THE SRAF/RRAF

One of the best written records we have of the service life of the SRAF Spitfires is David Barbour's *Personal Recollections* of his time as an SRAAF auxiliary pilot, supplemented by shorter but very useful accounts from a number of ex-Spitfire pilots. In addition to John Campbell's report there are also chronicles from Hardwicke Holderness, Charles Baillie, Alan O'Hara, Basil Hone and Dennis Bagnall. These written records, as well as recollections from some of the surviving pilots from that time, such as Air Vice-Marshal Chris Dams and Air Commodore Keith Kemsley, give us a good impression of how life was then on No. 1 SRAAF Squadron. The personal flying logbooks and the technical log—the F700—of PK355/SR65 (the sole surviving SRAF Spitfire), provide details of what flying was carried out and most usefully, the flying hours of the Spitfires can be determined.

Before delving into the detail of service life and in particular that of PK350, it may be wise briefly to review again the geo-politics of the time, and how these determined the structures and roles of the SRAF, and in particular No.1 Squadron.

Southern Rhodesia would remain a self-governing colony until 1 August 1953, when Southern Rhodesia, together with the protectorates of Northern Rhodesia and Nyasaland, formed the Federation of Rhodesia and Nyasaland, also known as the Central African Federation (CAF). Over a year later, on 15 October 1954, the SRAF became the Royal Rhodesian Air Force (RRAF).

This meant that, at last, the RRAF assumed a proper 'air force' identity in line with its bigger cousins in the Commonwealth—the Royal Canadian Air Force (RCAF) and the Royal Australian Air Force (RAAF). This was a most welcome event and, in accordance with tradition, serving members exchanged their khaki uniforms for air force slate blue uniforms and assumed the familiar RAF rank structure.

The creation of the Federation did not change the Commonwealth Defence Role and NATO commitment, in particular that of No. 1 Squadron SRAAF and a second squadron, when this became a reality. However, change came in the extent of regional support for law enforcement agencies and local government, this being required now for a much larger area. Sadly for the auxiliaries they were dispensed with in August 1953. This happened just as the SRAF was preparing to receive Vampires as part of her Commonwealth and NATO defence role. In keeping with these commitments, the Vampires, and later the Canberras, participated very successfully in exercises with the RAF out of Aden (in Yemen) and Akrotiri (on Crete).

While the Spitfires were never used in anger, in spite of their Commonwealth and NATO defence role, they were placed on standby for Korea in October 1951. As Dave Barbour understood things then:

> the structure of No. 1 Squadron was supported by regular ground crew, all the pilots were volunteers (initially fourteen strong)—all were qualified pilots mainly from the war time SRAF and RAF—senior pilots i.e. the CO, Deputy CO, Flight Commanders and say two or three others were fully operationally experienced; the balance were younger pilots such as myself with little or no operational experience—this gave the squadron an Immediate Operational Ability and also the know-how to pass on to the younger element. As I understand it, when we had grown to the NATO requirement of two squadrons, the senior personnel would retire in rotation as the juniors should be in a position to take over.
>
> Behind this, from almost the beginning, the regular SRAF undertook to train Auxiliary Volunteer Cadets from *ab initio* to wings so that they could provide the trainees and continue feeding the squadrons.

In addition to the NATO defence role played by 1 Sqn, it was also responsible for carrying out the operational training of graduates from the pilot courses on a high performance fighter with a strong emphasis on ground attack skills. The Harvard was used in conjunction with the Spitfire to carry out this role. Seated in the rear seat to simulate the longer nose of the Spitfire, the students would receive dual control and practise various skills on the Harvard: these included limit flying and aerobatics; battle formation; tail chases; quarter attacks and use of the gun-sight with cine film; gunnery and dive bombing. Once "buttoned up", to use Dave Barbour's words, these skills would be practised on the Spitfire. This was to save engine hours due to the surprisingly short engine life between engine overhauls. Rocketry was introduced only in July 1953, after the Spitfire had been fitted with a new gyro gun-sight, the "Wonder Sight" as Dave Barbour called it. The Inkomo Range, located about 25 miles north-west of Salisbury on the western side of the Salisbury/Kariba road, was utilised for weapons training.

Thus it was that No. 1 Squadron ended up training graduates from the two Auxiliary Courses—Corporal Mick McLaren, later Air Marshal OLM and Commander of the Rhodesian Air Force, was a member of the second Auxiliary Course—as well as the first three Short Service Unit (SSU) courses. Altogether 39 pilots were trained on the Auxiliary and SSU courses. Their names can be seen in Appendix C, which lists the names of most if not all 70 SRAAF/SRAF pilots who flew Spitfires. In addition, proficient auxiliaries with previous Spitfire experience were converted onto the Mk 22 in the months between the two ferries. According to Dave Barbour, in August 1953 when the auxiliaries and their services were withdrawn, 24 pilots had achieved operational status—enough to man two Spitfire squadrons and to start flying the Vampires. This was a substantial achievement: the skills and experience of the ex-WW2 pilots had been well and truly harnessed and utilised. However, it is worth noting that despite there being enough pilots to form a second Spitfire squadron, this never happened.

As would be expected, the Spitfires participated in numerous displays and fly-pasts to mark significant achievements and honour important ceremonial events. These included a synchronised display by Jack Malloch and Dave Barbour in anticipation of the intended closure of the RATG[12] at Thornhill in May 1951; the SRAF's first public display in front of 20,000 spectators on 7 June 1951 at Cranborne, on the occasion of the King's Birthday; followed by minor air displays at Karoi and Gatooma; another display at Cranborne on 1 December 1952; the first major air display at New Sarum on 13 and 14 June 1953, on the occasion of the Rhodes Centenary celebrations; flypasts on the occasion of Queen Elizabeth's accession to the throne in 1952; the annual Battle of Britain Commemorations; and wings parades for the pilots courses. It was on the occasion of the wings parade for No. 2 SSU, on 27 February 1952, that then Lieutenant Keith Kemsley flew SR64. In the six-aircraft formation flypast she was the first aircraft in the line astern position.

The air rally at New Sarum on 13 and 14 June 1953 was marred by a tragic mid-air collision between the Harvards from the RATG at Thornhill. However, as at the previous displays at Cranborne, the Spitfires produced some excellent displays. In particular Charles Paxton's low level aerobatics left the crowd breathless whilst the weapons demonstrations showed that the young guns had learned their skills well, with one of them managing to out-perform his older more experienced tutors and colleagues, notably John Mussell.

The regular Command element of the squadron, backed up by a very experienced core of ex-RAF pilots, the auxiliaries, and regular ground crew directed and supported all these efforts, supervising the gradual change from a reliance on auxiliaries to a fully-fledged air force made up of regular personnel. Major Hardwicke Holderness DSO, DFC and AFC, was the first Officer Commanding, backed up by Johnny Deall as a Flight Commander in charge of the Operational Conversion Unit (OCU) courses. Deall was by now a Captain and was held in very high regard. When Holderness retired in April 1952 he was replaced by Captain Bill (Charles) Baillie, another ex-RAF Typhoon pilot.

The auxiliaries made an invaluable contribution to No. 1 Squadron SRAAF. They flew over weekends and would meet on Friday evenings, before the weekend's flying, for briefings and talks to keep up with the latest happenings, including the Korean War. Of course there were the mess parties which were social highlights on their calendars. Alan O'Hara managed to accumulate 122 hours from 115 sorties on the Spitfire between June 1951 and August 1953; and his Harvard flying amounted to 67 hours from 76 sorties. This confirms how active the auxiliaries were during this time. Their disbanding in August 1953 upset them deeply. Some could not understand how their contribution, made without any financial recompense, was so summarily discarded, or why their involvement could not be extended to the Vampire, as was the case with the RAF's Royal Auxiliary Air Force (RAuxAF). According to Charles Baillie, the truth was that the SRAF could not afford them—it was a financial decision. Even the army's territorial units were dispensed with, and not all the graduates from the pilot courses were offered regular commissions in the SRAF once they had completed their OCUs on the Spitfire. For example, only three members from No. 3 SSU were offered permanent commissions, namely Chris Dams, Chris Hudson and Mike Saunders.

As for the ground crew, little is recorded of the unsung heroes who maintained the Spitfires. However, from the Ferry Op Order and Dave Barbour's records we have some of their names. The officer in charge of the ground crew was Captain Mick Gibbons. He was backed up by Sergeant Majors Frank Burton, Cyril Jones, Titch Nesbitt, and Pat Patrick, and Colour Sergeant Charlie Goodwin,[13] the men who maintained the aircraft on the ferry. Photos to hand from the squadron days show these other names: Dixie Dean, 'Taff' Evans, Jimmy Pringle (later Air Commodore), Bill Savage, Gus Simmons and Dave Whittingham.[14] Spike Owens was part of this team and features prominently in some of the photos we have today. Sadly, because these men were generally older than the pilots who flew the Spitfires, it has been particularly difficult to source their accounts and memories—many of them are no longer with us. Fortunately, Air Commodore Keith Kemsley, a member of No. 1 SSU and later Director General Support Services (DGSS) when PK350 was rebuilt, has provided this brief recollection:

> We had very few techs in those days and they all worked on all the aircraft types so there were very few dedicated especially to the Spitfires. The instrument fitters, radio fitters etc. all worked on all the aircraft. I don't recall the hangars being numbered—there was the Spitfire hangar or the Harvard hangar and so on. The Spitfires were in the hangar nearest the Control Tower at New Sarum; others were in the Aircraft Repair Section (ARS) hangar or the Engine Repair Section (ERS) hangar, etc. It was a very informal Air Force and all very friendly with everyone pitching in to help when there was a problem. For example when one of our chaps in the early days put an aircraft on its nose our course pitched in and stripped the fabric, helped straighten the bends and help replace the fabric. Good experience.

The Spitfires were initially based at Cranborne, close to Salisbury's city centre, but also used Belvedere. On 1 April 1952, the SRAF officially moved to the new Salisbury International Airport on the southern side of the city, having already had a presence there since October 1951. The airport had been built on a farm called Kentucky and so it was initially referred to as Kentucky. The SRAF Headquarters (HQ) moved there in October 1952, and the SRAF base became known as New Sarum—Sarum is the old Roman name for Salisbury in England. This was a modern Air Force base that was "too big and impersonal" in the view of Dave Barbour. This was not surprising, given that Cranborne had offered more of a flying club atmosphere. It was at New Sarum that the Spitfires would remain until they were withdrawn from service in December 1954.

All the ferry aircraft arrived in the standard RAF day fighter 'high speed' aluminium finish, with black anti-dazzle panels just forward of the windshield, with standard RAF flashes and numbers. The first ferry aircraft were quite quickly renumbered, starting with SR58 and ending with SR68—perhaps in an attempt to discourage the ferry pilots from 'claiming' their ferry aircraft. The original RAF number had been PK and the new SR was simply painted over the PK, and the new number was added.

Consequently, PK350 became SR64 and PK355 became SR65. The second group of ferry aircraft was renumbered SR80 to SR88, but not immediately. PK326 became SR80 and was still wearing her original RAF colours and number in September 1952 when she had a wheels-up landing at New Sarum, with Brian Horney of No. 1 SSU at the controls. It is noteworthy that, apart from only eight of the Spitfires, the records indicating which RAF tailfin number became which SRAF tailfin number no longer exist. Appendix D lists the relevant details for what we do know of each individual airframe and their SRAF numbers.

In all likelihood the aircraft would have been repainted over time using a gloss paint of high altitude blue colour[15] with similarly-coloured propeller spinners, which weathered in the harsh African sun. Apart from the substitution of SR for PK on the aircraft numbers, the SRAF markings were identical to the RAF markings, but with the addition of the green and yellow bars on either side of the fuselage roundels, denoting the national colours of Southern Rhodesia.

In mid-1953 the propeller spinners were repainted red to assist with gun camera assessments. This followed the input of two RAF weapons instructors, Dickie Dickenson and Sandy Mutch (later Air Commodore and DGSS), who had arrived with the latest techniques and training methods to assist with training in the OCU. Following the Air Force's change of name to the RRAF in October 1954, the green and yellow bars were removed and three assegais were painted over the red of the roundels, representing the three constituent countries of the Federation of Rhodesia and Nyasaland. Finally, at the instigation of Keith Kemsley, all the aircraft eventually had a 'Winged Assegai' painted on the port side of the cockpit. This was inspired by 266 Sqn's motto 'Stabbers of the Sky'.

All the colour schemes—and specifically those of SR64—can be seen in the section of colour photographs.

The quantum jump in performance of the Spitfire over the Harvard presented the pilots with plenty of opportunities to revel in the experience, especially taking only 20–25 minutes to climb to the aircraft's ceiling of just on 43,000 feet. Alan O'Hara, one of the auxiliaries, recorded that he took only 13 minutes to climb to 37,000 feet— effectively this was a climb of 32,000 feet, Salisbury being about 5,000 feet above sea level. Accounts from some of the surviving SRAAF and SRAF pilots (these appear later, in Chapter 10) clearly demonstrate the exhilaration felt by pilots. However, with its narrow undercarriage and heavy nose, the Spitfire had to be handled carefully on the ground. Two wheels-up landings occurred, as well as two 'nose-overs', but these were due to mechanical failures. It was fortunate that the aircraft were fitted with wooden propellers which helped minimise the damage during these events.

John Mussell's spectacular wheels-up landing was well recorded, as was the aftermath of Brian Horney's wheels-up, and the nose-over incident by Arthur Hodgson from No. 1 SSU.

There were two other major incidents. The first was in December 1953 when Lieutenant Ray Maritz from No. 2 SSU lost his life in a tragic accident during an eight-ship formation training sortie. The other occurred on 14 June 1954 when Lieutenant Chris Dams from No. 3 SSU, who later became an Air Vice-Marshal, experienced a severe vibration which led to the eventual scrapping of SR88. This event is described by Air Vice-Marshal Dams in Chapter 10.

According to one source, SR64 herself was possibly the early casualty of a malfunction when she landed wheels-up at Cranborne on 1 June 1951. The repairs cost £1,226 5s 6d. However, Air Commodore Keith Kemsley does not recall any wheels-up landings other than the two mentioned above. Nevertheless, SR64 must have given good service because in the end she was one of only two aircraft still flying in December 1954, when the Spitfires were grounded. She had 462:35 hours[16] on her airframe, not all of which had been in SRAF service.

It turns out that the best guide we have as to how many hours SR64 probably flew in SRAF service is the F700 of SR65,[17] the sole surviving SRAF Spitfire, today stored at the Military Museum in Gweru, Zimbabwe. It is the only F700 we have been able to access. According to her F700, SR65 had flown 220:20 hours on 8 July 1954, at the end of No. 3 SSU's OCU course.

However, according to the logbooks of Chris Dams and Chris Hudson, SR65 continued to fly until December 1954. Notwithstanding her missing final logbook it would be reasonable to conclude she ended up with around 223 hours. Therefore, assuming a similar utilisation in the SRAF/RRAF, PK350 probably accumulated around 240 hours in RAF service, most of which was on 73 Sqn—quite a high rate of utilisation.

Overall, the above figures indicate a fairly low rate of utilisation in the SRAF/RRAF, apart from the spikes of activity during the courses. For example during No. 3 SSU's training Chris Dams flew 55 hours in just under four months in ten different aircraft. The explanation for this relatively low rate of utilisation is the conservation of hours on the Spitfire.

WITHDRAWAL FROM SERVICE

No sooner had No. 3 SSU completed their Spitfire OCU training in early July 1954, than the bulk of the Spitfires still flying were withdrawn from service. Two aircraft, SR64 and SR65, were retained in a serviceable state and test flown by at least three pilots: Keith Kemsley, who had been an instructor on No. 3 SSU's OCU, Chris Dams and Chris Hudson. Furthermore, on 20 September 1954, Keith Kemsley in SR64 was part of a Battle of Britain commemoration flypast. This was the final operational duty of any RRAF Spitfire and one of the last for any Spitfire. This limited Spitfire flying continued until December 1954. Chris Dams takes up the story:

> On Saturday, 18 December 1954, I flew a thirty minute air test on SR64. It was serviceable. My previous Spit flight was on 26 November (SR65), and the one before that on 8 November (SR64)—both air tests. So you can see that they were being flown very infrequently. Luckily I was one of the few pilots still current on type. Even so, I see from the dates that I did not take part in every one of the Saturday morning air test events. After this last one and while still signing the F700, I was told, 'that's it.' They were being closed down all together. I guess someone at HQ had heard the Griffon sound and had asked himself whether it really was cost effective to press on. Another big factor was that the prop blades were coming loose in their mounting bosses, such that the tip of the blade could be rocked back and forth by some inches (we had not gone metric yet). The rocking was the result of the wooden blades swelling and shrinking repeatedly with the drastic changes in the moisture content, such that they began to move more and more within the metal bosses; typical of the reaction of wood in the tropics.

We now know that Chris Hudson flew SR65 the same day, a previously forgotten fact.

Whereas the propeller problem had precipitated the withdrawal from service of the Spitfires, in truth the authorities were bowing to progress with the RRAF's acquisition of jet-powered Vampires during the previous 12 months. However, there was still one more duty to perform. At first SR64 and SR65 remained parked outside, exposed to the elements at New Sarum, while the remaining seven aircraft were sold to the Syrian Air Force in 1955. See Appendix D. SR65 was later moved to Bulawayo and stored in a hangar at Woodville Airport, before eventually being returned to Thornhill for gate guard duties. Becoming a gate guard is a time-honoured tradition for military aircraft that have given stalwart service. SR64 remained outside at New Sarum until it was decided to use her also as a gate guard. Again Chris Dams recalls events from those days:

> Subsequently SR64 was mounted, engine and all, as the gate guard at Sarum, which might well still have been known as Kentucky at that time; I have no record of the date of the name change. Another Spit, number not known [SR65], was sent to Thornhill to serve the same purpose. It had the engine removed to simplify the mounting process. Doug Whyte was the Station Commander of the time. The engine, so far as my memory serves, was sold to a guy who used it in a boat on Kariba. I have a funny feeling that the boat later sank; no fault of the engine though.

The fact that SR64 was mounted "engine and all"[18] whereas SR65 was gutted, was to prove decisive in the future when consideration was given to restoring a Spitfire. In addition, SR64 had been painted in a silver colour scheme with RRAF markings, including the three assegais on the roundels to signify the status quo of the Federation at that time. This suggests that commencement of her gate guard duties was prior to cessation of the Federation in late 1963. As all who served in the RRAF and RhAF in the years since then will recall, she was mounted in a descending left-hand banking turn, and would be painted in three different colour schemes, altogether, before her removal in 1977. She silently dominated the view on arrival at the base via the Guard Room, a sharp reminder that she was still doing her duty, albeit frozen in space and time, as though waiting to take to the air again if given the chance.

Chapter 5
THE DECISION TO RESTORE SR64

Events and their associated activities moved quickly during this brief phase in the life of SR64. At the outset, SR64's silent vigil as gate guard suddenly came to an end. At the conclusion of this phase the Spitfire would be in private hands on a journey to full restoration. In the interim, the RRAF had since become the RhAF, following Rhodesia's Unilateral Declaration of Independence (UDI) in 1965. The Royal designation was dropped in 1970.

SR64 was removed from her plinth at New Sarum on 26 January 1977—22 years and 39 days after her last flight and some 14 years atop the plinth. Overseeing this exercise was Flight Lieutenant Bob Garrett, the Flying Wing Technical Officer (FWTO) from Thornhill Air Force Base. He was assisted by two senior NCO's, Flight Sergeant Stu Robertson and Sergeant Mike Rochat from No. 6 Squadron, based at Thornhill, as well as a number of junior technicians from the same squadron, including Les Booth, Howell Bowker, John Bulpit and Clive Dutton. Additional manpower was provided by prisoners and of course there was the crane. Remarkably this was operated by WO1 Jimmy Gordon-Brander who had placed SR64 on the plinth in the first place.[1] SR64 was lowered onto her undercarriage, which had recently been extended. The aircraft was then dismantled into four main pieces—the 11 foot propeller; the fuselage including her Griffon engine; and her two wings—and loaded onto a Bedford truck. She was then transported to Thornhill Air Base 300km away, outside Gwelo, Rhodesia's third largest city. Stu Robertson recalls the events:

> John Bulpit and myself were sent up to New Sarum by Spike Owens to remove the Spitfire and return it to Thornhill. It took about three days with the help of personnel from New Sarum to remove the wings, prop, and tail-plane, then load them onto a vehicle. When we disconnected the coolers under each wing the water glycol was as good as new, and the hydraulic system worked first time when extending the undercarriage. We had quite a trip back to Thornhill— each time we stopped the crowd asked us whether we were going to rebuild the Spitfire to join the bush war![2]

The decision to remove SR64 from her plinth and send her to Thornhill had been taken by Air HQ with the intention of restoring her for display at the Gwelo Military

Museum. WO1 Spike Owens, who was by now the warrant officer in charge of 6 Sqn[3] at Thornhill, had long been agitating for this.

Spike Owens had already enjoyed a long career in military service, having started out as an engines/airframe mechanic on Typhoons during WW2, but it is not clear on which RAF squadron he served. After the war, possibly because of his exposure to Rhodesians on 266 Sqn but certainly with the encouragement of an aunt[4] in South Africa, he decided to emigrate from Ireland to Rhodesia. He ended up serving as a technician on the Spitfires at New Sarum, evidence[5] of which is well captured in a photograph of the last squadron flight of Spitfires, starting up on grass runway 14/32 at Salisbury International Airport. Spike Owens had worked his way up the ranks to become a warrant officer on No. 4 Squadron[6] before moving to No. 6 Squadron[7] in the same capacity and eventually later to the ASF. In the process he had acquired a reputation for being resourceful and persuasive, having developed a very useful personal network. This he used to good effect to restore to flying condition a Provost known as 'Omega'. The story goes that he had even managed to 'hide' away a fully serviceable Leonides engine which was used in the rebuild of Omega.

Clear evidence that Spike Owens was passionate about restoring a Spitfire is revealed in correspondence from Captain John Desfountain. The latter, serving at Joint Services Photographic Interpretation Service (JSPIS) wrote a memorandum to Spike Owens dated 6 November 1974, more than two years before SR64 was removed from her plinth. He had his own passion—to restore a Harvard—and must have had numerous discussions about the Spitfire with Spike. In his memorandum he confessed that he did not "realise the completeness of the New Sarum Spitfire", and mentioned then Wing Commander Keith Kemsley, another pro-restoration personality and ex-Spitfire pilot, and "getting a restoration project off the ground". This, "either to get her airworthy" or "put it into a museum" was the essence of John's communication and discussion of options. Air Commodore Keith Kemsley had long advocated and lobbied Air HQ about a Spitfire restoration project, to the extent of incurring the displeasure of no less than Air Marshal Archie Wilson, when he was Officer Commanding No. 1 Ground Training School at New Sarum.

Bob Garrett takes up the story:

> The whole project was the idea of (the late) Spike Owens and he approached me as FWTO, to seek permission from Air HQ to remove the aircraft from the plinth at New Sarum and transport it to Thornhill for a long term rebuild.

Even though Bob Garrett mentions a long term rebuild, it seems pretty clear that at this stage Air HQ intended that the aircraft be restored for museum display only.

> After much deliberation Air HQ gave the OK and Spike, his hangar crew and I went up to New Sarum with suitable transport. Unfortunately, dismantling the aircraft was more complex than we realised, as parts had corroded and other parts had been 'modified' to take the framework which supported the aircraft on the plinth. Anyway, eventually job done, the aircraft was positioned in the hangar back at Thornhill, and the aircraft was roughly reassembled.

From the video *Spitfire—The Pursuit of Dream* we have the words of Spike Owens on this decision:

> I think it was early in 1977 that Jack Malloch, myself and a few other Air Force associates managed to persuade the right people to take the Spitfire for a flying medical. The aircraft was taken off the plinth at Sarum and carefully packed off to Thornhill where we gave her a thorough examination.

It says much for the influence exerted by Spike Owens, assisted by the likes of Keith Kemsley, that he was able to persuade Air HQ to let him remove the aircraft and restore her. According to Bob Garrett, confirmed by John Desfountain, Spike Owens had in fact conducted a survey which determined that SR64 was the better of the two airframes to restore—SR65 being the other airframe, also on a plinth, at Thornhill. Clearly, Spike wanted only to restore her to flying condition, but was willing to go along with a museum restoration as a compromise to get her off the plinth. It is also interesting that Spike should mention Jack Malloch's name, which suggests there was active communication between the two men—this is the only record of such communication.

Mindful of the completeness of SR64, the decision must have been straightforward. And Spike's judgement was quickly vindicated. After SR64 was reassembled at 6 Sqn tests were carried out on the undercarriage and flaps by Stu Robertson and John Bulpit. Using an independent hydraulic rig for the undercarriage and compressed air for the flap system, both systems worked, as is evident from official photographs taken at the time. This must have been hugely encouraging, but—there was a damper. As Bob Garrett recalls: "Spike was very keen to start overhauling and repairing the machine but still had a squadron to run, so it was obvious it was going to take a long, long time to show any progress."

Flight Lieutenant Dave Thorne, ex-10 Pilot Training Course (PTC), was acting Officer Commanding No. 6 Squadron at the time. Obviously he had been convinced by the revelations of the tests and completeness of the airframe to try and persuade Air HQ to have the aircraft restored to flying condition, rather than just a display condition for a museum. Writing on 7 February 1977 to the editor, Squadron Leader Alan Cockle, of the *Bateleur* magazine, the official Air Force publication, Dave Thorne had this to say:

> No. 6 Squadron is presently 'tarting up' the Spitfire that was on the New Sarum plinth. The intention is to present this splendid aircraft to the Gwelo Museum. While we appreciate the noble intentions of this gesture, we feel we must point out a few facts about this particular aeroplane ...

Whilst outlining a few facts about the aircraft already mentioned in the preceding chapters—her RAF number, her flying hours on cessation of flying in December 1954, who last flew her and signed her technical log—Dave begins building a convincing case to restore her to full flying condition:

> There are enough technicians and enthusiasts on station at Thornhill who are confident that this aircraft could be restored to a fully flyable condition at no expense to the Air Force while working out of working hours.
>
> All over the world enthusiasts beg, steal, and labour, using wrecks and odd bits and pieces to restore aircraft of similar vintage to make them airworthy. On our doorstep we have this complete historical gem which, with the means and technical knowhow available to us, could be restored to flying condition.
>
> WO1 Spike Owens who has over 35 years continuous Air Force service, a fair portion of which has been working on Spitfires including this particular one, has the technical expertise and enthusiasm to see this 'project off the ground'.
>
> We are certain that there are many aviation buffs throughout Rhodesia, from our Prime Minister down, who would get a tremendous kick seeing this symbol of Western air-supremacy in our skies again.
>
> Perhaps this letter will inspire those serving members who were closely involved with Spitfires in the past, to make this an official Air Force project and delay the final demise of the aeroplane, by persuading the Gwelo Museum that

its public value will be greater if it could be viewed by Rhodesians throughout the country as a flying example.

Any genuine aviator and enthusiast would agree with the sentiments expressed by Dave Thorne, which echoed Spike Owen's feelings and probably those of everyone on the base.

However, there was a pressing reality which had to be acknowledged. Rhodesia was at war and also under international sanctions as a result of its unilateral declaration of independence in November 1965. The Rhodesian Government of Ian Smith (ex-237 Rhodesia Squadron) was fighting an insurrection led by black nationalist movements, whilst having to contend with the considerable difficulties of acquiring spares and resources for repelling that insurrection. At this stage, numbers were already beginning to overwhelm the Rhodesian security forces of which the RhAF was a key element. The Air Force provided a unique degree of mobility and flexibility to the Army through its helicopters and transport units. In addition, through its Hunters and Canberras, backed up by the Lynx (Cessna 337) aircraft, it provided a potent striking force that reached well beyond the country's borders. These were its priority missions. Restoring a Spitfire would be a distraction in the view of Air HQ, despite the noble intentions expressed in Dave Thorne's letter.

This matter should have involved only Thornhill Air Base making an appeal direct to Air HQ, but somehow Squadron Leader Chris Dixon at New Sarum became involved, adding his weight to the project. As Officer Commanding No. 5 Squadron in 1979, Chris later gained international fame as 'Green Leader', leading a strike into Zambia in a Canberra bomber. On 23 February 1977 he sent an encouraging signal to Bob Garrett and Spike Owens, requesting a technical assessment of the aircraft on a low priority basis—but Government funds were not available and there were no manuals to hand.

Whilst Air HQ deliberated over Dave Thorne's recommendation and whatever influence Chris Dixon added from New Sarum, Spike Owens and his men started dismantling the aircraft inside and outside the ASF hangar, to carry out the technical assessment. This assessment was completed by 24 March. It determined that the airframe was free of corrosion but should be subjected to non-destructive testing (NDT) to be sure. The engine was seized and would need a complete overhaul. The canopy and all the wiring needed replacing. While the fuselage fuel tanks were in good condition, the wing fuel tanks were in poor condition and seals needed replacing.

Although the pneumatics and hydraulic systems had been operated satisfactorily, the components would need to be bay-serviced, and the oxygen system needed complete replacement. The oil tank and cooling system were in good condition but would need to be flushed and pressure tested. Finally, and critically, the propeller would need to be stripped to assess whether a rebuild was possible. Evidently a lot of work would be required to restore the aircraft, requiring loads of spares and a high level of skill. In addition, maintenance manuals and pilots notes were needed.

Bob Garrett must have contacted John Desfountain to offer assistance but apart from supplying a three view plan and photos of the Spitfire, he was not really able to help. It appeared that the manuals already were no longer available in the technical libraries. This was confirmed by Chris Dixon who nonetheless pointed out that the correct designation of this mark Spitfire was Mk 22 and not Mk XXII. The RAF had abandoned the use of Roman Numerals after the war.

Pat King was one of the hangar crew from 6 Sqn who had helped to strip the aircraft. His father, Vince King, had flown Spitfires on No. 2 SSU. Pat recalls:

> I can't remember too much about the beginnings of the restoration but I do remember the engine being removed along with all the various old (very old) wiring and components. It was quite amazing stripping an aircraft that old and especially one that my old man had flown in the past. I can remember that we stripped it in the open air outside the hangar initially. I can't even remember which hangar it was.

Air Marshal Mick McLaren, a cousin to Vince King, was the Rhodesian Air Force Commander at this time, although his tenure was soon to end in April 1977. Having started out as an auxiliary Air Force NCO pilot and one of the first to be trained on the Spitfire in the SRAF, he had witnessed much change and was now commanding an Air Force at war. Throughout his tenure, since 1973, there had been a steady escalation in that war with increasing casualties. His successor would be Air Marshal Frank Mussell, a No. 2 SSU member. Frank, like his brother John, now a Group Captain and Director of Administration in Air HQ, had also flown Spitfires. Mick McLaren does not remember much about deliberations to restore SR64 before he handed over to Frank Mussell. It was Air Vice-Marshal Chris Dams, as Chief of Staff, who dealt with the matter.

By mid-April the story had been leaked to the press. On 16 April 1977 the Defence

Correspondent with the *Rhodesia Herald* reported that a decision to restore the Spitfire had been made. The headline read: "Enthusiasts plan to put historic Spitfire back in the air". However, the article makes it clear that a firm decision had not been taken at that point to restore SR64 to flying condition. Rather, one is left wondering whether the article was being used to drum up support for this worthy project: "The decision has been taken to preserve SR64 for posterity. How much more worthy would be a project to see this so-historic aircraft flying in the Rhodesian skies again?" the Defence Reporter challenged. His words strongly resembled the language used by Dave Thorne when this clarion call went out to return SR64 to her former glory.

Bob Garrett continues:

> It was realised by Air HQ that it would be expensive and parts would need to be purchased out of the country, and as Affretair (ATA) was interested and had the manpower and finances and worldwide contacts, the project was handed over to them and the aircraft moved to their hangar back at New Sarum. End of story. Spike was upset but realised it was for the best.

Again from the video *Spitfire—The Pursuit of a Dream*, we have a statement from Spike Owens confirming his acceptance of the inevitable:

> Unfortunately, in those days our technicians were hard pressed and a rebuild seemed out of the question. So we reluctantly took it apart and stored all the pieces in the hangar. Jack Malloch had his own airline with a number of good contacts; he had the means to rebuild the aircraft and we were only too pleased to give the project to him. So all the parts were collected, canopy, panels, pipes, radiator and engine cowlings and finally the wings and fuselage.

It could easily have been perceived that the restoration project was "handed over to Affretair", which was owned by Malloch. But in fact a deal was struck between the RhAF and Malloch. Jack had served as a pilot on 237 (Rhodesia) Squadron in WW2, and had assisted in the ferry of the Spitfires in March 1951 as an auxiliary pilot. He was thus well known to the Air Force community. In the intervening years, since leaving the SRAAF in 1951, he had pursued a very successful career in civilian aviation. Plainly, in spite of his busy schedule directing his company's sanctions-busting activities, he still found time to keep his ear to the ground and was fully aware of the state of SR64 following her removal from the plinth.

Chris Dams continues with the story:

> I was Chief of Staff when it happened. Jack came to see me at HQ. His request
> was to put the Spit back in the air as a flying museum piece—at his own expense.
> We were very occupied with the war and could not devote or divert effort to a
> project like that. We chatted about it and essentially it boiled down to the aircraft
> remaining Government property with Jack earning the right to fly it after it
> became airworthy. There was no talk then about any air force pilots getting in
> on the act.
>
> As I recall, Jack was inspired by the report from Spike Owens who had
> done some dis-assembly at Thornhill and had found, remarkably, a reasonable
> condition in most parts. I remember he told me that he had found pressure still
> in one or two components (I forget which now).
>
> The upshot of our talks was a visit to the Ministry of Defence civil servants
> who organised a contract. Again I forget the details and who actually signed it,
> but I was part of that process.

We have no exact date as to when this contract was signed, but by all accounts
it was probably in late April or May 1977. It was clear, though, that Jack Malloch
would carry all the risk and provide the leadership and technical expertise from his
very capable engineering staff. His aircraft and sanctions-busting network would
be a substantial asset in acquiring spares, whilst the RhAF would provide facilities
for bay servicing of components and whatever else its substantial infrastructure and
expertise could provide.

Frank Mussell,[8] who took over command from Mick McLaren in April 1977, recalls
that the agreement made provision for an Air Force pilot to fly her and thought this
would be Chris Dams himself. He also revealed that Jack Malloch wanted to use
the aircraft in operations, once rebuilt, but that the RhAF flatly denied him that
opportunity. Clearly, Jack Malloch had a good sense for the feelings of the man on
the street. It will be recalled that when transporting the dismantled aircraft back to
Thornhill in January 1977, inquisitive observers had speculated whether the aircraft
was to be rebuilt for use in the bush war.

When asked whether Jack Malloch would manage to rebuild the Spitfire, Chris
Dams replied: "Yes and No. Yes, because of his reputation, but No due to all the
challenges of sanctions and acquiring spares."[9] He reflected that prior to negotiating
the contract for the rebuild he hadn't actually known Jack, but was very aware of

the man and his reputation. Nevertheless he found Jack easy to interact with and immediately connected with him. Jack Malloch himself had these words to say, recorded for posterity on the video, *Spitfire—The Pursuit of a Dream*:

> I did my full period of service in WW2 on Spitfire fighters and enjoyed this very much indeed. It was as a result of this background that I welcomed the opportunity of arranging for this aircraft to be rebuilt … fortunately the enthusiasm of the blokes in the hangar also made this a reality.

It is time to take a closer look at Jack Malloch, the man.

Chapter 6
CAPTAIN JACK

By the time Jack Malloch committed himself and his ATA staff to the restoration of SR64, in 1977, he had developed a substantial reputation. Not only had he demonstrated a high level of piloting skills on countless occasions, he had also demonstrated an exceptional ability to manage a sizeable degree of risk in his aviation business. Through these activities, ongoing since leaving the SRAF in 1951, he had gained the respect and admiration of his peers and the aviation community at large. He had also earned grudging respect from his 'opponents', who were also Rhodesia's opponents, regarding his sanctions-busting activities on behalf of the Rhodesian government. He even featured in United Nations debates on Rhodesia.

These latter activities had cast him as a patriot in the truest sense of the word. He was tireless in his support for his old RAF 237 Sqn comrade-in-arms, Ian Smith, now the Prime Minister of Rhodesia. However, for all his national and international renown, he was still plain Jack Malloch. He commanded respect, rather than demanded it. To his inner circle at ATA and his aviation peers he was Jack, but to the larger community of his employees and colleagues he was variously known as Captain Malloch, Captain Jack, Captain, Uncle Jack, JMM, the Old Man or The Boss. Underlying the respectful titles there was also patent affection for this man. It is easy to see why this was the case. Even though he was a man of few words, he was evidently one of the few men in life who consistently, and successfully, 'walked the talk'—he led by example and was assiduously fair and interested in the welfare of his staff. Alyson, his daughter, has given us key insight into this side of his character and his work ethic, recalling:

> According to my Gran he was always fair—painfully so—if he had a sweet he had to divide it up equally for everyone present. His Mom could be quite difficult, I believe, and I think he learnt how to be very sensitive to her moods and maybe that's why he was so good with people. He was quite incredible with us growing up—very sensitive and attentive to our feelings but very strong on hard work and treating people well and fairly. We could never be seen not to be doing our share of the work.[1]

Andy Wood,[2] one of the apprentices on the Spitfire project, remembers how surprised he was when Jack Malloch greeted him by his first name on his first day of work at ATA. He said Jack knew everybody by their first name and took a keen interest in everyone as individuals. Piet Bezuidenhout, a fellow apprentice with Andy Wood, confirmed that:

> Everyone pulled their weight for Jack Malloch. He was an amazing man. He knew everyone's name and always took the trouble to speak to us during his daily walks around the hangar, inquiring after our families and personal welfare. If ever I could find a Boss like him again ...![3]

Jack was well supported by Zoe, his wife, in seeing to the welfare of his staff. Zoe was known regularly to bring clothing for the African staff in the hangar and freight shed, according to George Paterson, a flight engineer with ATA. In addition Jack's willingness to extend credit to his staff and others at the airport was well known.

Jack Malloch's word was his honour and he diligently returned favours that others had done for him. ATA's Traffic Manager, Ian Hunt,[4] recalled that on occasion the 'Old Man' would task him to arrange a freight load on behalf of someone as a favour, in return for a past favour done for him. This confirms his daughter's recall of Jack's strict take on fairness, a lot like balancing the books.

Further insight into Jack Malloch's character predictably comes from a recently rediscovered story from WW2. This occurred after he was shot down in Italy in February 1945. Having found himself in the care of Italian partisans and some nuns who were helping him to recover from his injuries, he was able in March to write a letter to Flying Officer Bill Musgrave, a friend and colleague with 237 (Rhodesia) Squadron. A copy of this letter follows:

> Dear Bill
> Just a line to let you know that I am still in the land of the living, also to ask if you please forward the enclosed letter to my folks at home, by Air mail, you will find plenty of stamps in my wallet. If there is any money in the wallet please pay Bob Simpson 120 lire that I owe him.
> Please excuse this awful scrawl but I am in bed and the leg is treating me rather rough, as you probably know I have a broken ankle, which has just been put in plaster so am hoping that the pain will wear away.
> You might remember me to all the fellows at camp and are Keith and Arthur still getting as drunk as ever.

Tell my crew that I am very sorry about the good old 'M', but it was in such a mess with oil that I thought I had better not let them see it like that. Max has probably told you that I had quite a bit of trouble trying to leave her. There is nothing left of her now for people to scorn at.

I am wondering what the O.C. had to say to my effort. I hope he has not stopped you chaps doing this work ... if he has, then I don't know how I will square up with the C/O.

Well Bill this is just about as much as I can find to say for now except that I would be glad if you would keep my kit and wallet etc. For I will be seeing you in five to six week's time so don't you go off before I get back. I hope you and Keith had a good leave in Rome and that you behaved yourselves when there.

I am not sure that this note will reach you so I would be glad if you could slip past one day when up here (some of the boys were here last Sunday with the OC). I am in the big red building and if I see the 'T' on the kite I will know you got this letter, hence be pretty relieved regarding the letter home.

Well I am closing now, keep my mail if any. When I look back over the scrawl I don't know how you are going to read it.

Yours,

Jack

PS. If Pat hasn't left yet say hello to him for me.[5]

Jack Malloch's efforts to balance the books and think about others, despite his circumstances, is abundantly clear in this missive. Sometime after the war when the Musgraves and Mallochs met for a meal at a hotel, Bill Musgrave chose to remind Jack about the letter—which produced a very emotional response from this warrior now turned entrepreneur. According to Margery Musgrave, Bill Musgrave's widow, her husband most likely did manage to fly over Jack Malloch's hideaway to acknowledge receipt of the letter some three weeks after it was written. His logbook had an entry that read: "Jack returned to the Squadron with a bust ankle."[6]

ATA was something of a colossus in Rhodesia. It symbolised everything about the Rhodesian spirit—courage, resourcefulness and adaptability—as the country battled an increasingly difficult insurgency by nationalist guerrillas at the same time as trying to outsmart international sanctions. Jack Malloch was at the forefront of these battles. In January 1977, in an individual capacity, he was made a Flight Lieutenant in the Volunteer Reserve, which facilitated his participation in military operations with his aircraft. At a company level, ATA was at the forefront of Rhodesian sanctions-busting activities. His aircraft ranged far and wide, moving military personnel and equipment, delivering exports and importing precious imports. Even though it was essentially a civilian charter airline business, it displayed a military efficiency in the performance of a strategic role enacted with sublime tactical flexibility. It was rather like Rhodesia's Strategic Air Transport Command.

By 1977 Jack Malloch was operating four aircraft on two different registers. He utilised a Douglas DC-7F, a Canadair CL44 and a DC-8 on the Gabonese register with registrations TR-LNZ, TR-LVO and TR-LVK respectively. He also operated another DC-8 on the Omani register, registration A4O-PA.[7] This aircraft had been his first DC-8 on the Gabonese register, as TR-LQR, which he had acquired in October 1972.[8] This mix of aircraft provided ATA with plenty of flexibility being a mix of piston, turbo-prop and heavy jet aircraft.

Assisting ATA with its operations were two associate companies, set up with the help of the Rhodesian government. Affretair was the Gabonese company with offices in Libreville, and CargOman was the Omani company with offices in Muscat.[9]

ATA had a regular route structure into Africa and its destinations included Lubambashi and Kinshasa in then Zaire; Brazaville in Congo Brazaville; Franceville, Port Gentil and Libreville in Gabon; and Sao Tome and Abidjan in the Ivory Coast. The CL-44 and DC-8s operated these routes exporting prime beef, fresh produce and other products to these countries, most of which were ex-French colonies and willing to turn a blind eye to these sanctions-busting operations. The aircraft would route straight out of Salisbury in the early hours of the morning toward Lusaka in Zambia, using an Affretair call sign (DG) and onward to the aforementioned destinations taking special care to avoid Angolan airspace. In 1977, following a security breech, ATA started using the Air Gabon call sign (AG). The DC-8s and sometimes the CL-44 would then generally operate empty into Schipol and Amsterdam. Amsterdam was used mainly for charter work, a vital source of foreign currency, and one flight a week originated from there to Johannesburg. The Dutch tolerated ATA's flights into and out of Schipol as long the Rhodesians didn't embarrass them; there was one regular scheduled flight from Schipol to Johannesburg known as the 812. The French on the other hand, allowed military exports. This meant most of the military imports into Rhodesia originated from Paris.[10]

The route via Victoria Falls and due west along the border between South-west Africa and Angola to the Atlantic coast and then northbound to Libreville was only occasionally flown.

Another route was north-east via the Comores and Seychelles to Oman, and then back via the same routing. Even though the CargOman DC-8 had originally been intended to operate east-west, bringing high value cargo from the Far East into Europe via Muscat as a hub, this never really materialised into a regular operation. Instead, both DC-8s ended up operating similar routes which meant, at times, basing out of Paris and Palma de Majorca and operating into Africa on charter work.

ATA also operated flights northbound into Teheran and then onto Amsterdam.[11] These flights saw day-old-chicks from Arbor Acres being exported to Iran; Arbor Acres being part-owned by Ben Bellingan, an ex-SRAF Spitfire pilot.

A feature of ATA's operations was that the turnarounds had to be quick—to forestall any attempt by various authorities at the prompting of the British to clamp the aircraft.[12] This never occurred. Most countries turned a blind eye.

In the process, ATA managed some highly successful military imports. In 1977 the CL-44 imported the Siai Machetti SF260s to be used by 6 Sqn for pilot training, and the Agusta Bell 205s for 8 Sqn. The CargOman DC-8 imported complete Avon engines and spares from the Middle East for the Hunter fleet and spares for the Spitfire.

The DC-7 on the other hand was used internally and regionally into South Africa and South-west Africa on military operations. Using its RhAF number 7230, these operations ranged from deploying combat troops by parachute on major external operations, to air drops of fuel supplies for the 7 Sqn helicopters in remote areas, and shuttling troops backward and forward between Rhodesia and South Africa. Accompanying Jack Malloch on these military operations would be Squadron Leader George Alexander, Officer Commanding No. 3 Squadron RhAF, Flight Lieutenant Jerry Lynch and ATA's own John Hodges as the flight engineer.

These latter DC-7 operations served to confirm the closeness of the relationship between South Africa and Rhodesia. As the story later reveals, the DC-7 would also play a key part in the Spitfire story.

In retrospect it could be said that by 1977 Jack Malloch and ATA were fast approaching their zenith. It was a slick operation and a key element in the Rhodesian effort to thwart sanctions and remain militarily viable. All of this had been achieved on the back of a quarter of a century of Jack Malloch honing his operational and business skills in some of the hottest places in Africa. And—this was on the back of an RAF career as a fighter pilot packed with drama and loyal service, but which started inauspiciously because he struggled to be accepted as a pilot.

Jack Malloch was born in Durban, South Africa in October 1920 making him 56 when he took on the Spitfire project. He was the eldest child and only boy amongst four children born to John McVicar and Margaret (*née* Bremner) Malloch. He was named John McVicar after his father and grandfather, the latter being a Scottish immigrant to South Africa. Jack's father moved his family to Southern Rhodesia in 1925 and settled in Umtali in the scenic and mountainous Eastern Districts.[13] Work prospects were better in Rhodesia at this time, and this turned out to be the beginning of a strong affection for Jack Malloch's adopted country. In 1933 he was sent to boarding school in Somerset West in South Africa.

He was not an academic and was only ever happy driving and fixing the school tractor, having already demonstrated a love for machinery and driving at an early age. Thus on the recommendation of the headmaster, his parents withdrew him from school. In 1934 he went to work as an apprentice mechanic in Fort Victoria where his parents had moved from Umtali. Later, having gained his driver's licence, he became a driver for the Railways Mail Service, to avoid doing national service.

However, Jack Malloch was not content. Before leaving Helderberg College, his headmaster had given him a damning assessment by telling him that without an education he would never do better than becoming a road sweeper.[14] This spurred him on to be something better and with the outbreak of WW2 in 1939, he volunteered to become a pilot with the RAF. But his lack of education proved a hindrance and the RAF would offer him only an engineer's job. Jack would not give up. He reapplied and in spite of failing his entrance exam, he somehow managed to persuade the recruiting officer to give him another chance; quite an achievement for a man of few words and with a fear of public speaking.

The RAF eventually accepted Jack for pilot training. He struggled with the ground school and especially the maths, and in spite of his mother taking a wager that he would fail, he made it—admitting he had never worked so hard in his life.[15] He started his flying training at 25 EFTS based at Cranborne in Salisbury, on the Tiger Moth on 29 March 1943. Thirty-seven years later this date proved deeply significant: it was the date on which he flew PK350 for the first time, again, whether by design or accident is unknown.

Jack Malloch qualified as an RAF pilot in December 1943 with an Above Average assessment.[16] Not only had he proved his headmaster and his mother wrong, demonstrating tremendous resolve in the process, but he had now entered the profession of aviation which, apart from a short break after the war, he was never to leave. He had found his place. Instead of tractors it was now aircraft that were the focus of his life.

In February 1944, aged 23 years old, Jack Malloch was posted to No. 73 Operational Training Unit at Abu Sueir in Egypt to become a fighter pilot on Spitfires. He completed his training in March, having flown mostly Spitfire Mk Vs. In March 1944 he was posted to 237 (Rhodesia) Squadron which was operating Spitfire Mk IXs. He flew from Corsica in support of the land operations in Italy on ground attack operations which would have entailed bombing and strafing German targets. Shot down and wounded on 23 February 1945, he was hidden from the Germans by Italian partisans in similar circumstances to his 237 Sqn comrade-in-arms, Ian Smith.[17] Having received treatment for his broken legs by nuns at an orphanage, he was then relocated, having to endure a tough three-day journey through the mountains before receiving better treatment from a doctor who had to reset one of his legs. Eventually, after some weeks, he made a dramatic escape[18] when he was flown out of a mountain hideout in a captured Fieseler Storch. He reported back to the squadron on 15 May. By now the war had ended but he stayed with the squadron until 31 July 1945, flying Spitfire Mk IXs and Mk XIs. By this time he had accumulated a total of 536:40 hours of which 172:25 were on operations.[19]

On leaving the RAF, Jack Malloch returned to Rhodesia. He opened a garage in Marandellas with his gratuity and later started a transport business.[20] In 1948 he married Zoe Coventry. Together they were to have three children, Alyson, the eldest, followed by the boys, Ross and Greg, all three of whom would later enter the world of aviation. In the meantime he was eager to get back in the air.

Fortunately, the SRAF was desperate to utilise the experience and skills of ex-RAF servicemen like Jack Malloch to assist it in rebuilding the air force, so in 1949 Jack joined the recently re-formed SRAF as an auxiliary. He enjoyed the rank of Captain and flew a mix of aircraft until the decision to purchase the Spitfires was taken in late 1950. From then on it was all preparation and training on the Harvard for the task of ferrying the aircraft from England. As has already been related, the first ferry took place in March 1951 and Jack Malloch flew the sole surviving SRAF Mk 22 SR65 (PK355)[21] to Southern Rhodesia.

He continued to fly Spitfires as an auxiliary until 17 August 1951.[22] He flew mostly SR61 (PK514) and SR65 on a mixture of exercises including formation, quarter attacks, dive bombing and a synchronised display, with Dave Barbour at Thornhill on 24 May, to mark the end of the RATG's presence in Rhodesia. Jack never flew

SR64 (PK350) in SRAF colours, although he had flown her once in the UK on a formation practice. Jack Malloch ceased flying with the SRAF on 30 October 1951, his last flight being on a de Havilland Rapide transport aircraft.

Was he readying himself for life outside the air force? The SRAF was moving on by then, with a huge expansion programme that would sooner rather than later dispense with the auxiliaries. Likewise Jack Malloch was ready to move on with his life in commercial aviation.

In March 1952 he formed Fish Air in partnership with Jamie Marshall, utilising a de Havilland Rapide. They imported fresh fish to Salisbury from Paradise Island off the Mozambique coast and later would fly holiday makers to the island, on the outbound leg from Salisbury. In 1955 Fish Air was sold to Hunting Clan who retained Jack Malloch as a pilot.

In 1960 he founded a company known as Rhodesian Air Services (RAS), utilising a Douglas DC-3 Dakota. RAS offered both charter and schedule air services in Rhodesia. It later failed, probably in early 1965 having suffered the misfortune of a fatal accident at Salisbury airport in November 1961[23] and then the loss of another DC-3 in the Congo in July 1962, which was shot down by the United Nations. Jack had been involved in the Congo in support of Moise Tshombe, the secessionist leader in the Katanga province.

Never to say never, in early 1965 he established another charter company, Air Trans Africa (ATA), using a mix of aircraft including a Lockheed Super Constellation, a C-54 (military version of the DC-4) and a DH Heron. Once again he became involved in the Congo in support of Tshombe, now the prime minister of that country. Tshombe was trying to quell a rebellion led by the Simba rebels and relied upon Jack to transport mercenaries in support of these operations.

In the meantime, the Unilateral Declaration of Independence (UDI) was announced on 11 November 1965 by the prime minister of Rhodesia, Ian Smith. Shortly afterwards the United Nations (UN) instituted sanctions against Rhodesia, the country having been declared a 'rebel' nation. This state of affairs soon created a need amongst Rhodesians to circumvent those sanctions.

Jack Malloch continued his activities in the Congo until 1967, whereupon he became involved in the Biafran War, in Nigeria. Charter operations saw his aircraft flying into Port Harcourt on the Niger delta, under treacherous conditions, and then his DC-7 was impounded in Togo whilst carrying Nigerian banknotes. Jack was on board at the time and was imprisoned, together with his crew, for six months.

He and his men were subjected to daily threats of death by firing squad which he endured in his typically stoic way. The manner of Jack Malloch's response to this torment, together with his leadership skills, served to increase his eminence in and around Africa as well as further afield. He and his crew were eventually released in mid-1968.

In January 1970 Jack ceased operations in Biafra when the secessionists admitted defeat by Nigerian forces, and Biafra was reintegrated into Nigeria. In the meantime the L1049G Constellation TR-LNY was 'rescued' from Luanda and flown to Salisbury, in November 1969, where it was refurbished and registered as VP-WAW in the colours of Afro Continental Airways. It operated between Salisbury and Windhoek, in South-west Africa.

Given Jack Malloch's reputation and experience it was logical that he should become involved in sanctions-busting activities on behalf of the Rhodesian Government. To this end, and with assistance from the government, he obtained a fleet of five DC-7C and DC-7CF aircraft. These aircraft were all registered on the Gabonese register and thus became a major part of the sanctions-busting network. ATA's operations continued to flourish and evolve with the acquisition of two DC-8s and a CL-44. By 1977 the fleet had stabilised at four aircraft—along the way he had lost a DC-7 to a fire and the remaining three DC-7s were grounded and used for spares for the single aircraft, TR-LNZ.

Inevitably these sanctions-busting operations would attract scrutiny and interest. The *Sunday Times* in London printed an article titled 'Tango Romeo' in 1973, exposing his sanctions-busting activities and this signalled Jack's arrival on the international stage. Andy Wood[24] recalls that all these African exploits later earned Jack Malloch the nickname of 'Biggles of Africa' among some of the apprentices at ATA.

Of course Jack would not have sought such a light-hearted characterisation of his exploits, neither had he sought an international reputation. However, looking back on the previous decade of intense operations mixed with a very high level of risk, one is left wondering what drove Jack during those days? Financial gain must certainly have played a part, as well as a strong desire to succeed. To what extent his African exploits were driven by a desire for high adventure is hard to say, but it seems reasonable to conclude that his experience in the RAF instilled within him the ability to manage high risks. He dared to tread where most feared to tread. George Paterson, one of Jack's flight engineers at the time, recalls some of Jack's favourite sayings which seem to capture his drive and approach to life: 'Can't does not exist in my life and vocabulary,' and 'the impossible we will do now, miracles may take a little longer'.

Unquestionably though, it was Jack Malloch's sense of patriotism that played a big part in his sanctions-busting activities. His daughter Alyson recalls this side of her father:

> He always loved Rhodesia and lived there from the age of six. It was his country and after witnessing, often first-hand, what was happening in the rest of Africa, he seriously believed in that little country and that he was doing the right thing.[25]

Jack Malloch was not the only South African-born-Rhodesian to display a high level of patriotism. Air Marshal Mick McLaren, the Commander of the Air Force in early 1977, had come to Rhodesia as a young adult and then joined the Air Force as an auxiliary.[26] He also adopted Rhodesia as his own country, serving it very loyally at the highest level. Ian Smith, the Prime Minister, must have been very grateful for the calibre of these men, amongst many others, but especially for Jack Malloch's sense of patriotism. Jack Malloch and Ian Smith knew each other well from their wartime service on 237 Sqn, but what really defined their relationship was their mutual respect and admiration, and their respective families became close friends.

Colin Miller, who joined Jack in 1969 as a pilot and later became his Chief Pilot, gave this wonderfully succinct summary of Jack Malloch, his Boss and fellow professional:

> Jack was a legend in his own lifetime. He had contacts worldwide and faced adversity with incredible stoicism. He was highly respected by all who knew him. He was a gentleman of the highest morals and integrity; and would take on anyone and anything, so long as the end result benefitted his beloved Rhodesia.[27]

Jack Malloch shrewdly surrounded himself with very competent and trustworthy people, in particular his flight crew and engineers. According to Colin Miller he didn't stint on maintenance and crew training, and after the DC-8s arrived this meant aligning ATA's training and procedures with those of KLM, as well as utilising KLM's manuals. Without these men he could not have managed his various operations or developed the remarkable reputation that he enjoyed. Dave Hann, who was to oversee the rebuild of the Spitfire, remembers that Jack would never allow harsh words with his staff members to fester and create distance between him and his men—he would always resolve the situation, be it over a cup of tea or a glass of whisky. Also, he never failed to apologise if he had been at fault. George Paterson recalled that Jack would return to the individual within an hour, shake that person's hand and ask, 'Are we still friends?'[28]

It's no wonder then that when asked about the working relationship at ATA, Colin Miller had this to say: "As to the working relationships—all I can say is that Jack Malloch was Affretair. Without him, it was a non-entity. Everyone gave their all for him."[29]

At ATA everyone, from the Chief Pilot to the apprentices on the hangar floor, was unequivocal in their admiration of, respect for and loyalty to Jack Malloch. The arrival of the Spitfire at the ATA hangar in mid-1977 was to test this loyalty, although ultimately it again endorsed the quality of his leadership and management style.

Chapter 7
JMM'S ENGINEERS

ATA was part of a large aviation community at Salisbury Airport. The presence of the Air Force base and the passenger terminal had initially attracted business to the airport, but it was the configuration of the runways that determined the eventual position and layout of these businesses. Runway 06/24 (now 05/23) and the cross runway 14/32 (no longer in use) formed a distinct cross biased toward the north-eastern end of the main runway and thus produced a clustering effect. In fact most of the runways were centred around or along runway 14/32.

The New Sarum Air Force Base, the original home of Spitfire SR64, was positioned on the southern side of the main runway and the western side of 14/32. A substantial entity, it was the RhAF's principal base and housed Nos. 3, 5 and 7 Squadrons, as well as various supporting maintenance units such as the very capable Engine Repair Section (ERS) and Aircraft Servicing Flight (ASF). In 1977 the ASF was very busy with aircraft rebuilds and repairs necessitated by the increasingly demanding rigours of the bush war as well as 'smersh' jobs.[1] One of these smersh jobs was assembling the SF260s that ATA had imported for the RhAF. On the other hand, the ERS had developed a significant capability servicing Rolls-Royce engines for the Hunters and Canberras, as well as other power plants. In addition, there was No. 1 Ground Training School for the training of apprentice technicians; the Parachute Training School, utilised mainly for training army paratroopers; and Aircraft Movements, which supervised the frequent movements of passenger and military freight flights from 3 Sqn as well as those being carried out by ATA's DC-7. Finally, there were a number of well-equipped and skilled bay servicing units at the various sections that would prove most useful during the Spitfire rebuild project.

On the northern side of the main runway and along the eastern side of runway 14/32 were Air Rhodesia, another substantial entity; Airwork Services and RUAC, a charter business run by Group Captain Charles Paxton, now retired from the RhAF. It will be remembered that Charles Paxton had assisted with flying the Spitfires on the ferries from England, and had enthralled crowds at New Sarum with his Spitfire displays. Airwork Services had preserved a long association with the Air Force, carrying out maintenance work (minor and major services) on the Canberras, Hunters and Vampires.

Opposite Airwork and RUAC, on the western side of the cross runway, were Fields

Aircraft Services, which carried out maintenance work on helicopters for the RhAF, and finally ATA. ATA was housed in an imposing and substantial hangar close to the main runway, capable of accepting large aircraft like the DC-8. This modern hangar had been built by Lunny Construction in 1970. Lunny Construction was owned by a friend of Jack Malloch, according to Ross Malloch, his eldest son. Its towering profile was accentuated by large HF radio aerials essential to ATA's operations. These systems were operated by the likes of Cliff Slight and Doug Elliott, to keep contact with the aircraft as they roamed far and wide around the world. The hangar is still there today, as is the substantial cold room next to it, between Fields and ATA. On the western side of the hangar, across from a little used ramp, was the 'White House', which housed the company's administration offices and Jack's own office.

By 1977 ATA employed at least 200 employees. Over and above the 'approximately 42'[2] flight crew headed by Colin Miller as Chief Pilot and John Hodges as the Chief Flight Engineer, there were six loadmasters[3], operations and commercial staff, office staff, general workers and of course the engineers. There were no less than 90 engineers[4] in the hangar, plus at least two engineers based at Schipol, Amsterdam. The engineering section ranged from back room boys keeping essential records to frontline engineers. It fell to Jim Townsend as Engineering Manager,[5] backed by Al Binding,[6] to manage this substantial entity. Jim Townsend was also a Flight Engineer at the time and had enjoyed a long association with his Boss, Jack Malloch, He was also well known to Spike Owens.

With the arrival of the Spitfire in mid-1977 (exact date unknown), Jack Malloch and Jim Townsend appointed two senior engineers—Bob Dodds[7] backed by Dave Hann—to manage the project. Bob Dodds was the Quality Control Manager and was closely involved with the CL44 and its Rolls-Royce Tynes, whilst Dave Hann was the Chief Structural Engineer and hangar foreman.

During 1977 Jack Malloch tasked Jim Townsend to oversee a company called Rhobar, also known as Societe Robart[8] based at Roissy Airport outside Paris, which sourced spares for ATA, the RhAF and of course the Spitfire. As a consequence, from early 1978 to 1980 when Jim left Affretair to immigrate to the USA, he was largely absent apart from short visits to Rhodesia. In his absence, Bob Dodds became *de facto* Engineering Manager,[9] accepting the position formally when Jim Townsend left Affretair.

Bob Dodds was born in Peebles, Scotland and immigrated to Rhodesia with his parents and siblings when he was a young teenager. Educated at Alan Wilson High

School, famed for its technical curriculum, he entered aviation as an apprentice with the Central African Airways (CAA) and qualified as a licensed engineer. Following a sojourn in the UK where he worked for British Caledonian Airways, he returned to Rhodesia and joined the Department of Civil Aviation (DCA) as an inspector. In the process he had become a well-qualified and licensed engineer. He had licences for all the current aircraft power plants at Air Rhodesia and ATA, making him one of the most licensed engineers on the airfield according to Dave Hann. Dave described 'Doddie', as he was known, as a "walking mechanical encyclopaedia".[10] He joined ATA sometime in 1975 as the Quality Control Manager before eventually becoming Engineering Manager.

Dave Hann, who would eventually become the Spitfire Project Manager and Chief Engineer under Bob Dodds, joined ATA in late 1976, after being recruited by Jack Malloch. He had been working at Airwork on the opposite side of runway 14/32. His strength was his structural knowledge and experience and, according to Andy Wood,[11] his nickname among the apprentices was 'Mr Crack'—his reputation was such that he could spot a crack at 100 yards, whilst his work ethic would not allow a bottle of Coca-Cola near the workplace. If a bottle of Coke was found on a workbench, everyone knew what Mr Crack would do with it.

Born and bought up in the UK, Dave Hann had the unique experience of starting his apprenticeship in 1952 with Airspeed,[12] (originally owned by the famous author Neville Shute), the company that had pioneered retractable undercarriage on their aircraft. During his apprenticeship Airspeed was absorbed into de Havilland. This meant he experienced first-hand the old fashioned method of training which saw Sir Geoffrey de Havilland, of Mosquito fame, playing a direct part in the training of Dave Hann and his fellow apprentices. After completing his apprenticeship in 1957 he worked on the production line of the Sea Venoms and Vixens for two years. Preferring life in the colonies ahead of national service, he joined the RRAF in 1959. Serving on 1 and 5 Squadrons, he acquired excellent experience on the Vampires and Canberras before arriving in the stressed skin section. Dave Hann opted out of the RRAF at the break-up of the Federation of Rhodesia and Nyasaland in 1963 and returned to the UK to work for the *British Aircraft Corporation* (*BAC*). His plan was to join the CAA with the arrival of their BAC-111s but this did not materialise—the aircraft were never delivered to CAA. They were delivered instead to Nyasaland when Rhodesia made its Unilateral Declaration of Independence. So instead, Dave joined Airwork Services in Rhodesia and worked his way up to the level of charge hand, carrying out minor and major services on the Air Force's current fleet of aircraft, including Hunters and Canberras. During this time he played a major part in the rebuild of two Canberras from parts collected from Thornhill. One of these aircraft was test flown by Squadron Leader Peter Knobel who later flew the rebuilt Spitfire. Dave left Airwork for a short stint in Saudi Arabia as a crew chief on a Lightning squadron, before returning to Airwork from where he was recruited by ATA.

Jack Malloch had decided to carry out as much heavy maintenance as possible on his aircraft as he could at ATA itself. Dave Hann was one amongst a number, including Len George, whom he had recruited from Airwork for this programme. At this point the question must be asked: Did he have the Spitfire in mind when he recruited Dave Hann with his experience of rebuilds? Even if not, he now had an excellent skill base at ATA to deal with its day-to-day demands: maintaining a diverse fleet of aircraft 24 hours a day/7 days a week, with most of the movements being made at night time. It could be said that ATA's engineering strength was in the structural field.

In spite of the presence of Bob Dodds, with his knowledge of engines and in particular the Rolls-Royce Tynes, plus a number of engine fitters, ATA had no facilities to cater for the overhaul of engines. According to Jim Townsend:

> The eighteen-cylinder Wright R3350 Turbo-Compound engines on the DC-7c were mainly purchased zero time engines that were on the market, ex Air France, TAP, and Aerodex…a few of these engines were sent to an overhaul facility in the USA in Hondo, Texas. The Pratt and Whitney JT3D-3Bs on the DC-8s were overhauled in France and the Rolls-Royce Tynes on the CL44 were initially overhauled at Rolls-Royce in Canada, then at MTU in Germany.[13]

Despite ATA being able to draw upon Air Rhodesia's substantial engineering capability when necessary, Dave Hann recalls that the machine shop was a vital part of the engineering strength at ATA:

> The machine shop was staffed by a magician: John Nicholson could produce just about anything we needed at quite short notice. We had a lathe that was capable of throwing a DC-8 main wheel should we need to clean up sections of it, and a milling machine for handling quite large panels.[14]

The machine shop was backed up by stressed skin specialists, such as George Graham, with Des Pearce as a welder and sheet metal worker. Another vital skill was non-destructive testing (NDT), supervised by George Merritt and Len George.[15] These men would prove to be key assets when the Spitfire arrived. The Electrical & Instrument (E&I) section incorporated the radio section, headed by Phil Mason supported by numerous technicians, including Mick Kemsley, Jimmy Gibson and Johnny Norman, as well as John Davidson who was a radio specialist. John Clegg ran the wheel bay, hydraulic and ground power units. An experienced group of inspectors headed by Bill Rheeder scrutinised the standards of work. The back room boys included Rex Ovington and Doug Smith who maintained all the technical records. Ted Vine ran the tool store; he had at one time been in the SRAF and was remembered by Air Commodore Keith Kemsley as the man who spray-painted the Spitfires in their new colour schemes after the ferries. ATA's stores were run by Andy Wawn, who was also an engineer.

A number of the engineers at ATA had been sourced from the RhAF. Some had participated in a programme that allowed RhAF engineers to work part-time to earn extra cash, from late afternoon into the evening, assisting ATA to perform heavy maintenance on its aircraft. Heavy maintenance included the 300 hour and C and D checks.

In addition to its qualified engineers, ATA employed a number of apprentices at various stages of their training. Again, they would prove most useful when the Spitfire arrived. These included Piet and Louis Bezuidenhout, Russell Clements, Ben Darck, Carlos da Silva, Dave Lamb, Bob Lane, Morgan Maitland-Smith, Carlos Martins, Pete Massimiani, Dave Potgieter and Andy and Dave Wood.

Although not part of the skilled entity of ATA, there was also a notable contingent of general (African) workers in the hangar and freight shed, amongst whom was one Gideon. He and Jack had known each other since their days as youngsters. Even though he wasn't a foreman he clearly carried a lot of influence and had direct access to Jack. The story goes that when Tommy Minks, who had recruited a lot the workers from the Air Force, tried one day to fire Gideon for some reason, Jack quietly informed him that Tommy would go before Gideon.[16]

Finally, because SR64 was still an Air Force aircraft, ATA had automatic access to the resources of the Rhodesian Air Force. The key facilitator was WO1 Jimmy Gordon-Brander, who already had a close association with SR64. He was the RhAF's technical liaison officer, responsible for all the outsourced work for Airwork and

Fields at the airport, and thus by definition with ATA and the Spitfire project. He was to play a vital part in sourcing the windscreen, the port navigation light glass and providing access to the bay servicing units for various components at New Sarum. In addition, the Air HQ liaison officers included armaments specialist Flight Lieutenant Bertie May and another whose identity and position cannot be recalled.

A list of all the ATA engineers between 1977 and 1980 appears as Appendix E.[17] While this list is as inclusive as possible, it may be that one or two names do not appear on it, despite all the efforts to collect all the names and order them correctly.

Even though Bob Dodds and Dave Hann could draw on this substantial pool of engineers, practicalities determined that a relatively small group of engineers would do most of the work on the Spitfire. Carlos Martins was enthused enough to secure one of the pistons—the A1 piston—from the original Griffon engine on SR64, on which he engraved the names of 20 men who carried out most of the rebuild work. In the order in which they appear on the piston, these are: Peter Massimiani, Morgan Maitland-Smith (deceased), Ben Darck, Bob Brown, George Graham, Bob Dodds (deceased), Dave Wood, Ross Malloch, Trevor Blofield, Dave Lamb (who died in October 2004 in the MK Airlines crash at Halifax, Nova Scotia), Victor Pereira, Rob Myers, John Dodds, Mike Holmes, Andy Wood, Piet Bezuidenhout, Jim Gibson, Dave Hann and Carlos Martins. Undoubtedly there were others who worked on the aircraft and whose names do not appear on this list.

It is important to remember that without the substantial pool of engineering skills available to ATA at the time, the task of rebuilding the Spitfire could never have been completed. Recognition of this fact, and of the engineers who worked for Jack Malloch, would follow in time.

Chapter 8
NUTS AND BOLTS

The Spitfire project commenced when Air Vice-Marshal Chris Dams and Jack Malloch concluded the terms of agreement for the rebuild of SR64, sometime in mid-1977. It was signed shortly thereafter with the Ministry of Defence by both Jack Malloch and probably the then Secretary of Defence, Tony Parker.[1] This would have been followed by a signal from Air HQ to Thornhill, probably to the Officer Commanding Technical Wing (OCTW) at Thornhill, instructing him to arrange the relocation of SR64 to the ATA hangar at Salisbury Airport. In turn the task was delegated to Bob Garrett, the FWTO. Dave Hann recalls that Jack Malloch gave him and Bob Dodds little warning of the arrival of a Queen Mary low-bed truck belonging to the RhAF. The accompanying crew, with the help of ATA staff, off-loaded an aeroplane that was in pieces. Spike Owens and his 6 Sqn technicians had been in the process of stripping the aircraft when the decision was taken that Jack Malloch and ATA would rebuild her. Technicians had managed to strip the paint off the aircraft and were already disassembling its various components, but they were in no position to put it together again. Consequently it appeared to ATA's engineers as a rather shambolic mess—Bob and Dave both called it a "suspect load".

Bob Dodds recollected his reaction in the video *Spitfire—The Pursuit of a Dream*:[2]

> The first information we had that the Spitfire was no longer fiction but fact, was when Captain Malloch came and informed us that the Spitfire was arriving that particular day. It was with great trepidation, and horror, that we viewed the results of this long awaited event. We saw the state of the actual aircraft, accompanied on a low loader by a motley selection of boxes and suspect-looking aircraft parts and general paraphernalia.

Bob's words indicate that, despite the surprise arrival, he must have had some advance warning of Jack Malloch's intentions. This was not the case for Dave Hann, who recalled his feeling in the same video:

> It arrived in the hangar quite unannounced and it was much to everybody's surprise that we had this aircraft. We were very busy with our own aircraft trying to keep them together. There was no plan mentioned. There we were—

7,000 pounds of pieces of aluminium and copper what-have-you, just dumped in the corner of the hangar, occupying quite valuable space, I thought, at the time. No project arrangements; there it is, just get on with it and just build the Spitfire.

The manner of the arrival of the Spitfire 'wreck' set the tone of a loosely structured project. Other than a clear expectation that the aircraft would fly again, no firm target dates were established until close to the end of the rebuild, when Dave Hann and Bob Dodds nominated the first flight date to Jack Malloch. Dave Hann remembers the project as a 'fill-in job' and that the priority at the time was to keep ATA's aircraft operational. If they were working on the Spitfire and a DC-8 required repair, then all hands would attend to the DC-8's needs, leaving the Spitfire until the next quiet time.

The Spitfire wreck was initially greeted with a lot of resistance—understandably so. The senior engineers and especially some of the inspectors displayed the greatest disapproval, even refusing to get involved. It was felt that the Spitfire would interfere with their primary job of maintaining ATA aircraft and would absorb funds that could be better spent on those same aircraft. Yet, for all the potential distraction that the Spitfire represented, Ian Hunt recalls that Jack Malloch never took his eye off the ball while directing operations at ATA.[3]

It was the apprentices who displayed the greatest interest and curiosity. This probably persuaded Dave Hann, who by this time was the Project Manager, to utilise this pool of manpower. In fact, this turned out to be an inspired decision: the rebuild project became the ideal platform on which the apprentices could cut their teeth and learn the basics of an airframe and systems, and some of them proved very adept at their delegated tasks. For example, Carlos Martins is forever associated with the pneumatics, and Piet Bezuidenhout with structural work under George Graham. However, it was Dave Hann's leadership that was to prove so essential to the project. Dave Hann brought superlative technical knowledge, plus experience of a rebuild in the RRAF and he plainly led by example. Andy Wood recalls just how much Bob Dodds and Dave Hann poured into the youngsters on the project and he retains a very high regard for them to this day.

So it was that Jack Malloch's engineers grew into the job. Bob Dodds and Dave Hann knew they had Jack's full backing and that he could be relied upon to solve any spares and resource problems—and that no questions were to be asked as to the source of a spare. Dave remembers the wry smile on Jack's face when suddenly an important spare arrived in the hangar. He knew not to ask the obvious question and he quietly marvelled at Jack's ability to get things done. Jack seldom held any progress meetings but easily monitored developments during his daily walks around the hangar. Grant Domoney, who joined ATA in 1978 from the RhAF as an instruments (later known as avionics) technician, recalls efforts by The Boss to chivvy his engineers and accelerate progress:

> Another thing that sticks in my mind was that, whenever possible, Captain Jack would saunter across to the hangar and complain that the rebuild was taking too long and he was dead keen to get her into the air. After explanations that we were also busy keeping the two DC-8s and the dog of a CL-44 flying, which seemed to keep him quiet, he would stroll back to his office, mumbling.

Bob Dodds and Dave Hann did hold regular meetings and they developed a very solid professional working relationship. Sounding each other out at critical junctures and then deciding upon a course of action was critical to the successful outcome of the project.

Squadron Leader Chris Dixon was a regular visitor to the project and his visits were greatly appreciated. Fields and Airwork engineers were another source of regular and curious observers, as was Terry Eaton from the AF. These visits have been captured in photographs. In addition, the Rhodesian Department of Civil Aviation maintained a keen professional interest in the project.

PHASES

ATA's modern hangar was very capacious. Aligned northeast/southwest and thus parallel to what was then Salisbury's main runway 06/24, it could accommodate the DC-8 quite comfortably. SR64 was deposited on the hangar floor in the western corner. This marked the beginning of its movements around the hangar, as if on a rough production line. Just as 'X' metaphorically marks the spot, so it was that the aircraft would follow the outline of the letter X on its journey around the hangar keeping out of the way of important day-to-day maintenance activities. Each movement, however, would define a different state of disassembly, associated work activity, and later reassembly, thus making for four distinct phases that would cover the better part of three years.

The first phase lasted only a few months and was dedicated to sorting out the pieces and getting them into some order. The aircraft was then moved to the opposite eastern corner for the second phase—the time-consuming process of inspecting all the various components to determine their state and serviceability, and how to proceed with repairs. The aircraft probably remained here for well over a year. From there it was moved to the northern corner next to the line records office, for the third phase of its reconstruction. Here the aircraft was reassembled, but without its engine and aircraft systems. When the aircraft was back on its undercarriage it was moved to the southern corner next to the E&I office and a power supply, for her final assembly. This fourth and final phase incorporated the reinstallation of aircraft systems, replacement of all the electrical wiring, reinstallation of the instruments and, finally, the refitting of the engine and propeller. It was from this position in the hangar that the aircraft performed engine runs prior to her taxi tests and first flight. In fact, this southern corner became her permanent hangar position. These movements around the hangar lend themselves to identifying different phases in the rebuild chronology, which makes it easy for the reader to follow the story.

From here on the story will reflect the methodology followed by the engineers—inspection, rectification and reassembly with certain modifications. As it turned out, the bulk of the work was carried out in the last phase of final reassembly.

The Spitfire Mk 22 was structurally a relatively simple aircraft—see Appendix A for a cutaway drawing of a Mk 21, there being no cutaway drawings available for a Mk 22. Throughout its evolution to this advanced state, its most complex components were the Griffon V12 engine and the 5-bladed propeller; its most complex system was the pneumatics; and its most sophisticated component was the gyro gun sight. Its airframe was simple and bore all the hallmarks of British engineering with which Dave Hann was so familiar. With the experience he had gained over the years this project was like meat and drink to him. Whilst Jack Malloch would deal with the engine, propeller and sourcing of the canopy, it was left to Dave Hann to oversee the job that would take the longest time to restore – the airframe, including the undercarriage, flight controls and systems (hydraulic and pneumatic). Bearing in mind that there were no Air Force publications available to the engineers, this was the perfect platform for skilled engineers to display their expertise, and this is what they demonstrated in the weeks and months ahead as they tackled this unique rebuild task.

It is worth mentioning here that Jeffrey Quill, the famous Vickers Supermarine Spitfire test pilot, was well aware of this project. He had been approached to assist with manuals but was unable to do so as he was based in Munich working for Panavia at that time, in February 1978. A certain Chris Faber[4] had initiated the contact through a friend, Viv Bellamy, in his efforts to help Jack Malloch, his former Boss. Chris Faber was by this time flying Viscounts for Air Rhodesia. In a letter to Viv Bellamy (brother-in-law to John Fairey, who would assist Jack Malloch on the day of the first flight) Jeffrey Quill indicated that he "would like very much to help the enthusiasts in southern Africa who are rebuilding a Spitfire 22". Their efforts were rewarded with a copy of the Mk 21 Instruction Manual from the South Marston factory. Somehow, though, this manual never reached Dave Hann and his team, who were already well into the project. Nevertheless, Viv Bellamy and Chris Faber provided invaluable assistance to the project later on, as we shall see.

INSPECTION, ASSESSMENT & PRIORITISATION:
THE WEST AND EAST CORNERS

Once the engineers recovered from their shock at the imposition of the rebuild task, their first activity was to sort out all the bits and pieces and to separate the Spitfire components from the Vampire and Provost parts, inadvertently included with the Spitfire parts. Suitable ground equipment had to be sourced and, in some cases, manufactured. This meant using existing Vampire tripod jacks and Provost fuselage supports and modifying them, as well as fabricating wing formers and supports and slings; even a suitable towing arm had to be manufactured.

Once this was complete the aircraft could be moved to the eastern corner in an organised and accessible state for the next phase of activity. Here the laborious process of inspecting all the components was carried out, following which the components were classified according to their function, i.e. structural or system, and the level of damage, i.e. minor/major state of disrepair. This was necessary to determine whether the component could be replaced or repaired or needed to be remanufactured.

ATA's inspectors with military experience were chosen to perform the visual checks to determine a component's state of serviceability. In this context the engine was easy—it was seized—and was dispatched forthwith, probably on the ATA DC-7, to the SAAF for overhaul. The propeller assembly was totally unserviceable and required a complete remanufacture of the blades.

Apart from visual checks and the experience of the inspectors, the use of NDT by George Merritt and Len George was essential to the process of inspecting components, especially structural items. Non-destructive testing consists of three different techniques: X-ray, ultra sonic sound and dye penetrate. X-ray was widely used, not only to check for corrosion in key components such as the wing spars, but also to try to understand how components such as the oleo legs were constructed and assembled. Mindful of the fact that no publications were available to the project team, the X-ray technique proved invaluable in this area and showed that the spar was free of corrosion. The spar consisted of four sets of five square concentric tubes, each of diminishing size, fitting one inside the other. Two sets attached to a beam in the shape of an 'I' made for one wing spar. It was essential to check that there had been no water ingress between the laminations of the tubes.

Ultra sonic sound was not used as widely as X-ray, but it was used on a critical structural component—the main spar carry-through beam underneath the cockpit and fuselage fuel tanks. The use of ultra-sonic sound requires special skill as it is very easy to be confused by echoes which have emanated from a change of section rather than from a defect in the metal. Defects found by this method were subjected to further inspection by X-ray. The carry-through beam was found to be serviceable and free from corrosion.

Dye penetrate was used quite widely on hydraulic, pneumatic and coolant pipes to ascertain their integrity.

Once this process was completed, the rectification process was allocated to one of four courses of action:

1. Items that could be repaired or overhauled at ATA;
2. Items that the Air Force could bay service at New Sarum;
3. Items that could be replaced by equipment in the RhAF stores at New Sarum;
4. Items that would have to be outsourced (because neither ATA nor the RhAF had the capacity to handle their manufacture or repair).

Thus it was that ATA managed the bulk of the work on the airframe and undercarriage, the fuel tanks, the rewiring of all the electrical looms and modifications, the refitting of the pneumatic and hydraulic systems and the flight controls, as well as the entire final assembly.

The RhAF handled the bulk of the outsourced work and facilitated the engine overhaul. Together with stories relating to the propeller and other components, the process of rectification produced fascinating accounts that appear later in this chapter. These have all made it a richer narrative and they will be related as the rest of story unfolds.

IN-HOUSE RECTIFICATIONS

The process of rectification was well underway when it was realised that the task which took the longest time was replacing the fuselage rivets. Dave Hann estimated that 80% of the magnesium alloy rivets were eventually replaced, due to corrosion. This time-consuming task continued into the final reassembly phase and was an ideal task for apprentices under supervision. During WW2 when skill shortages were prevalent, women were employed in huge numbers on the Spitfire production line and proved to be most adept with finicky tasks such as the fitting of rivets.

The airframe was generally free from major corrosion, except for the magnesium alloy rivets and the outer portion of the port wing. The latter had been subjected to considerable corrosion by virtue of the fact that SR64 had been in a permanent left wing low position on the plinth at New Sarum. Water had gathered in the wingtip during each of the 13 rainy seasons of her silent vigil there and when the water evaporated so the corrosion set in. The final 30 inches of the wing was completely re-manufactured by the skin 'basher' George Graham, assisted by Piet Bezuidenhout.

Many of the 14 wing attachment bolts which secured the wing spars to the carry through beams needed to be replaced. This was not problematic as there were samples and material specifications and conditions could be ascertained. Jimmy Gordon-Brander of the AF saw to this job and probably had them made, either at New Sarum or by a sub-contractor in the Salisbury industrial area.

The fuel tanks proved to be quite a challenge and here Dave Hann's experience proved very useful. The Mk 22 had six fuel tanks: two fuselage tanks (totalling 85 gallons), being a lower and an upper tank between the firewall and the cockpit; and two in the leading edges of each wing (totalling 35 gallons) forward of the undercarriage. The AF was easily able to service and pressure-test the fuselage lower flexible self-sealing tank. ATA serviced the upper tank without too much of a problem; it was a rigid tank with a self-sealing cover and required flushing out and pressure-testing, only. The leading edge tanks had weathered badly. Manufacturing replacement tanks or dispensing with them altogether was considered and rejected. Rather, Dave Hann chose to use a PRC fuel tank sealant. The tanks were removed, PRC was 'sloshed' around the interior of each, and the tanks were then finished off with a sealing coat. Once the tanks were pressure tested they were replaced in the wings. The only drawback was that the colour of the PRC dye came out in the fuel but this leaching soon stopped after a few refuels. Calibration suggested no great loss of volume and fuel flows were satisfactory.

The engine oil tank was similar in construction to that of the fuselage ridged fuel tank, and after cleaning proved to be serviceable.

The cockpit windshield and canopy provided a substantial and interesting challenge. The distinctive teardrop canopy had been damaged beyond repair by the sun and had to be replaced. ATA tried hard to manufacture a replacement canopy and enlisted the help of Wing Commander Peter Knobel of the Air Force. He had successfully assisted the RhAF in manufacturing bubble canopies for the Canberra fleet. These were relatively simple in shape, whereas the Spitfire's canopy was a more complex tear-drop shape, which proved to be the undoing of the project. Peter Knobel was unable to get the finished product, when cooled, to assume the correct proportions. In Dave Hann's words: "Peter's canopy lacked the rise and fullness where it joined the windscreen frame. You could put your head against the canopy inside and just about see around the windscreen frame." Pictures taken by Peter Knobel certainly show a lower profile. Short of sourcing a genuine late mark Spitfire canopy, this fine one-off version would probably have been retained as the actual canopy, according to Dave Hann. In the end the project was saved by Jack Malloch and his network, the successful outcome of which will be related later.

The entire windshield consisted of four panels: the main windscreen was made of glass while the two forward side windscreen panels and the upper centre panel were made of Perspex. A replacement for the main windscreen replacement was successfully sourced by Jimmy Gordon-Brander from the Pilkington glass factory in Umtali. This company had already been manufacturing replacement windscreens for the 1 Sqn Hunter FGA 9s, so it was a fairly straightforward matter to manufacture one for the Spitfire, based on the available original. The only variance was that the glass had a slight green tint to it but this did not affect the most critical aspect of the windshield, being the optical quality of the glass.

The centre upper windscreen panel required the manufacture of a small male mould. The Perspex was free to form naturally over the mould when it reached moulding temperature and a measure of distortion was acceptable, as the aircraft was no longer a combat aircraft. The wing tip navigation lights were manufactured in the same manner. The forward side windscreen panels were the easiest to manufacture as they comprised nothing more than flat panels with rebated edges.

In the early stages sourcing the seals for the main undercarriage was a problem because neither the AF nor Fields locally had suitable spares. Quite by chance, Dave Hann was able to source a set of seals from Bestabel in the Salisbury industrial area.

He had gone there looking for something else and when he mentioned his problem the technical manager managed to rustle up a spare set of seals within a couple of minutes—at no cost other than a thank you.

On the subject of seals, the double Schrader valves in the flap selector had perished rendering the selector useless. The ATA workshops came to the rescue and produced the double valves, with spares.

The ATA workshops proved invaluable in making a complete set of seals for the pneumatic system. A local tyre manufacturer supplied the raw rubber and the method for curing the product. The workshops produced a small moulding tool that produced a dozen seals at a time. Once loaded with the raw rubber, the mould was closed and placed in an industrial oven to cure and bingo—seals were produced, with spares.

The flying controls were all managed in house at ATA, supervised by Tommy Fraser, a Short's trained apprentice. Having a set of old flying control cables for the ailerons and elevators meant that these could be duplicated without too much trouble. The original fittings were the same as those utilised on the Vampire and the AF stores had stock, so remanufacture was straightforward. The rudder cables and those of the rudder trim had to be manufactured from scratch as no samples were available. The rudder trim tab had an unusual configuration—when the trim was in the neutral position, the longer upper portion would be flush with the fin, whilst the lower portion was offset to the starboard, as seen from the rear. It was linked directly to the cockpit rudder trim wheel—the bias of the lower portion was to assist the pilot achieve the full left rudder trim required for take-off. The pilot needed to counter the swing to the right, caused by the anti-clockwise rotation of the propeller, by applying full left rudder. Dave Hann and the project engineers battled to rig the trim correctly and could not find anyone who had knowledge of how to rig it. Jack discovered the error later.

Many of these later fixes were accomplished in the last phase, i.e. during the final assembly phase.

OUT-SOURCED RECTIFICATIONS

The RhAF was responsible for the bulk of the out-sourced rectifications and for the provision of numerous spares from stores. This work was carried out at the various sections at New Sarum, across the runway from ATA where the bay-servicing of numerous components took place, including: the instruments, the hydraulic and pneumatic pumps, the oxygen system, the gun sight and the Hispano Suiza cannons with their associated Belt Feed Mechanisms (BFMs). Fortunately, there was a lot of commonality with components still in use by the AF which at the time was utilising mostly British manufactured aircraft. The Vampire, which had taken over from the Spitfire, was a typical example of this —the gyro stabilised gun-sight was similar to the one used on the FB9 Vampires, as were the Hispano Suiza 20mm cannons. The Spitfire's cannons were Mk 2s, as opposed to the Vampire's cannons which were Mk 5s. The oxygen system was the same and the flight instruments would have been very similar, if not the same. On the day of the first flight Phil Mason, head of the E&I section at ATA, commented that they had to source quite a few spares from the UK. While we don't know which specific instruments were sourced from the UK, we do know that finding them was thanks to Jack Malloch's network.

All this work would have been initiated by Dave Hann using standard Air Force paperwork, in particular Form 6, as it was known. Dave would have been very familiar with this from his RRAF and Airwork days and this system worked very well for him. It meant that all this work was carried out by the RhAF at no direct cost to Jack Malloch and ATA. This would have been a huge saving, but it has to be remembered it was still an RhAF aircraft and thus a simple matter to 'hide' the cost!

The RhAF also facilitated the overhaul of the Griffon engine. An excellent relationship existed between the Rhodesian and South African Air Forces at this time. Air Marshal Mick McLaren of the RhAF and Lieutenant General Bob Rogers of the SAAF knew each other personally. This provided excellent access for then Group Captain Keith Kemsley, as Counsellor to the Diplomatic Representative at the Rhodesian Diplomatic Mission in Pretoria. Keith Kemsley set this process in motion with a 'Secret' security classification,[5] so that when the engine arrived in Pretoria, in Jack's DC-7, AF number 7230, at the SAAF AFB Swartkop, it went straight to No. 1 Aircraft Depot (AD), just down the road from the base, to be overhauled. Most fortunately the SAAF still had Shackleton aircraft which utilised the Griffon 57A, as opposed to the Griffon 61 on the Spitfire. The major difference was that the Griffon 57A utilised fuel injection whereas the Spitfire's engine used a carburettor; in all other respects the engines were the same. Mr Moffs, who supervised the overhaul, commented that he could do this job in his sleep. He was assisted by Messrs R. den Boestert, Johan Locke,[6] G. P. Nel and P.S. Weyers. By all accounts the overhaul took the better part of two years to complete and an excellent job was accomplished. It has not been established how many man-hours it took, but it would have been a lengthier job than a standard overhaul as the engine had seized with corrosion. Most of the moving parts were replaced although the original block was used. Again the cost of this substantial 'secret' project was settled between the two Air Forces, probably just by hiding it as another SAAF Griffon overhaul. The engine was collected by Jack Malloch's DC-7, probably in January 1980.

The other major project to be out-sourced was the remanufacture of the propeller blades. This was to be an outstanding achievement, bearing in mind the state of sanctions imposed on Rhodesia at the time. Dave Hann arranged to transport the old propeller to Paris in a DC-8, where Jim Townsend, Jack Malloch's point man in Europe, who sourced spares for the airline and thus the Spitfire project, was instrumental in sourcing a new propeller.[7] Jim Townsend recalls his efforts to get the propeller repaired and reminds us why the Spitfires had been grounded in the first place:

> The Rotol five-bladed wooden propeller was badly deteriorated. The reason why most Mk 22 Spitfires were grounded, although few and far between, was due to the wooden blades shrinking and becoming loose in the metal root hub end acme threaded portion. There was a shortage of props so I contacted Rotol Propellers in the UK but they were not particularly helpful and their prices were high. I then contacted a company in Germany—Hoffmann—which specialised in wooden propellers. They made propellers for the German Air Force and for the Russian aerobatic team and recently for a refurbished Focke-Wulf 190 airplane. They agreed to help us. I took the metal parts (some time in 1978) and one partially intact blade to Hoffman in the boot of a rented car and had their engineers look at the parts. They stated that they could manufacture the prop using the metal parts and the blade as a template. The only information that Hoffman needed was the engine max horse power and the max RPM.
>
> They produced a propeller far superior to Rotol's, although it looked identical to the original. To prevent the previous recurring problems with the wooden blades, Hoffmann secured the blades with the original acme threads then pinned the metal hubs to the blades by inserting pins the length of the blades. Finally, to prevent moisture ingression the complete blade with each hub was completely fibre-glassed. The complete propeller costs came to the same price as Rotol would have charged us to make one blade.
>
> The propeller never gave a problem on installation or operationally: it was smooth running and vibration free, better than the original.

The cost of the propeller was documented as US$25,000. In today's values that would cost around US$60,000 (∈40,000.00) according to Stefan Bichlmeyr at Hoffman Propeller.[8] It took six weeks to complete and was a highlight in their company's history. Today they still manufacture mostly four-bladed propellers for Spitfires. The completed unit, in pieces, was returned to Rhodesia in late 1978 or early 1979, in one of ATA's DC-8s. According to Dave Hann, some smooth talking by Jack Malloch with customs officials was required to ensure the unit's trouble-free return to the country.

This was indeed an incredible achievement and steeped in irony as well—it had been a German company that had seen to the repair of the propeller on a British Spitfire.

The rectification of the under-wing radiators produced another story within the main story. They were stripped and inspected and it was decided that they needed to be flushed, cleaned internally and then pressure tested. This was beyond the capability of ATA so Dave sought assistance from a local company that specialised in industrial radiators. In discussions with the owner it transpired that he had worked for Holden in Australia during the war. Holden was one of the manufacturers of radiators for military aircraft and thus he had specific knowledge of these types of radiators. With the system running pressures and test pressures on the brass information plates on the radiators they were duly serviced and pressure tested and painted in the original grey finish. Dave remembers that when he collected them they were, to all intents and purposes, brand new. These under-wing radiators were vital components. The forward sections were dedicated to the cooling of the engine glycol. A thermostat was set at 115° C, at which point the ramp door opened fully automatically under pneumatic pressure sensed by thermal sensors downstream of the restricted flow. The rear port radiator contained the oil cooler and the rear starboard the supercharger intercooler, which also used glycol. The supercharger intercooler was positioned at the rear port side of the engine and it cooled the compressed gases before induction into the cylinders.

One of the idiosyncrasies of the Spitfire was that as the undercarriage was retracted one leg would lag behind the other. The lagging leg would hang in front of the radiator and would cause the temperature to rise rapidly. Dave Hann believed the introduction of a simple flow divider would have solved this problem but he was never able to make the modification.

MODIFICATIONS

One of the principal modifications was to the emergency extension system of the undercarriage, including the tail wheel. The Mk 22 had been designed with a retractable tail wheel—a feature which had been incorporated into the Spitfire family from the Mk VII onwards—which provided the aircraft with a few extra knots in speed. However, following practical experience and reliability issues, pipes within the tail wheel hydraulic system were disconnected. This was part of the Air Ministry Modification, along with the introduction of PK screws to secure the doors in the closed position. This meant that the tail wheel was permanently locked down.

When it came to the rebuild, the first challenge was how to recharge the single emergency extension cylinder. This was achieved by seeking assistance from an ice cream company in Salisbury, named Dairibord. Dave picks up the story:

> The emergency bottle had a CO_2 charge of 90 grams. Not a pressure, but a weight! Somehow the charge had to be captured in the bottle. The method of sealing the bottle was with a copper blank. This blank was retained under a sealing nut and during emergency selection it was pierced with a very heavy hypodermic needle. That satisfied the capturing and discharge of the bottle, but left us with the problem of refilling. Well, after several meetings regarding the filling the question remained, what pressure would be generated by 90 grams of CO_2 in a bottle of that volume? We had to find a practical solution. This is where the local ice cream factory came into the story. They used dry ice during the manufacture and transportation of their product, so off to the factory we went to acquire a lump of dry ice. Using a sensitive balance we weighed the empty bottle, the sealing nut and copper blank and then proceeded to fill the bottle with dry ice until we achieved datum weight plus 90 grams. Then, very quickly, we placed the copper blank and sealing nut in position and dumped the whole assembly into a bucket of water, well away from the hangar. We were not sure quite what would transpire, so better safe than sorry! After a suitable time, several hours in fact, there having been no explosion, the bottle was returned to the balance and checked for total mass. We achieved datum mass plus 90 grams. We used this bottle to satisfy emergency lowering of the undercarriage during our function testing, and we subsequently recharged it several times using the same procedure.

Dave Hann again picks up the story of how they maximised the opportunity to reinstate the original emergency lowering of the tail wheel with a more reliable system:

Originally the aircraft was fitted with emergency lowering for the main and tail wheel assemblies, but due to low capacity of the CO_2 bottle it was possible to end up with one main leg and the tail wheel being deployed, which made for a difficult landing configuration. To overcome this situation the RAF introduced a modification that eliminated the supply of CO_2 to the tail wheel, and, with the aid of self-tapping screws, secured the tail wheel doors.

If you see any photographs of PK350 flying after restoration with the tail wheel locked down, then these photographs would have been taken during the very early flights, possibly May or June 1980 (Note: this was actually around September 1980). Later flights show the tail wheel retracted. We reintroduced retraction, and the emergency lowering system to the tail wheel assembly; all the plumbing was still in the aircraft from the date of manufacture in 1945, and was redundant. In the event of having to lower the undercarriage in an emergency it required two operations: one for the main gear, and one for the tail. With the tail wheel retracted a few extra knots could be achieved. Our modification introduced a separate CO_2 bottle for the tail wheel system.

The main wheel tyres were easily replaced with Vampire main wheel tyres, which were the same size as the original Spitfire wheels. This was a good luck story, but replacing the tail wheel tyre was harder to resolve. All the original spare tail wheel tyres had found their way onto ground equipment in the AF and eventually a Cessna tail wheel tyre was used. It was first reprofiled by a local tyre retreading company so as to fit inside the tail wheel fork.

The original VHF radio was replaced completely. Utilising the original whip aerial position along the cut-down rear fuselage, the AF provided a new radio which was installed behind and to the left of the pilot's seat. This required the pilot to select a frequency or channel by feel only—not a very satisfactory solution. Dave Hann commented that this feature would have been rectified if the aircraft had not been lost.

The final modifications were to the electrical system. A lighter, greater capacity, fully aerobatic battery replaced the heavier, original model. The Coffman starter cartridge system, for which cartridges were no longer available, was replaced with an electric starter. An advantage of the electrical starter was that it produced a softer start for the engine; a disadvantage was that the aircraft now had to rely upon a 24 volt external power source for the start. To this end, a power socket had to be fitted in the starboard wing root fairing, similar to the one on the port side, for general servicing electrical power.

INITIAL REASSEMBLY: THE NORTH CORNER

When the bulk of the structural repairs to the airframe were complete it was time to partially reassemble the aircraft, utilising the majority of the structural parts. As already mentioned, this was carried out next to the line records office and took about a year, emphasising the 'fill-in' job characteristic of the entire project. The wings and empennage were refitted and all the plumbing for the pneumatics in the wings (cannon heating) and radiators were secured in place, making it possible for the aircraft to stand on her undercarriage once again. She was mobile up to a point, albeit with her weight distribution mostly on the tail wheel because of the lack of an engine and its attendant systems in the nose. She was extremely heavy at the tail and Dave was worried the tail wheel oleo would bottom out and be damaged. The workshops produced a clamp to prevent such damage but this did not work too well; it crumpled, leaving just enough movement to prevent damage.

While it must have raised everyone's spirits to see the aircraft on its wheels again there was still much work to be done. Several photographs record this phase of the project and it's easy to see why this achievement lifted morale—PK350 looked very striking in her plain metal finish, and once again was clearly recognisable as a Spitfire.

Andy Wood, one of the project apprentices, recalls that at this stage the RhAF suddenly became interested in the project. Perceptions at ATA were that the RhAF had shown zero attention to date, but now that the aircraft was recognisable as a Spitfire it became interested—and arranged for photographs to be taken. This professional jealousy was understandable: ATA's engineers had worked hard to get the aircraft back to this gleaming fledgling-like state[9] and probably resented the intrusion by the RhAF. Also, they believed the aircraft belonged to Jack and were not aware of the true status of its ownership or the extent of the RhAF's quiet but significant assistance with the project.

FINAL REASSEMBLY: THE SOUTH CORNER

Probably toward the end of 1979, practicalities demanded one final move around the hangar. A good power source was necessary, as was more space, now that the Spitfire had her wings reattached. This meant the southern corner was the ideal location. It was close to a little-used ramp outside and this became her permanent hangar position.

Dave Hann relates this final phase of assembly:

Once again, the airframe was lifted off the ground onto servicing jacks and trestles and the serious business of system installation started. The business of finding its feet again was very short-lived indeed and the distance travelled was short, just a few metres. The replacement of various corroded fasteners to the fuselage continued until such time that the task was completed. The electrical tradesmen, along with the airframe fitters, installed the various systems that had been removed for cleaning and bench testing. In the case of the electrical systems, the electricians replaced all the old cables with new. This task used the original routing and ensured that there would be no nasty surprises later on. A major modification to the electrical system was the introduction of an electrical starter for the engine: this modification required a heavy-duty cable to be fitted from the starboard wing root fairing, aft of the wing right up to the starter on the starboard side of the engine. To facilitate the required supply point a structural modification was carried out. This modification was the replication of the ground-servicing power point similar to the one found in the port wing root fairing. It allowed for the shortest cable, easy and safe access during engine starting.

Work on the pneumatic system was very slow at first as we were trying to install the system using the original pipe seals; but, no sooner was one leak fixed than another would appear. This problem was causing a delay with other work, as most of the pneumatic system piping was situated in the under-floor area of the cockpit. Once the airframe man started working there then the other trades were delayed in their work. A decision was taken that the pneumatic system would be reworked totally, thus freeing up the cockpit for a while, and ATA engineering would investigate the possibility of seal manufacture.

As has been related above, this problem was solved with the help of a local tyre manufacturer and ATA's machine shop. Between them they made a mould for seals to be produced to the correct specifications at ATA, with some spares left over.

Dave Hann continues:

During this time, the vast majority of the cockpit work of the other trades was well ahead. The under floor pneumatic system was refitted by Carlos Martins using our new seals and proved very successful. The flap selector was another problem area: the seals on the Schrader valves used in the mechanism had perished, which rendered the selector useless. Workshops tackled this problem and after several unsuccessful attempts produced the required double valves, and several more as spares. The hydraulic system was possibly the least troublesome, other than the undercarriage selector, which did give some problems, mainly because of our lack of knowledge of its full function and the correct assembly of the selector. During retraction tests the undercarriage would stow correctly and the fairing doors close; it was on the down selection that the problems started. The door 'shoot bolt' actuators were considerably smaller than the main actuators and in theory they should have retracted quicker than the movement of the main actuator. This, in fact was not happening; the main actuator was moving before the shoot bolts could retract and the wheel was resting heavily on the doors. This situation was causing the gear to hang up. The whole system would work correctly when a little upward pressure was applied on the doors during a downward selection but this obviously could not be the situation during a flight. Therefore, the decision was made to remove the troublesome doors for the first few flights and only with the refitting of the doors afterwards was the problem effectively resolved. Several flights later, during an investigation into this problem it was discovered that the selector valve was in fact incorrectly assembled. Correct reassembly and a full function test proved that the system was now working correctly and the undercarriage doors should be refitted for flight. Retraction tests were performed and the system was working well. After all is said and done, many earlier models of the Spitfire were flown without undercarriage doors, so there could be no harm in flying this particular aircraft minus the doors.

The fuel system was also rectified during this final assembly phase. While the RhAF had serviced the lower fuselage tank, it was ATA who successfully serviced the remaining upper fuel tank and repaired the four wing tanks (as has already been related above).

Dave Hann confessed that by Christmas 1979, when he took a well-deserved break in South Africa, the project had begun to drag. He resolved that on returning to Rhodesia he would get the project finished as quickly as resources and man power allowed.

By early February 1980 the Griffon engine had been fitted and its associated plumbing was in place. Pictures taken by Peter Knobel around this time clearly show his canopy fitted to the aircraft in an advanced state of assembly with work still being carried out on the fuel tanks and undercarriage. The instrument panel with all the flying and system instruments were also refitted at this time, thus completing most of the jobs. The RhAF had bay serviced all the instruments and the instrument panel.[10]

Phil Mason, with the help of Mick Kemsley and Jimmy Gibson, had repositioned the instruments in their respective places in the panel and attended to the plumbing of the pitot static system. Most of the rewiring and electrical work had been carried out by Mike Holmes, 'Dup' Du Plessis, and Andy Winter.[11]

Notwithstanding Peter Knobel's valiant efforts to manufacture a canopy in-house, acquiring a genuine canopy remained a pressing priority. It was time once again for Jack's network to kick in, this time through the son of Sir Richard Fairey of Fairey Aviation fame. John Fairey, a British citizen, had nobly joined the Rhodesian Air Force as a Dakota pilot on 3 Sqn. Steeped in aviation tradition he had also owned a share in a two-seat Spitfire in the UK and knew who to contact to locate a canopy. Chris Faber, previously mentioned in connection with trying to source manuals, related the story in the video *The Final Flight of the Spitfire MK 22* produced by Group Captain Bill Sykes. He and Viv Bellamy, an ex-Fleet Air Arm pilot and brother-in-law of John Fairey, managed to locate a brand new canopy owned by Doug Arnold at Blackbushe airport in the UK. Doug Arnold had sourced three brand new canopies from the Indian Air Force which had operated MK XVIIIs in the post war years. The acquisition of the canopy in February 1980, just six weeks before the first flight, was a massive coup, matching the successful outcome of the propeller repair and the overhauled Griffon engine. Without Jack's network and his regular flights into and out of Europe, the canopy and especially the propeller may well have stalled the project indefinitely.

Dave Hann and Bob Dodds were able now to reflect that:

> By this time the thought of actually having an aircraft coming together and being a flyable product created an up-surge in activity. The manufacture of flying control cables and the fitting and rigging of flying controls[12] was satisfactorily completed as if they were normal hangar functions, and this was nothing other than a routine hangar check. Now the pace was such that Doddie and I took the time to work on a finishing target date. The number of outstanding jobs now could be counted on one hand. Establishment of the centre of gravity, compass swing, preliminary engine ground runs, external finishing of the airframe and (not forgetting the all-important documentation) were all that remained to be done.

It was now coming to the end of February 1980. Bob Dodds and Dave Hann targeted 29 March as the date for the first flight, not realising that this date had any special significance as far Jack Malloch was concerned. It happened to be the anniversary of his very first flight in the RAF way back in 1943. Dave Hann is sure that he never attempted to manipulate this target date so it has to be assumed this was pure coincidence.

FUNCTION TESTS

The SAAF-serviced Griffon arrived back sometime late in 1979 or early 1980 and was stored out of the way in the ATA hangar. Together with the Hoffman propeller it was refitted in February without a hitch, the engine taking a full day to fit, followed by the vital ground runs. These were carried out by Bob Dodds.

Dave Hann recalls:

> At the ground running point on our hard standing there was a picketing point to which we tethered the tail of the aircraft (the strop was made by New Sarum Safety Equipment), and from the port wing we secured a concrete block on which Mick Kemsley sat to bring the total mass up to 700 lbs—yes, Mick was, shall we say, well built. Without this additional weight under the wing, the torque of the engine would induce roll, and at high power settings it would pick up that wing.

In total probably about five engine runs were performed. Dave Hann made the carburettor adjustments with the engine at idle, which no doubt put the fear of God into Bob Dodds. The only hiccup occurred when a 2.5 inch coolant pipe burst late one afternoon. Jack Malloch was a spectator on the day, wearing his familiar trademark white floppy hat, keeping an eye on things. He was clearly shocked and tried to stop Dave Hann who had raced forward to resecure the pipes, to save precious glycol fluid. Jack was sure Dave would burn himself. Fortunately he didn't and Bob Dodds rapidly shut down the engine, leaving a large pool of fluid under the aircraft. Even though a few days were lost, Jack was able to acquire a replacement supply—no doubt from the SAAF at the bidding of RhAF connections in Pretoria—which would have been collected by the venerable DC-7. Jack Malloch had the following to say in the video *Spitfire—The Pursuit of Dream*:

> This was a big disappointment as it was practically our entire stock of glycol at the time. The engine wasn't affected in any way but we did get a big fright,

in case we had overheated it. It didn't really set us back because I was able to get some more glycol and the engineers were in the meantime able to make adjustments that had come to notice.

It is worth pointing out, as a sharp-eyed observer would have seen, that in the video the aircraft was already painted in its new colour scheme when this particular ground run was carried out. The initial ground runs were carried out in the primer and the last two in her new paint scheme.

It is relevant at this stage to wonder if there were any Pilot's Notes to hand. We know there were no Air Force Publications (APs) to assist the engineers during the rebuild. However, there was a set of Pilot's Notes, the source of which is not entirely clear—they were probably sourced by Jim Townsend in the UK. However, it must be remembered that there were numerous surviving ex-Spitfire pilots, such as Air Vice-Marshal Chris Dams and Air Commodore Keith Kemsley, and it's also possible that a set was 'borrowed' from amongst their colleagues. In numerous photos Bob Dodds can be seen accompanying Jack Malloch performing pre-flight inspections and on the video he is seen with the Pilot's Notes. Dave Hann has confirmed their existence but not the source.

The AF supplied the safety equipment including the parachute and the seat straps as well as the oxygen system which was fully serviceable.

The four 20mm Mk 2 Hispano Suiza cannons were refitted as fully serviceable weapons together with the gunsight. Never one to pass up a good chance to teach the apprentices another useful lesson, Dave Hann demonstrated how to harmonise the cannons:

> as a practical exercise for the apprentices, using some of the maths they had learned at school. How far apart must the sighting marks be, and how far from the sighting marks should the aircraft be, when rigged in a flying condition. We harmonised for 600 feet, all the parameters required for the maths were available; it just needed a couple of plumb bobs and a tape measure. Lovely practical exercise. I bet not one of the apprentices has ever since done anything like that again.

Another practical exercise was determining the aircraft's Centre of gravity (C of G). Dave Hann continues:

When the aircraft was weighed and the C of G calculated, once again this was a practical exercise undertaken by the apprentices. Again, they had covered the necessary maths showing where the C of G should be; now it was a case of application. The C of G calculation proved the need to introduce 20 lbs of lead onto the mass balance bar. The reason for this additional weight was the fact that we had introduced modern batteries and a modern radio and required to pull the C of G back to within the limits, which were indicated on a brass plate on the port side of the fuselage just below the main fuel tank.

The final task, one that would reconnect SR64 with her original roots, was to repaint the aircraft. This was done over the weekend of 22–23 March, with the help of the apprentices. As Dave Hann recalls:

When we arrived at the position of having a mechanically complete serviceable aircraft, we had just one more problem, what paint colour scheme should be applied? Should we return the aircraft to the silver colour scheme of the original SR64, or take into consideration the current state of Rhodesia, where all military aircraft other than transport and communications machines were finished in camouflage? This was discussed in depth with Jack who, I'm sure, discussed it with higher authorities. Nothing came of this discussion and it was left to us to use our own discretion. I approached Plascon (Pvt) (Ltd) for the finishing paints in the colours as shown in the Airfix kit insert. Plascon was very generous and supplied the paint free, as far as I know. The aircraft was positioned on servicing jacks, the undercarriage retracted, and all panels secured. Plascon supplied ATA with a red primer undercoat, the undercoat looked essentially like 'red oxide', and it wasn't…but a primer undercoat for cellulous paint. The entire aircraft was painted with this primer paint and I honestly thought that she looked good in the colour. Next the application of the silver underside paint followed by the masking off to separate the upper structure from the lower. The upper surfaces were marked out using a chalk line for the separation of the two colours used in the camouflage scheme: application of the lighter of the colours followed by the second colour. We were aware of the aircraft registration number, that being SR64, but for the other numbers and call signs, we waited for guidance. I suggested that PK350 be applied in its original format and as nobody was prepared to commit to a call sign, I used JMM (John McVicar Malloch). Once the decision was taken, the apprentices then marked out the signs and masked off the area for painting. When Jack first saw the semi-finished aircraft there was an apprehensive look on his face—I was waiting for the order to remove the personal touch and would have done so quite willingly but somehow this artwork was accepted. The application of roundel and fin flashes along with the various warning and instruction sign followed. In a matter of some 48 hours, a bare finished aircraft had taken on the look of the majesty of the skies that she really was.

This must have been a tremendously exciting moment. Resplendent in her new colour scheme, the European Temperate Day Fighter scheme, PK350 was very similar in appearance to her launch from the production line in July 1945. The exceptions were the presence of the lettering on the fuselage, denoting Jack's initials, and the omission of the yellow stripes on the leading edge of the main wings, used for identification during the war. This latter omission caught the eye of a visiting RAF Technical Officer who was returning from a visit to the SAAF. His negative comments were not well received by the engineers. One can well imagine the comments that would have been made behind the back of this particular Group Captain. Dave Hann also received a call from a plane spotter in the UK, who pointed out that 'JM' was the call sign for an Operational Training Unit[13] at Lossiemouth in Scotland. Dave Hann's reaction was to ask under his breath if that had anything to do with the price of cheese. These negative remarks were countered somewhat by a call from Rolls-Royce enquiring about the performance of the engine during the ground runs. This call, according to Dave Hann, was unprompted by Jack Malloch or his engineers, and reconfirmed the interest taken by Rolls-Royce in significant aviation developments in far-away Rhodesia.

The paperwork was largely complete. This included compiling all the Forms 4800, 4801 (Airframe and Engine Logs) and 6 (Component Bay Service Record) used along the way and getting the F700 or technical log updated. This was very important, as Dave had to know who had signing powers for what. In the end Bob Dodds and Dave Hann were authorised by Air HQ to have full signing powers for the airworthiness side, which was the obvious practical solution. After all, they had been working on the aircraft for nearly three years and knew it inside out.

All that was left now was for Jack to carry out the taxi tests. ATA's proximity to the runway made for a quick taxi in the Spitfire, useful for keeping the engine temperature below the critical 120° C—the limit for take-off. It seems that Jack carried out only two taxi tests—the first along Runway 06 and a second, at high speed, along Runway 24. Jack was satisfied with the handling of the aircraft. However, Dave remembers an anxious moment when Jack nearly nosed over onto the propeller. It was likely that Jack had forgotten how quickly the tail became effective with the rush of a powerful propeller flow from the Griffon as he opened up the throttle. These taxi tests were carried out on 27 March, the Thursday prior to the first flight.

Finally, the scene was set for the first flight after the rebuild. Some two and half years after the 'wreck' of SR64 was deposited on the hangar floor at ATA, PK350 was ready to take to the skies again. No more silent vigils on a plinth watching vehicles and pedestrians passing in and out of the main gate at New Sarum. Now was the time for the skies around New Sarum to resonate once again with the unique powerful growl of the Griffon engine—25 years and 104 days since she had last flown on 18 December 1954—powering PK350 back into the sky, her rightful domain.

Chapter 9
THE GRIFFON GROWLS AGAIN

For all the risk involved there had been an increasing degree of certainty that PK350's first flight as a restored aircraft would be successful. This was very noticeable during the last phase of the rebuild. Despite the obstacles that Jack Malloch had to overcome and any doubt that the RhAF hierarchy may have had about a successful rebuild, 29 March 1980 saw PK350 parked on the ramp outside ATA's hangar, ready to fly. She was as good as the day she first flew on 25 July 1945, even if she was missing her undercarriage doors and the streamlined fairings on the inboard cannons. However, as with all first flights, be they of a prototype or a restored aircraft, a lot of anxiety and last minute nerves were part of the build-up to the moment when the aircraft actually became airborne. And then there was still the safe recovery of the aircraft once the air test had been completed. Only then could the success or otherwise truly be judged.

This phase was characterised by three distinct stages, ending, as it had begun, on a high note. But first let's enjoy the memories of PK350's first flight.[1]

Fortunately the day's events have been well recorded. Apart from newspaper reports of the event and the excellent photos taken by Paddy Gray[2] from *The Herald*, a video was made by the RhAF. Produced by Wing Commander Bill Sykes, it was titled *Spitfire—The Pursuit of a Dream*, and aimed to record the events that led to the rebuild, the rebuild itself and the first flight. In addition, Dave Hann later recorded the rebuild on an internet blog, principally from a technical stand point, but he also recorded his memories of the first flight, in particular the final hours before the flight. This is what Dave remembers:

> The evening before the day of the first test flight Bob, Jack, and I, after normal working hours when everybody had gone home—you know, that quiet time— we were walking around the finished aircraft, sort of doing our own pre- flight inspections, looking in here looking in there, checking a couple of items and clearing our minds for the morning. Nothing much was spoken but the atmosphere was quite something else, excitement, nerves, fear, happiness that we had achieved a goal—possibly surprise might even come into the equation. It was at this time that I found a problem with number two gun fairing and promptly replaced the item. That in fact took my mind off things for a while.

Bob said in the video that he hardly slept the night before the first flight—well he was not the only one. I had planned to be at the airport very early in the morning, just after five o'clock, just to have a last good look over the machine. I was at work before my planned arrival time. Apparently I was not the only one sleep walking: Jack, and Bob were there. The ground handling crew were there too, and they set about their individual trade pre-flights. In twelve hours, that airframe had more eyes looking at it than the centre page of *Playboy* magazine. Later, in Bob's office, Jack, Bob and I sat down and nervously went over the next few hours. In the video, I make a statement that we offered Jack the opportunity to 'cry wolf' and I would paper-wise declare the aircraft unserviceable. Put it away and fly another day. We had tried, quite unsuccessfully, to keep the flight date under wraps but I think Jack's network had been busy and there were a couple of hundred visitors expecting a flight. During the next hour or so I prepared the F700, checking out all the relevant sections and finally turned to section 3, I think it was, and declared the aircraft fit for use. Now we were down to the last signature, hell the tension was fantastic. Asking Jack if he was ready to sign off the flight—what a wonderful moment—we had arrived at a point where everything that could be done had been done and now it was that magic signature time. I had been here before with the Canberra but that was different somehow, this signature was the expression of trust in our work and trust in our ability to get a job done.

Memories of these tension-filled final hours related by Bob Dodds are recorded on the video; they seem to suggest he was more concerned about whether his Boss was up to the task or not:

My nerves before the first flight ... I think honestly started the night before the first flight. I mentally checked every nut, screw, washer and connection on this aeroplane through the period of the night. The next morning everybody was nervous. We were confident the aeroplane would perform, but there was always the element of doubt on the first flight of any aeroplane. Knowing that Captain Malloch hadn't flown a Spitfire for about 20 years just didn't help, at that stage of the game, from the point of view of giving us more confidence.

A respectable crowd of around 200 people had gathered at ATA. This had not been anticipated by Jack Malloch or his two chief engineers. Most of these spectators, including all of Jack Malloch's family, would later move down to the runway during the flight itself. Included in the crowd were eleven ex-Spitfire pilots, as well as the past and present commanders of the Air Force—Air Marshals Archie Wilson, Mick McLaren and the current commander, Frank Mussell. Amongst the ex-Spitfire pilots were Group Captains Johnny Deall, Charles Paxton and Ossie Penton, who had helped ferry the Spitfires way back in 1951, as well as Air Vice-Marshal Chris Dams who had negotiated the contract to restore the aircraft with Jack and who had last flown SR64 in December 1954. Paddy Gray took a wonderful photograph of all these men with Jack before the flight, which appeared in the 27 April edition of The *Sunday Mail*.

There was also a sizeable crowd on the New Sarum side, gathered mostly on the revetment wall and on the taxiway entrance (where the author was positioned), in front of the Flying Wing HQ building. This building had kept a silent vigil over the Air Force's activities since 1952 and housed the offices of the Base Commander and the Officer Commanding Flying Wing (OCFW). In addition, there were three aircraft that had flown up from Thornhill, the RhAF's other base, which had parked at New Sarum within view of ATA. These were a Lynx flown by Squadron Leader Steve Baldwin, then Officer Commanding No. 6 Squadron, with five enthusiastic passengers[3]; a Siai Marchetti SF260 which ATA had air-freighted into Rhodesia in 1977; and the restored Percival Provost 3160, 'Omega', with Spike Owens in the right seat as a passenger.[4] Spike Owens was by now WO1 in charge of ASF at Thornhill and he had come to see the result of his long standing efforts to restore SR64.

Finally, there were spectators on the viewing balcony of the passenger terminal and around the meteorological platform of the control tower. Inside the control tower was Leon Keyter, the Duty Tower Controller, assisted by Debbie Carmody (now Addison). Jack Malloch had earlier contacted Leon Keyter[5] to request the shortest possible taxi time, to assist with keeping the radiator temperatures down.

The presence of this crowd had injected an unanticipated dynamic. Both Jack Malloch and Dave Hann acknowledged this fact in the video. Jack admitted he was:

> petrified at the thought of taking off, and had there not been such a crowd of people I don't know whether my nerve might have weakened and I would have thought of some excuse to postpone it for another day or two. Also, ultimately I was determined I was going to get this aircraft airborne.

Dave Hann summed it up:

Well, this flight was supposed to take place with only half a dozen people present. Unfortunately, there were over 200 people there, the pressure was on and at the wrong time; there was a rather nervous pilot and two nervous blokes (Bob and Dave) and 200 people expecting something and so Captain Malloch said 'yes, he would take it.

Chris Dams recalls Jack Malloch looking very relaxed that morning despite his admission to the inevitable nerves. However, deep down, he must have connected to the inner strength he had demonstrated on countless occasions before this memorable day. This is very evident in his own words, once again, in the video:

As far as any feeling of writing the aircraft off, strangely enough this did not worry me. I was quite sure that if I got the thing airborne at all, then I would be able to get the thing back down again.

Jack Malloch's choice of words is interesting. The Spitfire was a 'thing' in his mind. Perhaps this was his way of not allowing himself to be unnerved by the thought that this was now a precious and unique aircraft. Rather it was just another aeroplane that he both wanted and had to fly—in spite of being nearly 60 years of age and not a young buck, as he was when last he flew a Spitfire. His last flight in a Spitfire prior to this was on 17 August 1951[6] on a formation sortie in SR65, the aircraft he had ferried all the way from the UK in March of that year. SR65 today is one of only four surviving Mk 22 Spitfires in the world. Jack had now committed himself to the flight. His huge experience as an airman, together with his courage and professionalism, would carry him through the next 45 minutes or so as he took PK350 into the air for this first time in 25 years three months and 12 days. This day, 29 March was also the anniversary of his first ever flight in the RAF in a Tiger Moth, numbered 530. Surely this was a positive omen, even if he had made absolutely no mention of it.

Expressing faith in his engineers Bob Dodds and Dave Hann and the men who had worked so hard to get to this point, Jack Malloch signed the F700. He had also sensibly arranged to have the late John Fairey present that day, equipped with a portable VHF radio. John Fairey had the benefit of recent experience on Spitfires, having recently sold his share in a two-seater TR IX, MT818 in which he still had an interest. It is believed that Jack Malloch had sought John Fairey's more current experience to help refamiliarise himself with the Spitfire. Even if Fairey had not flown a Griffon-powered Spitfire before, his presence on the radio would be very helpful to manage the checklists in the air and most importantly help deal with any abnormality. John Fairey was dressed in his Air Force uniform that day carrying the rank of Flight Lieutenant and is clearly visible in the video. Their dialogue over the radio would utilise two simple call-signs, 'Spitfire' and 'Ground'.

PK350 stood waiting for Jack Malloch, parked on a north-easterly heading on the main ATA ramp, on the eastern runway side of the hangar. Though lifeless at this powerless moment before start up, she bore all the hallmarks of a thoroughbred. Her streamlined and handsomely aggressive lines cast elongated shadows across the tarmac, mixed with the continually moving shadows of those attending to her last minute needs. Her lines were accentuated by her European Day Fighter colour scheme, reminiscent of the day she first flew, 25 July 1945, in the hands of Wing Commander Peter Ayerst from the Castle Bromwich Aeroplane Factory. Jack Malloch's trusted senior engineer Bob Dodds accompanied him during the pre-flight, referring to the Spitfire Pilot's Notes. He was dressed in his familiar older generation colonial style of dress, long trousers, long-sleeved white shirt for protection against the harsh African sun, and a black short-sleeved jersey. Bob also helped Jack strap himself into the beautifully restored cockpit and don his period leather flying helmet.

Jack obtained clearance from the tower controller, Leon Keyter, for both start up and taxi to the intersection of the taxiway from ATA to Runway 24. Dave Hann recalls the start-up and significance of the moment for him and his apprentices:

> After the engine was fired up, which it did after exactly four blades, Jack signalled for chocks away and there she was on her way to a flight never to be forgotten. It was the very first time I had witnessed a Spitfire getting airborne; the first time I had heard a Griffon pulling power in earnest. Actually, I was not the only one; all the apprentices who had worked so well were now getting the satisfaction from all the hours of graft. You seldom experience these moments in your working life when something extra special happens and this was one of them.

Two of the young apprentices, probably Carlos Martins and Morgan Maitland-Smith[7] pulled the chocks away from the wheels, freeing the throaty Griffon driving the massive 11 foot Hoffmann made propeller to pull PK350 away from her parked position. On their way to the runway Jack Malloch had to yield briefly, to allow a Viscount[8] to taxi past. He kept a watchful eye on the radiator temperature—the critical temperature was 125° C immediately after take-off in the climb.[9]

Having taxied for Runway 24 via intersection 06B[10] Jack Malloch performed a high speed run down 24, before receiving clearance for take-off from Runway 06 for local flying up to 15,000 feet (10,000 feet above ground level). According to the video, at 0544Z (07h44 local time) Jack opened up the throttle. The airspace above the airport was for the Spitfire's exclusive use for the next 30 minutes or so.

The sound and expression of power as Jack opened the throttle to 7 psi boost to get PK350 airborne, and then probably to 12 psi once airborne, was so very special for the fortunate few who witnessed this event, with countless cameras recording the event for posterity. The Griffon was growling once again. Two thousand metaphoric horses had been set free and in the process PK350 reclaimed her rightful station in the hands of a living legend.

As Jack Malloch eased PK350 into the air he began to have difficulties with the rudder trim. But this did not stop him from maintaining positive control of the Spitfire as he raised the undercarriage and flew off on a north-easterly heading, remaining in close vicinity to the airfield. He soon realised he had to maintain a positive left rudder input to keep the nose straight, but he couldn't trim out this force with the rudder trim wheel on the left side of the cockpit. Communication with John Fairey to verify the safe retraction of the undercarriage soon revealed that he had also lost pneumatic pressure, with the gauge reading 100 psi, enough only for the brakes on landing, and not enough for the flap extension. However, these problems didn't stop him from rediscovering his feel for the aircraft and establish that she was in pretty good shape despite her age. Jack Malloch had this to say on the video: "After ten minutes airborne with the aeroplane the Spitfire feeling came back, and by the time the flight was complete I was quite happy for the landing. I had no worries about the landing at all."

The flight lasted 35 minutes during which time he carried out a low speed handling check with a stall at 65 knots with no control problems and two high-speed low level passes down Runway 06 at 270 and 290 knots (still well below the maximum of 430 knots indicated), the last of which Paddy Gray captured on camera. The camera showed a young lad directly under the line of flight about twenty feet beneath the Spitfire. We don't know who that youngster was; what he remembers of that moment and if it perhaps led him into a career in aviation or not.

After the low level passes John Fairey briefed Jack Malloch to recover for a landing

The Spitfire ferry routes in March and December 1951.
Map by Phil Wright

SR64 on the plinth at New Sarum in her initial RRAF Federal colours.
RRAF/Bill Sykes

SR64 on the plinth at New Sarum now in her RRAF post-Federal colours.
RRAF/Steve Kesby

SR64 at New Sarum in RhAF colours prior to her removal from the plinth and
renumbered '64'. *RhAF/Rob Thurman*

SR64, in May 1977, being pushed into the 6 Sqn hangar at Thornill by 31 PTC cadet pilots. *Michel Seegmuller*

SR64 in pieces in the ATA hangar after her arrival in mid-1977. From left: unk., Pete Massimiani, Piet Bezuidenhout. *Dave Hann*

Final reassembly phase with panels off, exposing the engine bearing beams and a 5-gal leading-edge fuel tank on the wing. The flying controls and pneumatics were still being worked on at this stage. *Peter Knobel*

Chris Dixon and Jack Malloch outside ATA after the 'Green Leader' raid over Lusaka in October 1978. *Dave Hann*

Final reassembly phase 6–8 weeks before the ground runs. *Peter Knobel*

Final reassembly. Note the 'lower profile, less full' canopy made by Peter Knobel. *Peter Knobel*

Jack Malloch's most recognisable DC-8, A4O-PA, at Dusseldorf in 1977, which played a key part in importing spares such as the propeller and canopy.
By kind permission of AirTeamImages

Jack Malloch's DC-7F that transported the Griffon engine to South Africa and back, in her post-independence Affretair colours. *Dave Hann*

A nervous Bob Dodds carries out PK350's first engine ground run, still in her primer. *Dave Hann*

First ground run. Bob Dodds in the cockpit with Dave Hann on his right and Jimmy Gibson on his left. *Greg Malloch*

Jack Malloch shows great interest just prior to a ground run. Bob Dodds is in the cockpit. *Chris Faber*

Pre-flight for the first flight. *Greg Malloch*

Ready to go for the first flight. *By kind permission of Keith Foremann*

Taxiing for the first flight. *By kind permission of Keith Foremann*

Nick Meikle, on the New Sarum side of the runway, catches the Spitfire as it turns onto runway 24 for its high-speed run before taking off on 06. The ATA hangar is prominent, and so too the crowd of onlookers. *Nick Meikle*

Celebrations on the occasion of the first flight. From left: Andy Wood, Carlos Martins, Dave Potgieter, Jack Malloch, John Fairey behind Bob Dodds, Gideon, Ross Malloch (Jack's eldest son). *Greg Malloch*

PK350 outside the impressive Affretair hangar. *By kind permission of David Dodds*

Dave Hann and Jack Malloch review the F700 before a flight in April 1980.
By kind permission of David Dodds

Post-flight debrief. Dave Hann recalls a less-than-convincing slow roll that Jack had just performed. From left: Terry Eaton (AFZ), Bob Dodds, Dave Hann, unk., Jack Malloch.
By kind permission of David Dodds

After-flight. Bob Dodds, Dave Hann and Jack Malloch behind the fuselage; always in attendance Carlos Martins on the port wing and Morgan Maitland-Smith on the starboard.
By kind permission of David Dodds

Some of the Affretair engineers who rebuilt PK350. Behind the starboard wing from left: unk., unk., Mike Hill, unk., Dave Murtag, John Dodds. Back row in front of wing from left: unk., Carlos da Silva, Ben Darck, Scott Parkins, Morgan Maitland-Smith, Carlos Martins, Dave Wood, Andy Wood and Mick Kemsley (holding the propeller). Front row from left: Pete Massimiani, unk., Bob Dodds, Jimmy Gibson and Dave Hann *By kind permission of David Dodds*

Flypast along runway 06 at Salisbury International Airport on 3 May 1980. Jack Malloch returning from a local flight and flypast over the home of young Paul Maher in the suburbs of Salisbury. *Rich Sandercock*

Taxiing into its usual position at Affretair on 3 May 1980. *Rich Sandercock*

Parking after the same flight. *Rich Sandercock*

A good crowd greets the Spitfire while the engineers get on with the after-flight on 3 May 1980. *Rich Sandercock*

Cockpit with good detail and Jack Malloch's period leather flying helmet on 3 May 1980. *Rich Sandercock*

PK350 receiving her after-flight service with Rich Sandercock, a pilot with Affretair, in the foreground. *Rich Sandercock*

PK350 quietly parked and cooling down, 3 May 1980. *Rich Sandercock*

About to taxi for the flight to Thornhill on 22 May 1980. Morgan Maitland-Smith is at the left wing. *Greg Malloch*

Thornhill visit of 22 May 1980. Jack Malloch was met by two of No. 1 Squadron Hawker Hunters flown by Tony Oakley and Alf Wild over the Ngezi dam area. *Alf Wild*

Thornhill visit. Tony Oakley comes into formation with Jack Malloch at 250 knots. At relatively low speed the Hunter has a marked nose-up flying attitude compared with the Spitfire. *Alf Wild*

Thornhill visit. Chris Faber stands in front of his Dove VP-YKF on a breezy day at Thornhill. *Chris Faber*

Thornhill visit. PK350 is flanked by the Silver Provost 'Omega' and Chris Faber's DH Dove, prior to start-up for the Spitfire/Provost flypast. *Chris Faber*

Thornhill visit. PK350 taxies out behind the Provost flown by Steve Baldwin and accompanied by Bill Sykes. Morgan Maitland-Smith is in his usual position, riding on the port wing. *Alf Wild*

Thornhill visit. Jack Malloch and PK350 in a farewell formation flypast with the Provost before returning to Salisbury. *Alf Wild*

Above: PK350's visit to Charles Prince Airport The Spitfire was on display for the public with a chart of specifications taped to the aircraft's nose. *Keith Foremann*

PK350 is parked near Jack Malloch's old Constellation VP-WAW, at that time a clubhouse at Charles Prince Airport. Bob Dodds is doing a pre-flight while Jack looks on. *John Reid-Rowland.*

An unusual but striking view of PK350 at Charles Prince. *Keith Foremann*

Below: ... and starts up, with the ever-present Bob Dodds assisting. *John Reid-Rowland*

Top: Jack Malloch takes time to chat to onlookers during his pre-flight. *John Reid-Rowland*

Above: Jack straps on his parachute. *John Reid-Rowland*

Above: ... and takes off on runway 06. *John Reid-Rowland*

Left: A great view of the interior of the spacious Affretair hangar taken from atop the fuselage of a DC-8. The Spitfire is parked in her usual place. *Dave Hann*

Left: The view from the ground, with the Affretair logo prominent on the side of the hangar. *Dave Hann*

Top left: A normal day at work. Bob Dodds and Dave Hann in a relaxed mood, with the 'Whitehouse' in the background, September 1980. *Dave Hann*

Above: Jack Malloch with his eldest son, Ross. *Greg Malloch*

Left: Jack Malloch and Bob Dodds. *Greg Malloch*

Jack Malloch never missed a chance for a photo opportunity. PK350 in front of a Luftwaffe Boeing 707 sometime in 1981 outside Affretair with two Zimbabwean aviation legends, Ian Harvey and Jack Malloch, looking on.
By kind permission of Clive Ward

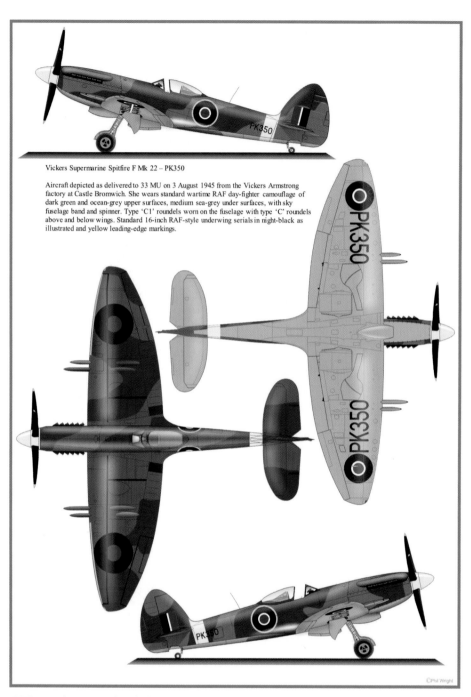

Vickers Supermarine Spitfire F Mk 22 – PK350

Aircraft depicted as delivered to 33 MU on 3 August 1945 from the Vickers Armstrong factory at Castle Bromwich. She wears standard wartime RAF day-fighter camouflage of dark green and ocean-grey upper surfaces, medium sea-grey under surfaces, with sky fuselage band and spinner. Type 'C1' roundels worn on the fuselage with type 'C' roundels above and below wings. Standard 16-inch RAF-style underwing serials in night-black as illustrated and yellow leading-edge markings.

PK350 in her RAF day-fighter colour scheme in July 1945. *Drawing by Phil Wright*

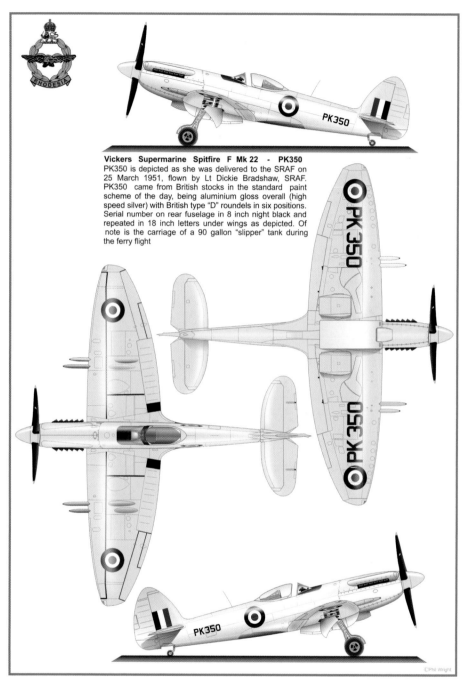

Vickers Supermarine Spitfire F Mk 22 - PK350

PK350 is depicted as she was delivered to the SRAF on 25 March 1951, flown by Lt Dickie Bradshaw, SRAF. PK350 came from British stocks in the standard paint scheme of the day, being aluminium gloss overall (high speed silver) with British type "D" roundels in six positions. Serial number on rear fuselage in 8 inch night black and repeated in 18 inch letters under wings as depicted. Of note is the carriage of a 90 gallon "slipper" tank during the ferry flight

PK350 in her RAF day-fighter colour scheme, as worn during the first SRAF ferry to Southern Rhodesia in March 1951. *Drawing by Phil Wright*

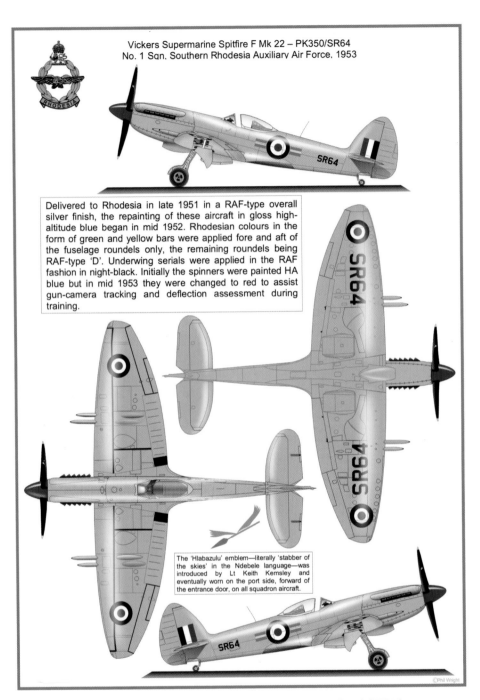

Vickers Supermarine Spitfire F Mk 22 – PK350/SR64
No. 1 Sqn, Southern Rhodesia Auxiliary Air Force, 1953

Delivered to Rhodesia in late 1951 in a RAF-type overall silver finish, the repainting of these aircraft in gloss high-altitude blue began in mid 1952. Rhodesian colours in the form of green and yellow bars were applied fore and aft of the fuselage roundels only, the remaining roundels being RAF-type 'D'. Underwing serials were applied in the RAF fashion in night-black. Initially the spinners were painted HA blue but in mid 1953 they were changed to red to assist gun-camera tracking and deflection assessment during training.

The 'Hlabazulu' emblem—literally 'stabber of the skies' in the Ndebele language—was introduced by Lt Keith Kemsley and eventually worn on the port side, forward of the entrance door, on all squadron aircraft.

SR64 in her SRAF colour scheme, 1951 to mid-1953. *Drawing by Phil Wright*

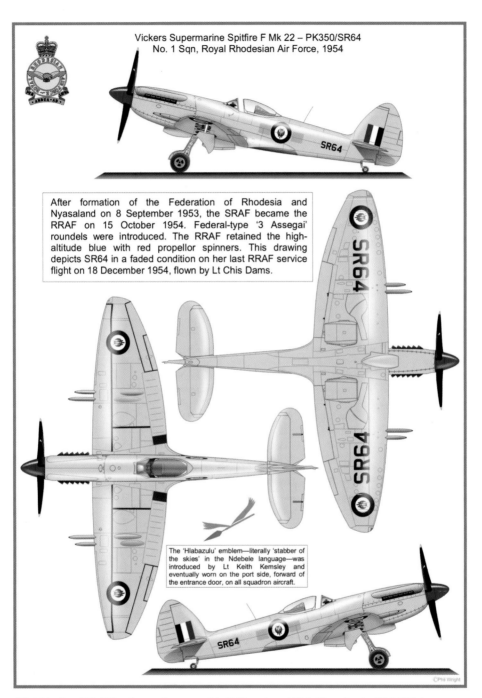

Vickers Supermarine Spitfire F Mk 22 – PK350/SR64
No. 1 Sqn, Royal Rhodesian Air Force, 1954

After formation of the Federation of Rhodesia and Nyasaland on 8 September 1953, the SRAF became the RRAF on 15 October 1954. Federal-type '3 Assegai' roundels were introduced. The RRAF retained the high-altitude blue with red propellor spinners. This drawing depicts SR64 in a faded condition on her last RRAF service flight on 18 December 1954, flown by Lt Chis Dams.

The 'Hlabazulu' emblem—literally 'stabber of the skies' in the Ndebele language—was introduced by Lt Keith Kemsley and eventually worn on the port side, forward of the entrance door, on all squadron aircraft.

SR64 in her RRAF colour scheme, mid-1953 to late 1954. *Drawing by Phil Wright*

Supermarine Spitfire F Mk 22 – PK 350

After manufacture PK350 was initially issued by a Maintenance Unit to No. 73 Squadron Royal Air Force before being returned to the MU and then sold to the Southern Rhodesia Air Force in late 1951. She is depicted here as she would have looked on 73 Squadron.

Gate guardian colour schemes – New Sarum

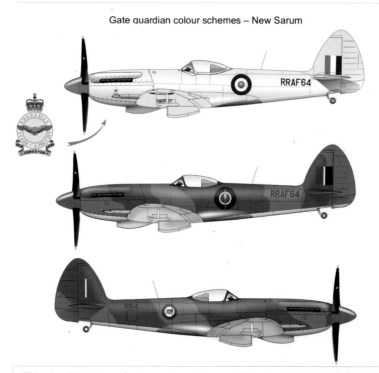

This aircraft had three spurious colour schemes while mounted on her plinth at New Sarum air force base, Salisbury, before commencement of her refurbishment in 1977. Each camouflage scheme represented the camouflage and markings of the air force at the time of painting. Initially she was painted in aluminium (silver), representing the RRAF Federal period of service, then in autumn brown, olive green and sky camouflage, representing the RRAF post Federal period and finally the same camouflage but with Rhodesian Air Force national markings and an 'R' prefixed serial number representing the RhAF period.

SR64 in her possible RAF 73 Sqn colours, 1947–48, and SRAF/RRAF/RhAF gate guard colour schemes, 1964–77. *Drawing by Phil Wright*

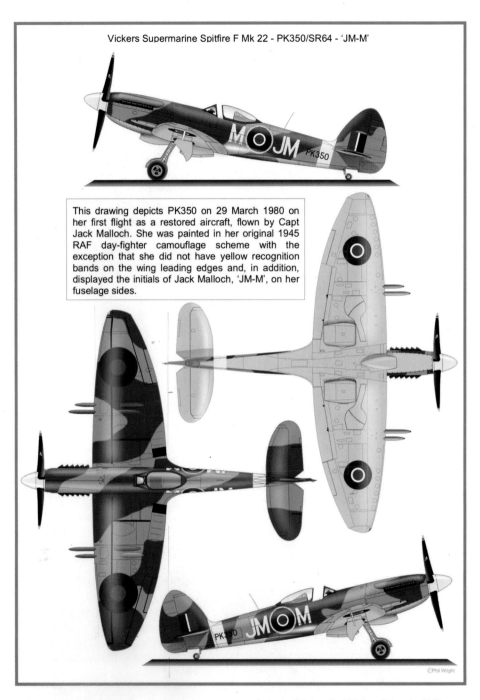

Vickers Supermarine Spitfire F Mk 22 - PK350/SR64 - 'JM-M'

This drawing depicts PK350 on 29 March 1980 on her first flight as a restored aircraft, flown by Capt Jack Malloch. She was painted in her original 1945 RAF day-fighter camouflage scheme with the exception that she did not have yellow recognition bands on the wing leading edges and, in addition, displayed the initials of Jack Malloch, 'JM-M', on her fuselage sides.

PK350/SR64 in her colour scheme as a restored aircraft March 1980 to March 1982.
Drawing by Phil Wright

The painting, *The Last Moments Together*, of the Spitfire and the Vampire on 26 February 1982. *Painting by William Sykes (son of Bill Sykes)*

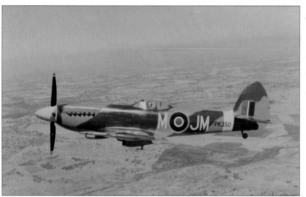

Jack Malloch wearing his period flying helmet on his first photographic sortie with a Bell 205. The tail wheel is still locked down. *Phil Scott/Nick Meikle*

A rare shot of the port side of the Spitfire, taken from the Bell 205, September 1980. As opposed to the Dakota, the helicopter affords the cameraman a choice of angle. *Phil Scott/Nick Meikle*

Jack Malloch, taken from a Dakota flown by Squadron Leader Clive Ward with Mark Vernon, on 23 October 1981, the day before the Air Force '81 air show. This iconic photograph was used extensively by the media for many years. *AFZ photographer*

Taken by Peter Knobel from a Dakota flown by Clive Ward and Norman Ingledew, on 3 February 1982. *AFZ photographer*

Peter Knobel joined the Air Force specifically to fly Spitfires, only to be denied at the last moment, in 1954, when the squadron was taken off line. *AFZ photographer*

... and this is why it is so unique that Peter was given the chance to fly one of those same Spitfires nearly thirty years later, and so fulfil his life's dream. *AFZ photographer*

These three photographs—the most evocative and beautiful of all the photos—show Wing Commander Steve Kesby flying PK350 on 11 January 1982, taken from a Dakota flown by Clive Ward and Sid Buxton. *AFZ photographer*

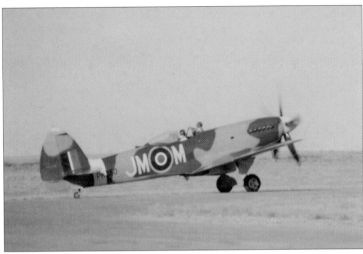

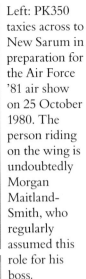

Left: PK350 taxies across to New Sarum in preparation for the Air Force '81 air show on 25 October 1980. The person riding on the wing is undoubtedly Morgan Maitland-Smith, who regularly assumed this role for his boss.

Left: PK350 parks close to the intersection of runways 06/24 and 14/32 in readiness for the Air Force '81 air show.

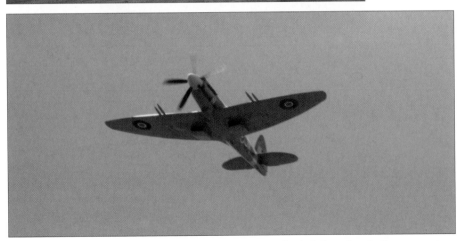

The Air Force '81 air show on 25 October 1981. For the Spitfire, the air show was the culmination of all the hard work and dedication that had been put into the rebuild of PK350. Poignantly, this was its one and only full public display.
AFZ photographer/Steve Harvey.

To have caught Jack as he sped past at over 300 mph is a masterpiece of photographic timing. *AFZ photographer/Steve Harvey*

Jack Malloch with Bill Musgrave, his old No. 237 (Rhodesia) Sqn friend and colleague, in January 1982. *Greg Malloch*

The Vampire, flown by Nick Meikle and Bill Sykes, taxies out with the Spitfire, at Salisbury International Airport, on the second of three filming sorties, 26 February 1982. *Visiting Airwork Executive/Bill Sykes*

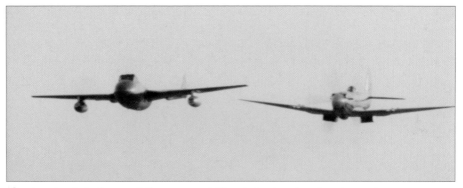

The low-level, high-speed flypast past Affretair, before 'breaking' into the circuit, 26 February 1982. The flyby was a tad low and extremely fast.
Visiting Airwork UK Executive/Bill Sykes

The modified port drop tank to protect the 16mm cine camera on Vampire T11 4220. *Bill Sykes*

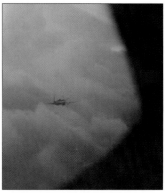

The last photograph of Jack Malloch and PK350 on 26 February 1980, taken shortly before the aircraft disappeared into the storm cloud on the left. *Bill Sykes*

A close-up of nature's awesome energy within a cumulonimbus storm, very similar to the scene recalled by Bill Sykes and Nev Weir whilst in pursuit of the Spitfire. *Bill Sykes*

One of the last photographs taken of Jack Malloch in PK350. The crash occurred ten minutes later. *Bill Sykes*

The most distinguishable mountain feature along the flight path just prior to the crash— Nyahungwe— recognised by Bill Sykes during the visit to the crash site. *Bill Sykes*

The final walk to the crash site. Peter Ngulu is visible in the foreground, with Ken Burmeister and Nick Meikle in the background. *Bill Sykes*

Above: Bill Sykes with Peter Ngulu. The young tree which marks the site has grown since the crash. *Nick Meikle*

Left: This battery fragment showing its number, make and aerobatics capability, was an instantly recognisable item among a number of other bits of wreckage at the crash site. *Bill Sykes*

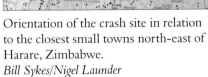

Orientation of the crash site in relation to the closest small towns north-east of Harare, Zimbabwe.
Bill Sykes/Nigel Launder

The accident site and flight paths of the Spitfire and Vampire on a Zimbabwe 125:000 map so familiar to RhAF pilots.
Bill Sykes/Nigel Launder

on Runway 06 via a left hand downwind.[11] Jack had to carry out a flapless landing.[12] The loss of pneumatic pressure precluded the use of the one position 75 degrees of flap for landing—but it would have taken very keen eyesight to pick this up. Fortunately, neither the problem with the flap, nor the propeller being stuck in coarse pitch, were to cause Jack Malloch any great difficulty and he successfully landed the aircraft on one of the world's longest runways. There must have been a collective sigh of relief both inside the cockpit, as well as outside amongst the spectators, but especially from Bob, Dave and Jack's family. However, having only 100 psi for the brakes and a slight uphill taxi onto the ATA ramp, Jack had to use his brakes very judiciously.

Jack Malloch was also very aware of the presence of Spike Owens. Just before he left the runway to taxi back, Master Sergeant Pete Besant from No. 2 Squadron at Thornhill sitting in the SF260 recalled the following:

> Both Spike and I flew up from Thornhill, Spike in the Provost and me in an SF260 Warrior, in formation. I can't remember who the pilots were. We taxied into Sarum and positioned facing Affretair so we could see the start-up, taxi, take-off and landing of the Spitfire. As soon as Jack Malloch saw us he slowed down and greeted us over the radio and we sent our congratulations before taxiing back to Affretair.

This speaks volumes about Jack Malloch being quick to acknowledge others, in particular the man who started it all, Spike Owens. In a sense the baton had been successfully passed from one guardian to another; the baton comprising the care of a nation's heirloom—not to keep, but to safeguard. Whilst congratulations were already becoming audible over the radio, Jack still had to complete a tricky taxi—and then deal with the congratulations for and recognition of this incredible achievement.

Bob Dodds takes up the story in his own words:

> When the aircraft came in and stopped, I got up onto the wing to help Captain Malloch undo his harness. Here was our aeroplane back. He was back. Everybody was watching. The feeling was absolutely tremendous; everything had been successful and it was all worthwhile.

Bob Dodds had felt the least confidence about the outcome. He had not been sure of Jack's level of confidence and ability, his boss not having flown a Spitfire for so long.

However, he was quick to recognise the accomplishment and had this to say:

> The feeling of achievement then, that we had actually taken this antiquated piece
> of equipment, nursed it, cursed it, kicked it and eventually got it to this stage; it
> was a real challenge to overcome these problems and see the thing actually fly.
> The initial feeling was one of a sense of achievement, of exhilaration, that we
> had actually got the aircraft off the ground. Two and a half years of work had
> paid off. I think at that moment in time we were very pleased with ourselves.

Dave Hann could only express pride in the apprentices—they handled the aircraft
in a manner that would have brought pride to the expression of any AF warrant
officer, including Spike Owens:

> When the aircraft returned to base after that flight, the after flight checks and
> refuelling were carried out with such professionalism you would have thought
> that those apprentices had been doing the job for years. No oil spilt, no fuel
> dribbled over the paintwork, the windscreen cleaned, Jack's parachute neatly
> laid out on the horizontal as if waiting for the next sortie.

When asked what he remembered of the day, Chris Dams said he was "totally
impressed". It was the quality of the workmanship that had caught his eye. He
would have remembered the well-used state of SR64 at the end of its operational
career with the Air Force. Now here, 25 odd years later, was the same aeroplane in
an excellent state of repair. He caused Jack Malloch to hesitate momentarily when
he jokingly told him it was his turn to fly the aircraft, but his humour only lightly
hid the understandable envy that he and all the other ex-Spitfire pilots would have
felt on that day. It must be remembered that this aircraft was unique in that it was
both fully aerobatic and had four serviceable 20mm cannons. But the overwhelming
sentiment was one of huge admiration for Jack Malloch and the accomplishment of
his engineers.

Now it was time to savour the delight of this incredible achievement. So the bubbly
was poured and as bottles of Cold Duck sparkling wine were handed around, the
significance of their achievement began to sink in for Jack Malloch and his engineers.
The congratulations flowed and the inevitable questions had to be asked. In the video
Jack Malloch is asked: "Has this been worth all the money, effort and pain?" His reply
is simple and unequivocal: "Oh yes, it's been worth every bit of it, every bit of it."

His answer is followed by another question: "Why did you go for the last 18 in the world?" This is a reference to there being only 18 Spitfires flying at the time, and Jack's answer again is simple: "It wasn't a case of the last 18, I think it was just a Spitfire that needed renovating and we were in a position to do it."

To which the same interrogator asks the inevitable question: "If somebody was to come along with an offer for this what is the minimum price, Jack?" The reply is enough to end the questions when Malloch answers: "Oh, there isn't a price; we wouldn't ever sell it." Most of the surviving 40-plus airworthy Spitfires today are probably priceless, especially those with a wartime record in the Battle of Britain Flight. The late John Fairey's TR IX, MT818 is said to be worth £2 million. At the time of its first (restored) flight, PK350 was said to be worth $1 million.

Ian Smith, the ex-Prime Minister and a wartime colleague and friend of Jack Malloch could not attend on the day. This disappointed him enormously according to Janet, his wife, who did attend and who chatted to Jack afterwards whilst extending her congratulations and acknowledging his achievement. The impact of the huge political changes occurring in Rhodesia had drawn Ian Smith away to a political meeting in the Midlands of the country. We cannot know this for sure, but one senses that Jack was only too happy to have achieved this lifetime dream of rebuilding the Spitfire before the country became Zimbabwe, 19 days hence.

The significance of the achievement would actually take some years to sink in. Andy Wood, who had spent many hours working on the Spitfire, and was there boots and all to help Dave Hann paint the Spitfire over the previous weekend, admitted to experiencing just that realisation years after the event.[13] The break that followed the first flight at least allowed everyone to start that process of appreciating their achievement.

PK350 SPREADS HER WINGS

In the weeks and months that followed this momentous day we have numerous newspaper articles and photographs, and Jack Malloch's logbook, which enable us to track PK350's movements. Now that the war was over and Rhodesia was about to become Zimbabwe on 18 April 1980, it gave Jack a chance to savour the delights of flying the Spitfire at a leisurely pace. These flights perhaps provided some relief from the new demands that his company, soon to become known as Affretair, was beginning to make. Affretair was entering a new phase, operating in an openly competitive market place without the strictures of sanctions and the need to be secretive about everything. Senior officers of the soon to be renamed Air Force of Zimbabwe also recognised the implications of the onset of peace time conditions. They were keen to use the Spitfire to wave the flag, so that people from other centres could see and hear the Spitfire in flight. It was made clear by Air HQ's spokesman, as reported in *The Herald* of 23 April 1980, that until the aircraft was fully serviceable, she would not tour the country.

We turn now to Jack Malloch's logbook and it is sad to discover that it stops recording his flying after 7 November 1980. There is not a single entry, after that date, of any flying. Jack's logbook entries are not written in his own hand, and after the Thornhill visit in May, no detail is indicated against the flights entered. It has been confirmed that Nicky Pearce (*née* Elphinstone), an operations clerk with Affretair, made the remaining entries.[14]

There was a two week break after the first flight during which the pitch control unit on the propeller was repaired and the gasket on the pneumatic pump replaced. According to Dave Hann, the pitch control unit had become clogged with sludge, which stopped oil pressure getting to the propeller hub to change the pitch of the propeller. The unit was completely stripped and cleaned, and ground runs were conducted to check its operation. In Jack Malloch's log book the next six flights were dedicated to four aileron trim checks and two mixture control and auto pitch control checks. In actual fact these were rudder trim checks, as it was the rudder trim that had given Dave Hann and his team quite a headache, trying to work out the rigging, before the aircraft flew. Obviously, the initial rigging was incorrect and so they repositioned the neutral position and eventually provided the necessary rudder trim authority.

These flights took place between 12 and 24 April and Jack Malloch didn't miss a chance to get attention. Two of these flights made the newspapers, with photographs. On 15 April, upon the arrival of the Russian delegation for the Independence celebrations, he buzzed the Illyushin 62 passenger jet aircraft as it parked on the international terminal. On Independence Day, 18 April, at the request of the Governor, Lord Soames, he performed an unofficial flypast for Prince Charles and Lord Soames as they left the country, signifying Britain's handover of Zimbabwe to Prime Minister Mugabe and his government.

During this time Dave Dodds,[15] (no relation to Bob Dodds) who was living in Ruwa outside Salisbury, took a large number of photographs of the Spitfire at ATA. PK350 made a spectacular subject with photos taken from some unusual angles.

These clearly show the excellent workmanship that contributed to the robust state of the aircraft, soon after the first flight. Dave Dodds was a staff photographer at the now defunct *Scope* magazine; Dave Mullany, a Rhodesian, was the editor. Dave Mullany had attended Chaplin High School in Gweru, the same school attended by Ian Smith in the early 1930s.

It was probably on the next flight[16] on Saturday 3 May, that Jack Malloch provided a 12-year-old lad by the name of Paul Maher with the biggest surprise of his young life. The weather was overcast and drizzly, but it didn't deter him from carrying out a flypast in a wide sweeping turn beneath the 1,000-foot cloud base over Paul Maher's home. Jack Malloch had promised the young lad a flypast in response to a letter he had sent to Jack, congratulating him on the first flight of the Spitfire. Paul Maher's father, Dave Maher, also held a private pilot's licence and was a committee member of the Mashonaland Flying Club.

It is worth dwelling on this event as it illustrates so powerfully the enthusiasm and expertise prevalent in the aviation industry in the newly born Zimbabwe. Paul Maher was in love with aircraft and flying. His room was decorated with posters of aircraft including one of Jack Malloch's DC-8s. Spitfires were as much a centrepiece to his love affair with aircraft as they would have been to most young boys at that time. He recalls this boyhood passion and how it led him to meet Jack Malloch:

As a kid besotted with aeroplanes and the son of a keen amateur aviator, weekend visits to the Flying Club were what life was all about. Aeroplanes were all-consuming to me, even at the expense of education. Undaunted by occasional bouts of airsickness, I was always hitching rides in aeroplanes with any pilot who could not avoid either my intense 'take me for a ride' telepathic stare or endless questions about their aeroplanes. This was a cause of grave concern for my Dad who knew the reputations of some of the pilots in whom I placed my blind, youthful faith. He always made me promise to ask him before accepting an offer of a ride. Sometimes, however, connivance and defiance of this order was necessary to get that ride.

One pilot my Dad had no such concern over was Alyson Malloch, a Flying Club Instructor. To this 11-year-old (at that stage), not only was Alyson a very competent pilot in my Dad's opinion, and worthy of the hero status she achieved in my eyes, but she was also the daughter of one of the most talked about legends in the aviation community, Captain Jack Malloch. Alyson was infinitely patient with her little shadow. Amongst many flights I had with her was my first flight in a Piper Cub, an aeroplane I developed a great fondness for over the years. Such was her patience and understanding of my passion she would pick me up from my parent's house and take me out to the flying club on the days my Dad wasn't able to take me.

Stories about 'Captain Jack' were abundant. My friends all had pictures of sports and pop-stars plastered to their wall. I had pictures of aeroplanes with a poster of an Affretair DC-8 flown by Captain Jack in pride of place. One evening, after one of Alyson's kind conveyances to the Club, she stopped at the Malloch family home before dropping me off at mine. This afforded me my first meeting with Captain Jack. The individual, whose picture was painted larger than life in my imagination, shook my hand, in person, in an unforgettable moment.

Jack Malloch's legendary status was confined mainly within the aviation community until the day the Spitfire project hit the news headlines. Suddenly everyone knew 'Captain Jack' and I was elevated to the status of the guy at school who knew his daughter and had actually met him. Seemingly silly in an adult perspective, but in a school circle of eleven-going-on-twelve-year-olds, the pride of this association was significant. Within days, pictures and news cuttings of Spitfire JMM adorned the wall around the DC-8 poster. Not only did I love Spitfires but now I knew someone who owned one! Poor Alyson had to endure my endless questions about it.

The first time I heard it fly in the distance over the Harare suburbs on one of its first flights, I felt indescribable excitement. There were likely a few home furnishings damaged in my scramble to get outside to catch a glimpse. Such was my enthusiasm with the Spitfire and the project that I sat in maths class that week surreptitiously penning a letter of congratulations to Captain Jack instead of tackling my fractions. I drew a picture of JMM at the end. I handed the letter, slightly embarrassed, to Alyson at the Flying Club that weekend. When you are twelve everything is embarrassing and what I did seemed cringe-worthy immediately after the fact. I didn't expect a response. Captain Jack was surely too busy and famous to bother with a twelve-year-old fan.

How wrong I was. I got home from rugby practice a couple of evenings later and my Dad nonchalantly said 'there was a phone call for you'. 'Who was it?' I said with matching indifference. 'Jack Malloch,' he said. My heart nearly jumped out of my chest. 'What did he want?' I asked. My Dad told me he said thank you for the letter and he was going to fly the Spitfire over our house the next day at 10h00. Once the adrenalin and disbelief had died down, I phoned every kid in the neighbourhood to come to my house to see 'my' flypast. I remember many of my friends' parents reacting by saying I was talking nonsense. My Dad had to intervene in several phone calls to save my credibility.

Jack Malloch, as we have already learned, was good to his promise and thus guaranteed another professional career pilot. Today, Paul Maher works for Boeing as an instructor pilot on Boeing 747s, 777s and 787s, having spent much of his airline career to date flying DC-8s, DC-9s, Boeing 727s and 747s[17] as well. The catalyst in all of this was Alyson Malloch, who helped nurture those boyhood dreams.

SENTIMENTAL JOURNEY

Jack Malloch flew once more (details unknown) on 14 May before undertaking what has to be seen as a sentimental journey to Thornhill on 22 May. It was sentimental for two reasons. First, it was two days short of exactly 29 years since he was last at Thornhill, on 24 May 1951 in Spitfire SR61, when he and Dave Barbour had been asked to give a synchronised display to mark the closure of the RATG at Thornhill. Secondly, Thornhill was where Spike Owens and the 6 Sqn technicians had brought SR64 in January 1977, in their unsuccessful efforts to restore her on the base. SR64 had now returned in pristine condition as PK350, to take her rightful place on the ramp outside Flying Wing HQ, and to rub shoulders with the Hunter, the Air Force's current frontline fighter. In the process, Jack was saluting and acknowledging Spike Owens for having started the amazing journey to a very successful restoration.

Air HQ would have fully sanctioned and no doubt encouraged this trip, as part of its policy for the Spitfire to wave the flag. It was not a formal military occasion but the AFZ and thus Thornhill gave the Spitfire the warmest possible reception. The Hunter FGA 9s from No. 1 Squadron welcomed the Spitfire at the airspace border near Ngezi Dam and escorted her to Thornhill. They were flown by Squadron Leader Alf Wild,[18] a weapons instructor attached to 1 Sqn, and Flight Lieutenant Tony Oakley, a flight commander on 1 Sqn. Alf Wild recorded the occasion with some fine colour photos which are included with this story. He recalled that the Hunters had to use two notches of flap whilst formating with the Spitfire at 250 kts as they escorted Jack Malloch to Thornhill.

To make a day of it, and to ensure technical support away from his base, Jack Malloch arranged for Chris Faber to fly to Thornhill in his de Havilland Dove VP-YKF[19] with eight Affretair engineers. Dave Hann recalls that the party included himself, Bob Dodds, Morgan Maitland-Smith, Carlos Martins, Phil Mason, Mick Kemsley, and two others whose names he cannot remember.

The Base came out in strength and photographs taken on the day abound in both colour and black and white, taken by many of the spectators. However, it was Jeff Hagemann, one of the photographers with Thornhill Photographic Section who took the official photographs. He had also taken the memorable photos of SR64 in early 1977, during the early investigative phase into the feasibility of a rebuild. Spike Owens is featured in these photographs which include the Provost. Colour photos supplied by Chris Faber show the Dove on the ramp with the Spitfire and Provost. It is possible that a homebuilt bi-plane belonging to an Italian friend of Flight Lieutenant Basil Miles, the Flying Wing Adjutant, known to all as Basil 'Brush', also managed to ease its way onto the ramp for a photo opportunity.

This was truly a nostalgic day for Thornhill. The story made it into *The Herald* the next day, reporting that Spike Owens was the first person to greet Jack when he parked the Spitfire outside Flying Wing Headquarters (FWHQ). Bill Sykes would have arranged for the reporter with *The Herald* to be there, but we do not know his name or if Paddy Gray again took the photos for the newspaper. The photograph taken by *The Herald*'s photographer from the roof of FWHQ shows the better part of 150 base personnel swarming around the aircraft; it was probably taken shortly after Jack arrived around mid-day.

The Dove arrived after the Spitfire so that the ground crew could attend to the Spitfire before its return flight later in the day. A rather bibulous lunch followed and then the Spitfire left, followed by the Dove and the rest of the visitors. Jack Malloch's logbook shows a one hour ten minute return flight, for what would normally have been only 40 minutes or so. This was because the Spitfire accompanied the Provost 'Omega' flown by Steve Baldwin,[20] accompanied by Bill Sykes, on a flypast over the base before he set course for Salisbury (the capital city had not yet been renamed). Dave Hann also recalled Jack Malloch surprising the Dove on the way back with a mock quarter-attack in the late afternoon. Clearly he was enjoying himself and savouring the moment.

After the Thornhill visit the flying diminished substantially over the next three months. The Spitfire flew only three times, once in June and twice in August, with no details shown in Jack's logbook. It is possible that during this time Jack flew one of at least two air-to-air photographic sorties with a Bell 205 helicopter from 8 Sqn.[21] There is a very famous photo taken from the right side of a Bell over the

Seki area, which shows the Spitfire's tail wheel still locked down, the background clearly indicating that it was the dry time of the year. However, it was not possible to determine exactly which flight this was. There were three lengthy flights during August, September and October—any one of which could have been the air-to-air flight.

The flying picked up in September when the Spitfire flew four times, which possibly included a flypast for the Battle of Britain commemoration, followed by a visit to Charles Prince Airport when Jack flew the Spitfire on 19 and 20 September.[22] It is likely that Jack performed a flypast and then landed at Charles Prince. According to Sean Carson,[23] a member of the Mashonaland Flying Club Committee with Dave Maher, Jack Malloch had been invited to fly the Spitfire into Charles Prince, with an offer to pay toward the cost of the fuel. He recalled the shock when they were told the Spitfire consumed a gallon a minute.

Wing Commander Peter Knobel remembers Jack Malloch experiencing a flat tyre and thought this had occurred on landing at Charles Prince. Jack had demonstrated superb airmanship to stop the aircraft from being damaged in a nose-over incident. However, Dave Hann thought this incident had occurred at Harare; in all likelihood this is what actually happened, but on the return flight from Charles Prince to Salisbury the next day, caused by a tyre valve failure. A similar failure led to Arthur Hodson suffering a nose-over in Spitfire SR85 during the SRAF days. Des Anderson, a former Spitfire pilot and course mate of Mick McLaren's, was airport manager and confirmed Dave Hann's recall. He received a telephone call from Jack after he landed at Salisbury Main, thinking he had picked up a nail at Charles Prince.

The Spitfire remained at Charles Prince overnight, possibly as part of the original invitation or because of a technical problem; in any case these movements match Jack's logbook entries for relatively short flight times—35 minutes on 19 September and 15 on the 20th, a Friday and Saturday respectively. Photos to hand taken by Brian Carson, Sean's brother, and John Reid Rowland, clearly show the dry grass alongside the runway and warm conditions—everyone is dressed in summer attire.

A respectable crowd with a sentimental flavour to it again gathered to greet the Spitfire. Jack Malloch had probably last flown into Charles Prince airport in his Lockheed Constellation VP-WAW on 28 September 1974,[24] with Colin Miller and John Hodges. The 'Connie' then became a bar near the flying club. It featured in some of the photos taken of the visit and was also used to get a good vantage point from which to take photos of the Spitfire.

It is pertinent to point out that by this stage the undercarriage doors had been replaced as can be seen in photos, whereas at Thornhill they were still absent. However, the tail wheel was still locked down which is evident in photos captured after take-off at Charles Prince, during a short demo given by Jack before returning to Salisbury Main. Obviously, during the quiet preceding months, Bob Dodds and Dave Hann had resolved the gear selector valve problem which had necessitated the removal of the gear doors.

CHANGE AT THE OFFICE

In September 1980 a significant event occurred: Wing Commander Peter Knobel[25] (PeterK to his friends and colleagues) started his conversion onto the Spitfire. His first official flight was on 30 September and this was followed by four more. These will be covered in more detail in the next chapter, but it is relevant to dwell on this change.

It will be recalled that according to Air Vice-Marshal Chris Dams, the agreement signed by Jack and the Ministry of Defence made no reference to any of the AF pilots flying the aircraft once she had been restored. On the other hand, Air Marshal Frank Mussell remembered that Chris Dams was the delegated pilot.[26] However, times had moved on, the war was over and peace time conditions prevailed. If Chris Dams was the delegated pilot, he had retired from the AFZ in May 1980. The aircraft was, as agreed, the property of the Ministry of Defence, with the AFZ being ultimately responsible for its operation. Further, within the context of this 'ownership', it would appear that AFZ had in mind a finite flying life for the Spitfire.[27] Once the air-to-air photography (at this point scheduled for some time in the future) had been completed, the Spitfire was to be grounded and placed in the Military Museum in Gweru. Whether or not Jack Malloch was aware of this is unknown. Dave Hann confirms that he had tasked his engineers to look at the manufacture of a long range tank similar to the one used on the ferry. This leads to the obvious question: Did he have a plan to fly the Spitfire out of the country? However, Dave Hann also recalls that Jack Malloch never pressed them for the long range tank.

Interestingly, Air Commodore Keith Kemsley recalls[28] that the agreement did make provision for AF pilots to fly the Spitfire. However it is clear that Keith Kemsley, a key agitator for the rebuild, was now advocating for Wing Commander Peter Knobel to fly the aircraft. Knobel had been desperately keen to fly Spitfires for years. Keith Kemsley recalls that he shuttled between the Commander (Frank Mussell) and Jack

Malloch to arrange this 'change at the office' (cockpit) respecting the fact that Jack did not want a queue of "gung-ho AF pilots lining up to fly the Spitfire", as Frank Mussell put it. Even if Jack was a little reluctant,[29] one can only conclude that he must have decided that if the AFZ wanted one of their pilots to fly the Spitfire then there was not much that he could do about it. He would have accepted it in the gentlemanly way he had always done business. However, Jack was not prepared to do the conversion and this fell to Keith Kemsley, who had 'disqualified' himself from flying the Spitfire due to a lack of flying currency.[30] At this time Kemsley was DGSS at HQ, and this conversion was one of his last duties before leaving the AFZ at the end of the year.

It has to be said that this change at the office was, in retrospect, handled very well. We must remember that when the contract was negotiated and signed in April 1977, the RhAF had very pressing business to attend to with the prosecution of the war. The subject of an RhAF pilot flying the Spitfire was never raised, according to Air Vice-Marshal Chris Dams. Whilst Chris Dams, and no doubt the RhAF, never doubted Jack Malloch's commitment to restore the Spitfire, the huge challenges involved introduced an element of doubt as to whether he would be able to pull it off. Now that he had, and the aeroplane was flying in peace time conditions, the situation was completely different. The matter had to be addressed and resolved. The existing considerable mutual respect between the AFZ and Jack Malloch was never in any doubt, but again we sense that it was Jack Malloch who made sure it happened—in a dignified and trouble-free manner. A key criterion was experience on aircraft with tail wheels, which Peter Knobel had. Finally, either at this time or later, the criterion was narrowed to the two OCFWs at New Sarum and Thornhill, each of whom had to have 1,000 hours tail wheel experience. This ensured there would be no queue of gung-ho pilots and it seems to have satisfied Jack Malloch, as we shall see in the next chapter.

October was a busy month for the Spitfire: seven sorties were flown, two by Peter Knobel and five by Jack Malloch. November saw two sorties being flown between the two of them, on 7 and 10 November respectively. Sadly, as has been previously mentioned, after Jack Malloch's last logbook entry on 7 November we have only the records of those Air Force pilots who flew with him during air-to-air photography flights, plus the recall of witnesses to determine further flights by the Spitfire. Dave Hann confirmed that Jack continued to fly the Spitfire on Saturday mornings, but on an infrequent basis.

RECOGNITION AND ACCOLADES

Perhaps by this time Jack Malloch was becoming too absorbed in the day-to-day affairs of Affretair to be able to give more attention to the Spitfire. However, it was during November that he and his engineers were recognised for their achievements. On Thursday 20 November 1980, at a function hosted by the Zimbabwe Division of the Royal Aeronautical Society, two trophies were presented—the Pat Judson Trophy and the Rolls-Royce Trophy. The Pat Judson Trophy was presented to Jack Malloch for "meritorious service by an individual or organisation to aviation or the community as a whole, where flying has been the predominant feature of that service". The Rolls-Royce Trophy was presented to the Affretair engineers for their work in restoring the Spitfire, in recognition of their "technical achievement in aeronautics". Most appropriately, the trophies were presented by Mr A.G. Newton, the Engineering Director at Rolls-Royce.[31]

Rolls-Royce had already displayed a keen interest over the years. Initially their attention was given to the SRAF Spitfires, and later to the RhAF's technical expertise in maintaining their Rolls-Royce engines. It is useful to recall that before the first ferry in 1951, Rolls-Royce and the RAF had agreed that such a long distance ferry was fraught with risk. Yet Rolls-Royce was quick to congratulate the SRAF on the successful outcome of the ferry, in April of 1951. Yet again, after the first ground runs performed on the Spitfire in early 1980, Rolls-Royce had contacted ATA to enquire as to its progress. Once more they were quick to recognise engineering excellence and achievement, and elected to present the trophies. This interest was emphasised by their efforts immediately after Independence when they contacted the AFZ to see how the RhAF had maintained their engines during the recently-ended civil war. Air Commodore Keith Kemsley, as DGSS, accompanied the Rolls-Royce party during its tour of the AFZ facilities at New Sarum, in particular the ERS where his son was working.[32]

Both of these awards were fully deserved. Jack Malloch had served his adopted country loyally and with great distinction through the activities of his company, Affretair. His engineers had provided the best possible pool of skills with which to rebuild the Spitfire.

Even though the bulk of the work was carried out by about 20 of the 90 or so engineers at ATA/Affretair at the time, almost everyone had a hand in the project at some time or the other, and this award could not have been more deserved. As mentioned previously, Appendix E includes a comprehensive a list of all the engineers at ATA/Affretair during the rebuild project, which positively associates them with the Rolls-Royce Trophy.

A replacement Rolls-Royce Trophy is currently held in safe-keeping at the Mashonaland Flying Club[33] at Charles Prince Airport, having been retrieved from the old International Terminal at Harare International Airport. The original trophy disappeared and Mr A.G. Newton of Rolls-Royce replaced this in 1981, presenting it to the Royal Aeronautical Society (RAeS), Zimbabwe Division. Unfortunately no mention is made of Affretair's engineers on the replacement trophy: the date of the award to the first recipient is 1982. The whereabouts of the Pat Judson Trophy is unknown. Sadly, the particulars of these trophies indicate that little of the aviation culture so evident in 1980 has survived in present-day Zimbabwe. There is physical evidence of aviation enterprises—Jack Malloch's hangar, Air Zimbabwe's sprawling complex, and the substantial AFZ base (now called Manyame). Nevertheless, conspicuous by its absence is the vital human element; the tremendous spirit fed by the enthusiasm and skill of each human component; the fervour that made things tick in those days has long faded from the realm of aviation.

The award of the trophies and the change at the office signalled the end of the exciting and achievement-filled first phase of PK350's restored life. As if to confirm this change, there appears to be little or no coverage of the Spitfire and its flying in the print media, the Air Force '81 Air Show notwithstanding, until the devastating news reports on 27 March 1982. Public interest also, sadly, had waned.

Chapter 10

THE OTHER MEN IN HER LIFE

One of the more interesting discoveries while researching this story was the fact that Peter Knobel also flew PK350 in her restored state.[1] Most ex-AF colleagues, including me, remember that Group Captain Steve Kesby was the only person other than Jack Malloch to fly her. But a well-posed photograph of PK350, commonly available on the internet, shows a pilot with a white 'bone dome' (flying helmet), identified as Peter Knobel, confirmed by Keith Kemsley. The photograph was taken from a Dakota in February 1982. Thus it is that we are introduced to the other men in her life—that is, the restored life of PK350.

Their time in the cockpit of PK350 virtually bracketed the remaining time the aircraft spent aloft. Peter Knobel flew most of his sorties in late 1980. All of Steve Kesby's sorties[2] were flown in late 1981 and early 1982.

However, there are still the other men in PK350's life who need to be mentioned, those from her previous life when she was a service aircraft known as SR64. As has been related, she had accumulated 462:35 hours by the time she was grounded in December 1954. Taking into account her time on No. 73 Sqn RAF, she must have been a well-utilised, if not one of the most utilised, aircraft in the SRAF service. She was one of the last two Spitfires to be flying at the end of 1954. Consequently she was probably flown by most of the pilots assigned for duty on No. 1 SRAAF/SRAF/RRAF Squadron between 1951 and 1954.

Jack Malloch was one of the very first auxiliaries to fly PK350, on 22 February 1951.[3] Dickie Bradshaw flew her for most of the ferry and, by virtue of the 23:25 hours[4] that he accumulated on SR64 on the ferry flight, it seems reasonable to credit him with the most hours on SR64/PK350. Thereafter, we have records only of the men who served on the squadron, including the members of the five pilot courses trained on the Spitfire. We classify these as the other men in her life—as a service aeroplane. I will shortly recount the memories of all the other pilots who flew her. Interestingly, the only pilot of those whose memories appear below, who did not fly SR64, was Air Marshal Mick McLaren.

Appendix C lists all the names of the SRAF pilots who flew Spitfires.[5] A substantial number of the approximately 70 men who were privileged to fly the Spitfires have since passed away, but at the time of writing about 15 of these men are still alive. It is time to hear some of their memories of flying these ultimate Spitfires.

Mick McLaren from No. 2 SRAAF Auxiliary Course was one of the earlier pilots of the fledgling SRAF to train on the Spitfire. Having received his Wings on 21 August 1952 from the Governor of Southern Rhodesia, he started his Spitfire flying on 15 September 1952 and finished flying nearly a year later, on 05 August 1953, with 42:20 hours to his credit. His first flight was in SR66 and against this entry is a short comment: "OK, JC, I've got her!" This suggests a fair measure of trepidation about getting the aircraft airborne, verified when he was asked what it was like to fly the Spitfire. Again his response was brief but succinct: "Beauty in the air, a bitch on the ground". He loved flying her, and along with everyone who flew Spitfires he wished he could have flown her more frequently. But he had pressing duties to perform as an instructor, growing the SRAF into the future.[6]

Keith Kemsley, like Mick McLaren, was also born and brought up in South Africa. He continued a trend, established by a number of his colleagues and friends, including the late Air Marshal Norman Walsh, and travelled north to serve in the Rhodesian military, initially joining the army as a corporal. His interest in flying led to his recruitment into the SRAF as a Lieutenant on No. 1 SSU. For a brief time he had the unique status of being a commissioned officer in the air force as well as an NCO in the army. He started his training in September 1951 and completed it in September 1953. He excelled on the Spitfire, winning the Low Level and High Dive Bombing prizes and went on to accumulate 115:55 hours, possibly the most hours on Spitfires amongst the SSU pilots. This included time instructing the pilots on No. 3 SSU's Spitfire course. He also flew SR64 on a number of memorable occasions including No. 2 SSU's Wing Parade on 27 February 1953 and the Battle of Britain Flypast on 20 September 1954. Keith Kemsley's last flight in a Spitfire was on 08 November 1954 when he had accumulated a total of 5:25 hours on SR64. Together with Air Vice-Marshal Chris Dams, Chris Hudson and possibly one or two others, he had helped keep SR64 and SR65 airworthy in the sunset months of the service life of the Spitfires, after the completion of No. 3 SSU's course in July. Keith Kemsley's last flight on a Spitfire has been captured on camera by Sandy Mutch. The aircraft features the famous Flying Assegai 'Hlaba Zulu' inherited from 266 Sqn, painted onto SR64's fuselage. Johnny Deall, his hero at the time, then Flight Commander and previously Officer Commanding No. 266 (Typhoons) Squadron in the Second World War, had happily given his consent for this piece of decorative history to continue its life on another famous fighter.

Recollecting his experience of flying Spitfires, Keith echoed Mick McLaren's succinct description above, and added that it was "bloody cold" as well, when flying at altitude![7]

John Mussell was also a member of No. 1 SSU. His memories of his first flight on a Spitfire amply demonstrate why pilots were so wary of the aircraft whilst on the ground:

> My first flight in a Spitfire (SR 85) was on 15 September 1952. It's interesting to recall that I had three incidents in my first three times in a Spitfire, two of which were my fault. First, at Cranborne, a week or so before we moved operations to Kentucky (New Sarum) we all had to start our Spitfire experience by doing a fast taxi run to tail-up and then throttle back and stop before reaching the end of the runway. In retrospect, an easier procedure—considering the shortness of Cranborne's runway—would have been to let us get airborne and do a circuit and landing. The reasoning for this fast taxi run was to teach us how to cope with the huge torque of the engine that required lots of counteractive rudder and judicious use of the throttle. All of this with almost no view of the runway. Well, I wasn't used to the larger range of movement of the Spitfire throttle compared with the Harvard and when I came to throttle back I did not close it fully. I should have been aware that the engine note was higher than it would have been at idling rpm, but I wasn't. Its residual power kept me heading for the overshoot. I increased the braking while trying not to topple the aircraft forward. Anyway, that's exactly what happened. Just short of the boundary, when the aircraft had almost stopped, my left wheel struck a small anthill and over it went on its nose. The damage was mainly broken prop blades and one very shame-faced sprog.

John Mussell continues, recalling a landing incident, his few flights on SR64 and gives us a fascinating insight into prevailing philosophies around day-to-day aircraft utilisation and the honour code:

> Then we moved to Kentucky where I enjoyed my first airborne and event-free experience on type. My second flight was in SR68 which had to be aborted because the undercarriage would not retract; that ended with a circuit and landing. I was then allocated SR60 and had a great time doing stalls, steep turns and aerobatics. Those tight turns ... fantastic. When I returned to base the wheels failed to lower. I tried the emergency device—an air pressure bottle—and that failed to operate. So I was left to do a belly landing on grass Runway 14. We had been led to believe that the Spitfire could flip onto its back when belly landing,

but that must have been applicable to marks with smaller engines and shorter noses. The landing went off without a hitch, as pictures in *A Pride of Eagles* show. Oddly, although I see most of the numbers in various places in my logbook I don't see mention of SR64 until 30 June 1953, some nine months after I started flying Spitfires. On that flight I did a 35-minute rocket-firing sortie at Inkomo. The weapons were fitted with locally made practice concrete heads (60 pounders I think). I repeated that exercise at Inkomo on 2 July in SR64 on a 40-minute flight. That was my second and last time in SR64. Perhaps she was off the line during that nine-month period. No doubt the logbooks will reveal if that was so. There is another possible reason for the absence of SR64 from my logbook: I recall that we were given the luxury of being allocated a Spitfire of our own. Mine was SR67 (a number I use often these days, when selecting raffle tickets, etc.—not that it has brought any dividends!).

The reason for this policy was to encourage a feeling of ownership and of needing to give our allocated aircraft plenty of tender loving care. For instance, we were instructed never to put the throttle through the gate. The twelve-psi that was available at the standard full throttle position was ample for all purposes that we might encounter. Extra boost up to 18 psi could be obtained by pushing the throttle through the gate. Our instructors, particularly John Deall, appealed to our sense of honour not to use all the available boost, on the basis that it could put unnecessary strain on the engines. John and others knew from their war experiences that reserving the extra boost for use only in extreme emergency could be a lifesaver. On the matter of honour and teamwork, we were drilled and disciplined almost remorselessly, as you know. Instilling honour even came down to the prohibition of the padlocking of our flying lockers, the contents— our purses etc., being out of bounds to anyone else.

And it worked.

John Mussell went on to win the Gunnery Prize and flew altogether 111:15 hours on Spitfires. Even though Keith Kemsley took the bombing prizes on No. 1 SSU, John managed to outshine his three ship formation war-experienced colleagues in a low level bombing demonstration at the Rhodes Centenary Air Display on 13–14 June 1953: he was the only one to hit the target with a marker bomb. The target was in the area where ATA's hangar was later built. However, their training and the guidance provided by old hands who had endured the harshness of war ensured they never became overconfident.

On another occasion John joined up with a four ship formation in bit of a hurry:

Over Seki (south of Salisbury Airport) I was joining a formation of four Spitfires flown by reserve pilots and instructors. I came up behind Ben Bellingan into the astern position a bit too fast. I throttled back fully and fortunately the drag of the five-bladed propeller slowed me rapidly enough to allow me to get into position behind Ben—but not before the effect of my prop was felt by him on his elevator. When we landed I got the full treatment. He told me that he had not gone through operational service in Europe just to be scribbled later by a careless sprog!

Like all Spitfire pilots he reflected "how privileged we were to fly an aircraft that was so outstanding. After the Spitfire, nothing I flew was its match."[8] John grew up in Bulawayo, in Southern Rhodesia. He recalls how, as an eleven-year-old, their home on the corner of Eleventh and Main streets was a home-from-home for some of the RAF personnel in their khaki uniforms. Sadly, many of these men would not return home, but John believed that many survived because of the handling qualities of the Spitfire. This is precisely the view expressed by Jeffrey Quill in his autobiography.

Frank Mussell was a member of No. 2 SSU. Clearly he revelled in the Spitfire experience but also had some hairy incidents to relate:

My logbook shows that I flew 72:10 hours in the Spitfire with five flights in SR64 (including my second-last Spit flight, a rocket firing exercise at the Inkomo range). I was a member of the battle formation exercise during which Ray Maritz was killed. Apart from that sad incident, OCU was largely straightforward, except that I experienced a flat spin from about 25,000 feet down to recovery at tree-top level (and poor old John Deall had to attempt to induce the same idiosyncratic behaviour next day—without drama, thank goodness). And I managed to bust all my haemorrhoids during a high dive bombing exercise when, during pull-out from each of the last two dives, the seat became unlatched and headed south, momentarily increasing g forces beyond my personal limit. In those days we wore white silk flying suits and several and various ground crew were seen to go very pale when I got out of the aircraft, then they rapidly disappeared in all directions! I still consider the Spitfire to have been the most exciting and rewarding aircraft I flew. Even now, I can hear the noise of a couple of them returning to base at very high speed and trying to scare Ossie Penton off the top of the runway safety van before breaking into the circuit for landing. Amazing! Ossie was a great talker, in the bar or out. During an early conversion phase onto Spitfires, Bob d'Hotman was subjected to the 'too high, too low, too fast, too slow' routine and was finally heard to shout in desperation, 'Shut up! I'm landing!'[9]

Wing Commander Roy Morris was also a member of No. 2 SSU and managed 71 hours on Spitfires. In addition he flew SR64 ten times during his course, totalling 11:20 hours on her, between October 1953 and February 1954. His memories throw light on the tragic circumstances of Ray Maritz's accident, as well as other dramatic moments like John Mussell's wheels-up landing;

My memory of Ray Maritz's crash is this: we were flying a 'Battle 8' with Captain John Deall in the lead (two sections of 4). Ray was No. 4 of the second section and on a cross under turn to starboard (right) he made contact with the ground whilst looking up at the rest of the formation. I was considered Ray's best friend so I was asked to head the funeral procession from the Dutch Reformed Church (near present day Monomatapa Hotel in Harare) to the cemetery on the far side of the *kopje* (hill), near the power station cooling towers. Some walk with part slow time!

I remember John Mussell's belly landing, when we were instructed to line the grass runway so we could get in quickly to help John out. Well, John was out by himself in a flash, and kissed the ground whilst I was still recovering from having to dodge bits of prop.

I remember the spin recovery of John Cameron. John could not recover from the spin and as the ground got closer, he pushed the rudder even harder until at last the aircraft responded. What happened is that the heel of his shoe had caught against a 'lip' on the floor of the cockpit and was preventing full rudder deflection. In the end he pushed so hard that he tore his heel right off!

The Spitfire was certainly purpose-built for performance and once airborne it was a delight to fly. On the ground it was difficult, to say the least. Another problem was that we did not have the pleasure of flying at night due to the non-availability of 'Flame' eliminators for the exhausts.[10]

Even though night landings were carried out successfully during the first ferry, Roy Morris confirms that night flying was not practised in the SRAF with the Spitfire because the aircraft did not have flame eliminators; and once again the Spitfire's tricky ground handling is mentioned.

Wing Commander Rex Taylor, a course mate with Roy Morris on No. 2 SSU, flew SR64 six times on a variety of exercises for a total of 5:35 hours and 67:25 on Spitfires. His memories suggest he had more than one lady to tame at the time and had to make a choice:

In March 1952, I was one of twenty brash, conceited, vain, and supremely over confident young lads; after all, we had emerged as successful pilot trainees after what we thought was a gruelling selection process. Before the year was over the vanity, conceit, over confidence and other vile shortcomings were knocked out of us, often with embarrassment and pain. Our drill and PT instructors, our classroom and flying instructors made us into twenty humble, polite and spirited cadets. We had come to realise that we were 'shark shit' at the very bottom of the planet's chain of life. However, at the ocean floor there is only one way to go—and so, ever so slowly, we climbed upwards to shallow water and after a year of dedication and trepidation we earned our Wings and self-respect. Another six months of classroom theory followed by gunnery, rocket and bombing practice and we were finally cleared as 'Qualified for Operations'. Ahead lay the daunting three-tonne prospect of a five-bladed propeller and 2,000 horsepower under a flexible lever in the left hand, and a comfortable joystick in the right hand. (Never let my instructors hear me refer to the control column as a 'joystick'. Yeeuch!)

In 1951 the Southern Rhodesian Government had purchased 22 Spitfire Mk 22s which was the penultimate Mark of the Spitfire line. It had a 2,000 horse-power two-stage supercharged Griffon engine, 12 cylinders driving five massive blades on a variable-pitch propeller hub. The cockpit was too narrow for the pilot to spread his elbows, but otherwise not cramped for a brat like me whose inflated ideas of self-importance had been well and truly expunged. The cockpit closed in around me as if it had been moulded for my body. All the instruments and controls were within reach, even though I sometimes felt I was a four-eyed octopus.

The main undercarriage wheels on the Spitfire were remarkably long and set close together; it was a 'tail dragger' which is pilot jargon for an aircraft fitted with a tail wheel. The long nose obscured the pilot's view as he taxied, leading to an exaggerated weave along the taxi-way. (Some of it was especially for the eagle-eyes of the duty instructor at the take-off point.) Run-up and take-off checks were a precise drill with no waste of time, as the engine temperatures climbed rapidly on the ground and the Spit needed to get air flowing through the radiators without delay. During take-off there were a number of forces acting on the aircraft to make each take-off exciting to the spectators but demanding on the rookie pilot. The powerful engine and huge propeller caused one wheel to lift and the other to be pressed firmly into the tarmac and full rudder was needed to counteract this torque and the spiralling airflow from the propeller. The stick had to be kept fully back to keep the tail down until flying speed was reached. By then the Spit had crabbed from the right-hand side of the runway to somewhere near the centre and it was time to ease the stick forward and lower the nose to almost the flying attitude. This simple two-dimensional trick evoked amusement among the onlookers as the monster gyroscopic forces kicked the aircraft in three dimensions faster than the pilot, rudder and brakes could stop it.

The next performance was much appreciated by our bunch of critics. The throttle was on the left cockpit wall, but the under-carriage UP lever was on the opposite side. There two ways of raising the undercarriage:

Method One: With his left hand, the pilot could release the throttle and quickly stretch across the control column to move the stiff undercarriage lever, and whip his hand back to the throttle before it closed down completely.

Method Two: Juggle the left hand quickly from throttle to control column, keeping wings and nose approximately level while the right hand heaved on the undercarriage lever. The pilot's hands then execute a reverse shuffle to regain control. The procedure was made more interesting as the undercarriage legs never came up in unison, which caused the aircraft to yaw and roll until the wheels were neatly tucked away into their tiny bays.

We all watched every take-off and laughed, smiled or giggled as we saw the Spit dance, wobble and weave as the wheels came up. At landing and take-off speeds, the controls were understandably sloppy, made more critical because, to counteract the torque of the propeller, the port wing was set at a greater angle of attack than the starboard wing. However, at speed, the Spit behaved just as a fighter aircraft should.

An amusing characteristic of the two-stage supercharger was that the pilot didn't have to take his concentration away from the enemy to change supercharger speed at high altitudes; a pressure switch did it for him. At about 20,000 feet, as the supercharger engaged a faster speed, the Griffon spat and coughed loudly, while the Spit would leap and lurch. Even when the pilot was anticipating the change, it would always catch him unawares and bring a wry smile to his lips (and a stain in his underpants!).

On 8 September 1953, sixteen months since my first ever flight, after signing the Authorisation Book, I strapped three tonnes of Duralumin, wood, steel and parachute silk to my backside for a one-hour sortie in Spitfire XXII, serial SR63. I was briefed for flight in the sector to the north-east of the field, towards Shamva where a special lady friend's family was farming. I knew Naomi was on the farm at the time …

My very first take-off seemed smooth enough. I didn't clip the prop tips, I kept to the runway, two green lights assured me that my wheels were tucked away, the wings were approximately level, the earth was below, sky above and the Griffon was purring in front of me. In fact the whole manoeuvre had been a resounding success. I knew the way to Shamva, but I glanced at the folded map strapped to my knee without seeing it, for Lion's Head *kopje* was already well behind me and the cockpit was full of smoke. I smelt burnt varnish. Immediately I recognised the unique smell, but too late I switched off the booster pump, which should have been part of my Thousand-foot Checks. The acrid smoke and burnt smell cleared immediately and knowing what it was, I continued with my first solo in the mighty Spit Twenty-Two. (A booster pump ensures that should the normal fuel pump fail at a critical time, the booster pump will keep the engine running. It is designed to run only for short periods.) Overhead Shamva in a twinkle I descended to well less than 1,000 feet above the ground and circled the de Kock's farmhouse in as tight a turn as I could. I did a few more steep turns and waggled the aircraft's wing on a low pass when I saw Naomi in the yard.

It was time to leave the farm's airspace to practise a few stalls and recoveries and to set up a dummy approach at altitude to get the feel of the Spit at landing speeds with wheels and flaps down. Some sixty minutes later, which appeared to pass in less than thirty seconds, I rejoined the circuit and like all the other new Spit pilots, carried out a textbook approach and landing. I was even more elated than I had been on my first solo.

Captain Deall, the Spitfire Squadron flight commander, berated me for not returning to land immediately. I had a fire on the aircraft, and with incredible constraint he dismissed my egotistical claim that I knew it was just the booster pump coils that had burnt out, that fuel pressures were normal and therefore the booster pump would not be vital for the circuit and landing. In the light of some thirty years of flying, I now know what could have happened because of my over-confidence and sympathise with his concern for one of his cocky junior pilots.

All too quickly our days on No. 2 SSU were over. Within a week of returning to civilian life I developed itchy feet and missed all the excitement, camaraderie and probably most of all, the glory of a Spit! A Spitfire in the air, and even on the ground, is undoubtedly the most beautiful aircraft ever built. Its slim and streamlined shape is the epitome of beauty, an everlasting icon in the history of aviation. The combined smell of avgas 100, burnt oil and Dural evokes passions and feelings like no other odour. The sounds, too, of a 2,000 horse power Griffon turning a monster wooden propeller is enough to bring any aviator leaping from the boudoir of a mistress to gaze upon the mistress of the air.

In a contest with Naomi, on a count of two out of three, the Spit wins.[11]

Wing Commander Wally Hinrichs was one of Rex Taylor's course mates. He accumulated 74 hours and flew SR64 eleven times between October 1953 and February 1954. He remembers vividly the blindfold checks before his first solo, and the starting hassles with the Coffmann cartridges. He managed a clean first start on his first solo, whereas Frank Mussell and Roy did not and had to wait a couple of hours for the starter to cool down. We can just imagine how, in the crew room afterwards, these young buck pilots would be ribbing each other over something like this. This, it will be remembered, challenged the ferry pilots frequently with hot engines. Wally remembers also the need for a quick taxi to keep a decent airflow through the radiators, as well as the need to keep weaving along the taxi-track and how the supercharger kicked in during the climb. Again, he loved flying the Spitfire, especially doing aerobatics, formation, and all forms of weapons delivery.[12]

Chris Dams on No. 3 SSU accumulated 57 hours and flew SR64 ten times, including her last flight. He recalls his first flight:

> I was on No. 3 SSU and we went on to Spits in March of 1954. By that time, they had done a lot of hard work, also in a very harsh environment compared to their design climate. My first solo was 12 March 1954 and that had a story (as most flights did). After take-off, the gear did not show 'up' on the lights. Consequently, I came round past the tower for a visual check. I was given the OK to press on. But this diversion and the performance of the Spit itself had prevented me getting through the after take-off checks completely. I began them again after starting the climb away from the visual check By the time I got to the end I was already at, say, 10,000 feet above mean sea level. The last check was Clean air to Ram air. To do this you flipped a switch which was mounted on top of the undercarriage mechanism. This moved a flap in the intake duct/ trunking, which you see under the nose, which then allowed air directly to the

supercharger, bypassing the filter. With plenty of boost on and the two stage/two speed supercharger doing its thing, this sudden extra gulp of air caused the engine to miss a couple of beats (maybe just one). The engine was such a dominant part of what was going on (with every flight) that I was half way over the side (at least mentally) during the very brief moment that it took for the Rolls-Royce Griffon to regain its composure.

The position of that switch reminds me of the curious fact that the undercarriage controls were on the starboard wall of the cockpit and only operable with your right hand, so to begin with it was almost inevitable that the wings would waggle while you changed hands and flew—possibly for the first time ever—left handed. Raising the gear was not just a matter of pressing a switch; you moved a lever down out of a gate, which engaged the hydraulic pump, then slightly inboard, then rotate up and forward through maybe 120 degrees. This last movement rotated two bolts/catches which were chamfered at their ends like door catches and which engaged with a hole cast on the edge of the oleo legs. Now with hydraulic pressure and with the bolt reversed the leg pushed the bolt out of the way and began retracting. When it was fully up the bolt went into a separate hole to hold the leg up. Lowering was the reverse rotation of the bolt, so that the chamfered side allowed the leg (with hydraulic pressure in the jack) again to push the bolt out of the way; very simple and very effective, but there was no room for such a mechanism on the port wall of the cockpit.

There is another thing about the undercarriage. Because it retracted with the wheels moving outboard, the track with the gear down was very narrow. This gave rise to a skittish character on the ground and also, because the leg which balanced the torque of the motor and prop (starboard leg) was so close inboard, it had to be pumped a lot harder than the other leg and tyre.

I flew 57 hours on the Spit. Far too few. The beauty of the Spit was that when you went about your normal flying business, you almost unconsciously corrected for unwanted changes in attitude or bank. This was because you sat half way back towards the tail and the wing tips were in your peripheral vision. So errors in nose position and bank were corrected for without thinking about it. Keeping a lookout was the easiest thing in the world. But that is just one example of its virtues.[13]

It is not every day that a pilot has a short, eventful flight and a successful, safe landing, only to be told soon afterwards that the aircraft has been classified as having

Category 5 damage (beyond economic repair) and has been written off. Chris Dams had exactly that experience and relates the circumstances as if it were yesterday:

> The SR88 story went as follows. I was on the Operational Training Unit (OTU) part of training and we were having a day of rocket firing at Inkomo, flying off New Sarum. I had had an aborted sortie earlier, due probably to the rockets (RPs) hanging up. I was then tacked onto the end of the programme and urged to jump around in order to complete the number of sorties due before lunch. I took off along Runway 06 and turned out starboard round Prince Edward dam and across towards Inkomo, underneath the approach path to Belvedere. The aircraft was running rough, as it had a reputation for doing. I tried opening up the power to clear the plugs but without much effect. When I came to set up the weapons and sight, I found the sighting line to be shaking around so violently that I seriously doubted that it would be possible to use it to fire rockets— remember that in the dive the gyro would be uncaged and would be even more prone to outside interference. So, unwillingly, after the flight commander's urgings, I decided to turn back. However, in the turn the aircraft smoothed out a bit so I continued round on a full 360 back towards Inkomo. Very shortly thereafter the roughness increased still more than before.
>
> This time I became concerned for the aircraft as a whole—to hell with the sighting problem. I decided to give up and turned back once and for all. I remember, having made the decision, that I then had a moment of real apprehension about the possible outcome of the flight. So I went the whole hog, declared an emergency and asked for a straight in approach to 06. I had a look at Belvedere as well, but decided to take it home.
>
> The story lacks some drama after this, except for the punch line. The landing went without incident and I cut the engine on touchdown and rolled off the runway across the grass towards the hardstanding. (In those days 06 began just before the taxi-track from our side entered the runway.) I left it facing parallel to 06 for the rockets to be made safe. There stood an apparently serviceable aircraft with me waddling down off the wing encumbered by the parachute. I was full of apologies to the flight commander, Flight Lieutenant Dickenson, who was at the time seconded to us from the RAF. (Sandy Mutch joined us at about the same time having been posted in on a similar basis.)
>
> It seems there could not have been such a hellfire rush with the programme, because my logbook shows that we continued flying weapons to Inkomo for the next three days.

Later in the day I was advised that the aircraft was Cat 5, the reason being that the reduction gear between the engine and the prop had been chewing itself to bits and was found to be on its very last legs.[14]

As we learned in Chapter 4, Chris Dams continued to fly Spitfires until they were grounded. His last sortie was on 18 December 1954 in SR64. Eight of his ten sorties in SR64 were flown during the OCU and the last two on SR64 were detailed as Air Tests.

Chris Hudson, a course mate with Chris Dams on No. 3 SSU, managed to log 54:45 hours on the Spitfires and flew SR64 three times. Chris also flew SR65 on 18 December 1954, the same day as SR64 had last flown. This was unknown until he was contacted and asked to recount his memories for this book. He had no idea that SR65 had been retained by the RRAF and thought she had been sold to the Syrians. Chris remembers the Spitfire as a beautiful aircraft. He described himself "as a very average pilot and as long as one treated her right, she was an absolute delight to fly." He confessed to being caught out by the enormous torque one day when being in a hurry to get airborne:

I opened the throttle without holding full left rudder and in a flash found myself beginning a ground loop. I caught it immediately but by then she was facing across the runway. The tower was less than complimentary, enquiring if I didn't need the normal length of runway for my take-off.

Chris also remembers well the descriptions of their first flights from Brian Horney and Solly Ferreira. Brian's words were reminiscent of Mick McLaren's account: "At 1,000 feet, I said, 'OK Lord, I've got her now!'" Solly was seen sitting on his parachute after climbing out of the cockpit in a state of ecstasy, uttering strong expletives: "F..k it! F..k it! F..k it!" Even though the words were not very original, his course mates knew what he meant.[15]

Squadron Leader Mike Saunders, another No. 3 SSU member, accumulated 38.4 hours on the Spitfire and flew SR64 three times. His memories balance the good and bad about the aircraft and give us an idea about how the guns were operated:

It was indeed a very challenging aircraft to fly, especially when you have what today would be considered very few hours—I had less than 200 hours solo at the time. However, it demonstrates the quality of our training here, that despite the complexity of the Spitfire, accidents were very few.

Being a classic machine does not mean it had no faults – it had some faults and some vices.

Fault one was the idiotic positioning, and action, of the landing gear control. It was on the right side of the cockpit and this meant changing hands immediately after lift-off in order to select UP. At this critical point this meant leaving the throttle to its own devices and flying the aircraft with the left hand; this was fine if you had remembered to apply plenty of throttle friction, but if you had forgotten to do this the throttle would snap shut and everything would go quiet. Now the dilemma was to re-open the throttle with the left hand while the right hand went back to flying the lurching brute. Now the friction lever had to be adjusted prior to a second attempt to raise the gear. If you had a very long pinkie on your left hand this could be achieved otherwise you struggled for valuable seconds. Meanwhile the gear remained down and since the Spit gear neatly banked off a lot of radiator area, so the coolant temp would enter the red sector. Incidentally the landing gear control lever was in a C shaped quadrant so in order to raise the gear you actually selected DOWN first, then UP and finally DOWN again. There was an incredible length of bicycle chain—I'm serious— leading from this lever to the gear locks which held the gear up and down. The whole weird process was reversed when lowering the gear for landing

Another strange idea was to fire the cannon using compressed air. The gun button on the stick was in fact an air valve and the effect of this was an appreciable delay between pressing the button and the cannon actually firing. This meant the pilot had to estimate the delay in the sighting picture as the nose swung on to the target in any turbulence and press well in advance of the actual firing point. And yet we won the Battle of Britain!

The brakes, of course, were pneumatic as well, which meant a hand lever controlling the amount of pressure while your feet on the rudders determined where this pressure might go. The Provost was like this as well.

I'm sure every pilot who flew the Spit here did the same thing, climb as high as you could go—well over 30,000 feet—open the throttle and stuff the nose down, thrilling and stupid, but fun, fun, fun! Compressibility? What was that in 1954?

Big thrill? Following Chris Dams across Lake McIlwaine (now Chivero, west of Salisbury) on a super calm morning and watching the wake caused by the prop wash.

Good days in a great aircraft.[16]

Today, the image that Mike Saunders describes as a big thrill would probably have been caught on a digital camera by someone in the formation, or even better, by a digital video that would have found its way onto YouTube. Mike can share it with us today only as a written memory. However, the spirit of flight, the romance of that spirit and the excitement of observing something which very few people witness and experience, is there for us to savour, inspiring us to imagine what it must have been like.

John Campbell, one of the SRAAF auxiliaries, offers a slightly different perspective Having flown all the main Merlin-powered fighter versions of the Spitfire, he was in a unique position to offer a comparative view when recalling his days on the Griffon-powered Mk 22 with the SRAAF. Interestingly, John's assessment was very much in line with the appraisal of late Mark Spitfires given by the test pilot, Alex Henshaw. John flew 123 hours on the Mk 22 and commented as follows:

> I much preferred the earlier Spitfire types. They handled like a feather, were dainty, but one could never get the thing to sit on the ground. The Mk 22 was heavier, not as pleasant to handle but was easier to land. I never cared for the Griffon; it coughed and spluttered compared to the smooth purr of the Merlin.[17]

All but one of the above ex-SRAF Spitfire pilots who shared their memories were describing a stage in their lives when they were stepping into a demanding and sometimes harsh profession as air force pilots. It was also a time of transition for the SRAF/RRAF as it moved from the piston age into the jet age. These changes followed the hard lessons of war which were relentlessly drilled into the new pilots by their flight commanders and commanding officers. Some of these men played a substantial role in moulding the SRAF into one of the finest small air forces the world has seen—the Rhodesian Air Force. The Spitfire was a vital component in that process and all these men were unanimous in acknowledging their sense of privilege at having been able to fly this legendary machine.

Peter Knobel and Steve Kesby, the last two men to savour the delight of flying the Spitfire, were at different stages in their flying careers as air force pilots; both had enjoyed very satisfying careers to date and flying PK350 was the icing on the cake. Keith Kemsley has already provided insight into the process that led to Peter Knobel getting his chance to fly a Mk 22.

Peter Knobel, like Keith Kemsley, was born in South Africa and started his aviation career there. Aeroplanes were his passion and Spitfires were at the very core of that zeal. Sadly for him, in his younger days he often just missed the chance to fly Spitfires. Having joined the SAAF and volunteered for pilot training during the Korean War, his chances of flying the Spitfire were dashed when the SAAF grounded their aircraft in 1954. Peter turned to a career in civilian aviation, migrated to Rhodesia and later joined the RRAF only to find that they had also grounded their Spitfires. Not to be outdone, he arranged to fly John Fairey's Spitfire G-AIDN, but unhappily this came to nought when the aircraft had a wheels-up landing the day before he was due to fly. The only thing left to him was to build a Spitfire himself. In 1965 Peter started the design phase of his project and in 1969 he began building a Spitfire to a three-fifths scale. The skills he developed on this project led him to work closely with the technicians in the RhAF and when he commanded 5 Sqn, he assisted technicians successfully to 'blow' Canberra canopies. This skill enabled the RhAF to bypass the sanctions imposed on Rhodesia. In the early 1970s, during his time as Officer Commanding No. 2 Ground Training School (in charge of the pilot cadets) at Thornhill, he found another outlet for his love of Spitfires—he arranged for the pilot cadets to polish SR65 on the plinth at the entrance to the Base. Sadly, Peter Knobel has recently passed away, but he has left us his memories and one can picture him recalling the Spitfire-polishing episode with his characteristic wry smile:

My standard punishment for any cadets who misbehaved was to polish the Spitfire. I was returning one afternoon from the swimming pool with the family, having awarded the cadets course the task of polishing the Spitfire, to find Dennis Spence[18] leading the team with four electric floor polishers on huge cables coming from the Admin Centre. That was Spence's version of hard labour. But I must say that Spitfire glistened—matt camouflage or no."[19]

Later, as we have seen, Peter Knobel did his best to assist the Spitfire rebuild project with his efforts to blow a canopy. In 1979 he had assumed a test flying role for the RhAF and was well positioned for consideration as the Spitfire's pilot when Keith Kemsley lobbied for him to fly PK350 in late 1980. Peter takes up the story in his own inimitable way:

Flying the Spitfire was traumatic in that it was of course a single-seat aircraft and there weren't that many Spitfire pilots around. Although John Fairey was extremely helpful, his two-seater Spitfire G-AIDN had of course only half the power of the Griffon engine, but he was a great supporter. I interviewed John Deall who had a lot of time on Spitfires and of course Uncle Jack, who, until this day I still consider one of the most magnificent people, never mind pilots, I have ever met: a great big cheerful, wonderful guy. It's a very pleasant thought that everyone I ever met at Affretair, if I asked them who they worked for, they said 'Uncle Jack'. No 'Captain Malloch' or 'Affretair', always Uncle Jack. An absolute wonder of a man. Needless to say, I interrogated him mercilessly over technical details, flying characteristics and so on and so forth, all the while being monitored by Keith Kemsley who had been nominated Instructor. This entailed putting on a blindfold and sitting in the cockpit with Keith Kemsley asking me to point out the oil temperature gauge, the undercarriage retract, etc. If I made just one error he said, 'Right, see you back here in two hours,' and I would do it again. But when nearly ready to fly, I did a final interrogation with Uncle Jack. He would sit with his seat tilted back, feet on his desk, eyes closed and we would run through the start procedure, the run ups and the take-off and the loops and rolls, etc. I said to him, 'Uncle Jack, the one thing that is bothering me is getting the tail wheel down in the event of an undercarriage malfunction.' The reason being that they had reconnected the retractable tail wheel but the emergency 'blown down system' didn't apply to that. (See the comment above.) Uncle Jack, the most cheerful of all people, said to me, stony faced, 'in which case you land it in Lake McIlwaine'. Click goes my limited computer. 'But Jack, it floats for only two-and a-half seconds.' And he says, 'Exactly, don't come back,' which scared me spitless. Not so much of hurting myself, but the thought of damaging the sole remaining Spit 22 in the whole world was dead scary.

It is worth pointing out that Dave Hann believes it was around this time that a second emergency CO_2 bottle for the tail wheel, the size of a dumpy beer bottle, was fitted next to the main undercarriage CO_2 bottle on the right rear cockpit wall. Photos of the aircraft at this time are few and far between, until the Air Force '81 Air Show in late October. However, in the last phases of PK350's life it is clear that the tail wheel was being retracted, confirming there was an emergency facility in the event of a normal hydraulic failure. The hydraulic supply could be reconnected as easily as it was disconnected. This was a unique but very practical modification.

Peter Knobel continues:

I heard all the stories about how one kept straight by applying full rudder on take-off and then varying the throttle, as you couldn't use full throttle from a standstill. I asked John Deall how much power was actually needed to get airborne and he confirmed actually very little, it would quite happily get airborne with half power. So for my first take-off I was an absolute wet and used half power and wound up taking off in an aircraft with the performance of a Harvard. However, soon, soon, I learned to apply full power by the time we got take off speed and then she was a pussycat. In the air she had a strange characteristic whereby one followed the engine like the tail behind a dog. In turbulence the engine would remain static almost like a gyro, whilst the aeroplane and I were bounced around it. One got the distinct impression that you were taking a bulldog for a walk on a leash, and you went where the engine wanted to go. A loop was tricky because as speed built up to the bottom of the loop, one applied full rudder. At the top of the loop, because of the torque, you had full opposite rudder and then the reverse on the way down again. Landing, of course required wheel landings, remembering on final never to let the speed get much below 85-90 knots, without a good deal of thought, because application of full power meant that the airplane rolled in the opposite direction to the propeller, due to the ineffective ailerons at that low speed. Landings as 'wheelers' (on both main wheels as opposed to a three pointer landing, characteristic of a tail-dragger aircraft) were remarkably easy, provided one kept up the speed and of course kept the tail up. The touch-down itself on a fairly rigid undercarriage was gentle and surprisingly without a great tendency to swing. I must say I never landed it in any severe cross wind when the story would have been rather different. Once on the ground one didn't mess about taxiing because the undercarriage leg protruded in front of the radiators and any prolonged taxiing resulted in gross overheating. I recall that the Spitfire had one curiosity after touch-down: if the stick was left totally neutral it would tend to tip over on its nose due to the very forward centre of gravity.

I remember a brilliant piece of flying by Jack Malloch, landing at Charles Prince (Note: this was actually at Salisbury Main). The valve stem had pulled out of the one tyre which was therefore flat, and as he touched down the drag of the flat tyre was causing him to nose-over and even with stick hard back the nose-over continued until he gave a blast of power sufficient to get the tail back down again and without damaging the aircraft—a remarkable display of airmanship.

All in all, flying the Spitfire was an incredible experience; a little scarier than I anticipated, and sadly the charm of the early Spitfires was definitely missing.

When I went to enter my log book Spitfire Mk 22, PK350, etc., it occurred to me that I could quite happily stop flying at that time. Today I am reminded of what the lady Captain of Concorde said when they were grounded: she asked the question, 'Where do I go from here?

Finally, after all his efforts over the years, Peter Knobel got his wish in the best possible way—flying this full scale, ultimate Spitfire. Again, his respect and admiration for Jack Malloch come through very strongly, together with the feeling that nothing else would ever compare with this experience. He flew five sorties altogether; his first having been aborted. The first four were flown in fairly quick succession between 30 September and 10 November 1980. One of these sorties was a display at the Salisbury Sports Club which is right next to State House, and Peter used North Avenue as the display line for his aerobatic sequence. Admittedly, these were early days in Zimbabwe's Independence; giving a display like this today is inconceivable, not only with the President living so close to the Harare Sports Club, but because displays over built up areas are unlikely to be permitted. On this occasion the only person whose displeasure was incurred was a friend of Peter's who had a penthouse flat overlooking the sports club; he complained that the sound of the Griffon had woken him from his afternoon nap. He worked at the Department of Civil Aviation.[20]

Peter's last flight was on 3 February 1982,[21] well over a year later, for an air-to-air photographic sortie with a Dakota. This was when the excellent photograph of the Spitfire, mentioned earlier, was taken. Captain of the Dakota (7053) was Squadron Leader Clive Ward, then Officer Commanding No. 3 Squadron, and with him in the cockpit was Norman Ingledew as his co-pilot.

By February 1982, Steve Kesby was also current on the Spitfire and by all accounts was doing most of the flying. Steve was OCFW at New Sarum and was in an excellent position for easy access to Affretair and thus the Spitfire. He was a member of 18 PTC and had enjoyed an excellent career thus far, flying mostly Hunters or Vampires as a weapons instructor. He had also spent time on 6 Sqn as a flying instructor and crucially had accumulated a lot of time on the Provost, with a piston engine and a tail wheel configuration. Substantial time on tail-draggers was a major criterion in determining which other AFZ pilots, apart from Peter Knobel, were to fly the Spitfire.

Steve takes up the story:

I presume that being OCFW would have been one of the factors under consideration when assessing a candidate to represent the Air Force. In addition I had a reasonable amount of experience as a Qualified Flying Instructor (QFI), Pilot Attack Instructor (PAI) and Instrument Rating Examiner (IRE), with around 1,000 hours on tail wheel aircraft. Whatever the reason, I was the person chosen. Being at New Sarum was certainly convenient as I was able to cross the runway to visit Affretair whenever possible, and indeed I did.

The first step was to meet with Jack Malloch. He was a fine man and I felt privileged to meet and get to know him. He made me very welcome and I spent quite a few hours in his company, first through briefing and then socially, joining him in drinking fine whisky. During this time I got to know how he felt and loved the Spitfire and he regaled me with his experiences on this aircraft. Jack introduced me to Bob Dodds and Dave Hann. Both of these men made me very welcome and again I spent many happy hours in their company and with their engineers. After their own individual briefings they put me with particular engineers who then shared their respective knowledge of the aircraft. And so, slowly but surely, I was able to get a good background on all parts of the aircraft. There were no written notes on the Spitfire, apart from an old set of Pilot's Notes, so this part was invaluable. Especially as I got to know the Affretair crew and how they all felt about the Spitfire (I was not going to be the one that damaged the aircraft in any way if I could help it!). At the appropriate stage I even did engine runs with Bob Dodds standing on the wing, giving instructions.

Finally, the aircraft was ready and Jack Malloch carried out engine runs and taxi checks before the big day. With Jack Malloch at the controls this went remarkably well and everyone was hugely relieved and pleased. Now it was my turn. By this time I was familiar with the aircraft and had done cockpit drills on normal and emergency checks and felt very comfortable.

I remember the first flight very well. It was late in the afternoon. There were a number of huge cumulus clouds but with a gap directly over the airfield. The sun was quite low; its rays shone visibly through gaps in the clouds, and there was a haze in the air.

The Griffon engine was water/glycol-cooled and needed airflow to stop the temperature rising too rapidly whilst on the ground. Due to the long taxi distance to the threshold of Runway 06 I waited until no aircraft movements were due before starting.

Taxiing was different due to the long nose and reasonably short wheel base.

In order to see ahead you had to weave from side to side whilst on the taxi way. This presented no problems but I could see the glycol temperature rising rapidly and so was pleased to finally reach the take-off position.

Pre-take off checks were completed. Part of these included full rudder trim to the left, the Griffon engine produced 2,000 horsepower with huge torque forces. These, together with a relatively small rudder area, made for interesting take-offs and go-arounds.

As the throttle was advanced the rudder was slowly increased. The aircraft accelerated very quickly and the tail was quickly raised. Keeping straight was not as difficult as I expected and the aircraft soon became airborne.

The climb rate was good and whilst slowly circling the airfield I climbed to 15,000 feet, about 10,000 feet above ground level. The aircraft was put through a series of turns and I experimented with 'G' stalls. (The aircraft quickly recovered by releasing the back pressure.)

Then a short session of stalling—both clean and dirty. There was a slight tendency to drop a wing but nothing untoward and easily recoverable. I found I was playing all the time with the throttle /engine, getting used to the power/ rudder combinations.

The Griffon engine was the most powerful piston engine I had flown and was a delight. It operated smoothly and efficiently and was very responsive. You could feel it through the airframe. The engine had a supercharger and operated in low and high gear, which changed automatically on passing through 11,000 feet (during a loop through this altitude the engine changed gears—very interesting).

After going through these exercises I felt comfortable enough to do aerobatics. The aircraft was very responsive and willing. The controls were light and again, very responsive—in fact it was a delight to fly. After a number of individual aerobatics I started sequencing them and had a great time for about 15 minutes. Generally cavorting around the clouds: rolling, looping, turning, climbing and descending in all combinations—fantastic!

The clouds, the sun's rays, the haze, the engine noise, the visibility—it was magic and I will never forget that time. It still lives in my mind's eye.

However, all good things must come to an end and I had to descend to carry out a few circuits and overshoots.

A particular point of interest is that this aircraft was rebuilt to a very high standard and there were no restrictions on engine and airframe other than those imposed by the Pilot's Notes. (For example; a 6 G limit and a maximum speed of 450 knots, both of which I achieved.) In the circuit, once again, the aircraft handled well. Visibility was good, (except on short finals) and speed control simple. One-wheeler landing and go round was practiced; this required some concentration with rudder/power application but was easily controlled. The full stop landing was in the three-point position and the aircraft behaved well.

So finally, my first flight in a Spitfire was complete. It was great! It was a wonderful experience and I eagerly looked forward to my next flight.

The de-brief with the engineers went smoothly, with little to complain about but lots to talk about. Finally, Jack took me back to his office for a flying de-brief to be followed by a large toast from his special whisky bottle.

An amusing episode occurred during one of my subsequent flights. Due to the overheating problem we always got permission from Air Traffic Control (ATC) before start. On one occasion we were delayed due to a small problem and when we finally started there was a Lufthansa 747 just starting to taxi. ATC asked him if we could have priority—which was granted. On passing just in front of the 747 a guttural German voice shouted 'Achtung Spitfeur' which produced laughter—a light moment.

At some stage there was a decision to film the rebuild of the Spitfire and Jack's particular part in it. As part of this Jack did a few filming flights but the main part was left to me.

In the filming process the camera was carried in the Huey, the Dakota and the Vampire. A full brief was conducted prior to any flying sequence but had to be modified in the air by the camera crew in order to get the best shot taking into account cloud, sun, aircraft attitude, etc. This necessitated frequent retakes to achieve the aircraft's best angle, speed, direction and attitude. It obviously worked because the film was finally made and was well received.

One aspect of the filming that was particularly delightful was when I was asked to carry out low level aerobatics and low flying for a camera that was placed on a prominent *kopje* in the Domboshawa area. It was a beautiful day and a wonderful experience.

I was able to do a number of flights in the Spitfire before Jack was tragically killed whilst flying the aircraft he loved.[22]

Steve Kesby has given us an excellent account of his memories in PK350, or SR64 as he entered her in his logbook. We have to remember she was still an Air Force aircraft, and SR64 was her correct service number as entered in the F700, even though Dave Hann had taken the liberty of painting her in her original RAF colours.

In fact it was from Steve Kesby's summary of his hours that this fact was revealed; it was confirmed by Dave Hann.

It is very easy to identify each of the three pilots of PK350 amongst the numerous photographs and video footage taken of her: first there was Jack Malloch with his WW2 leather flying helmet; Peter Knobel with his white bone dome; and finally, Steve Kesby, in his pale blue bone dome. It was subsequently pointed out by Steve that he flew a few sorties wearing his 6 Sqn helmet, which had a 6 superimposed on a black diamond, which is visible on his bone dome after his first flight.[23]

Steve Kesby started flying PK350 on 23 November 1981, and flew altogether nine sorties for a total of 11:40 hours, mostly to help Bill Sykes produce footage for the video on the first flight. His next memorable flight was when he flew with Dakota 7303 on 10 December. On this occasion his flying left a huge impression on the Dakota crew. Once again Clive Ward was the Captain, accompanied this time by Sid Buxton. They were very impressed at the accuracy and smoothness of the manoeuvres[24] executed by Steve Kesby.

Steve's next notable flight, on 15 January 1982, was in the Domboshawa area (north-east of Salisbury) and was clearly a memorable flight for him. Indeed it was also a very memorable day for Bill Sykes who had overseen the filming out at Domboshawa and who has provided a detailed account of this flight:

> After the most captivating, scintillating and enchanting afternoon of being beaten up by a Spitfire Mk 22 for fifteen minutes in the hills of Domboshawa, north of the capital city, it was difficult to come back down to earth again. In fact, it took many days. Had it really happened, or was it all a dream …
>
> Fortunately it had all been captured on celluloid, and we had the privilege of being able to relive the experience again and again, watching the film, accompanied by the moving music chosen by the film editor, Grettl Hughes.
>
> We were all on a high, and as we walked to the squadron after landing, I remarked to the helicopter technician that this was an experience never to be forgotten, and that it was wonderful to have been part of such an historical day. His attitude was surprising in that he had obviously not been impressed with the afternoon's flying. His reply to me was curt, "I would rather it had been a Messerschmitt 109."
>
> Stunned by this statement, I turned to the pilot of the Bell and said, "That's strange, why would anyone wish to have been beaten up by an Me 109?"
>
> "Maybe it's because his name is Kleinschmidt …"

The Domboshawa flight was followed by a flight with the Bell 205 helicopter on 20 January 1982. Bud Cockcroft was flying the Bell with Squadron Leader Ian Harvey, to watch proceedings. Bud recalls he had on board a gyro-stabilised camera to film a take-off and numerous air-to-air shots. This flight lasted 1:15 hours and recorded important sequences for the video *Spitfire—The Pursuit of a Dream*.[25] It was followed by a display at New Sarum in mid-February, for whom we don't know, and Steve's last flight was on 25 February, a month before Jack Malloch's last tragic flight and the same day on which the Vampire sorties began.[26]

Steve Kesby reminds us how special this opportunity was to him: "I have always felt honoured and privileged to have been given this opportunity. As an added bonus I was able to meet and get to know an aviation legend—Jack Malloch."

Finally, back to Jack Malloch's flying. In view of the lack of logbook entries and having no access to the F700, it's very useful to have Steve Kesby recall that Jack Malloch was also active in efforts to help Bill Sykes gather good footage for the film.

Before detailing those flights that can be conclusively linked to the photographic programme, a special flight was undertaken by Jack Malloch in 1981 that is well remembered by Dave Hann.[27] On this occasion the Spitfire carried its 'one and only passenger' on a Saturday morning (date unknown) and once again Jack Malloch's generosity of spirit was demonstrated. This was in response to a very personal request from the late Geoff Pullan of the Shell oil company, to scatter his ashes over the runway at Salisbury airport when he passed away. Geoff Pullan had assisted the Spitfire project by identifying the various lubricants for the Griffon, in particular for the auxiliary gearbox. He had also been closely associated with the Zimbabwe Division of the RAeS, as its Vice-President, and the previous November had supervised the recognition of Jack Malloch and the contribution of his engineers to aviation in Zimbabwe.

We know of the last three well-documented flights that formed part of the photographic programme. However, in addition there were at least two air-to-air photographic sorties with a Bell 205. One was originally thought to have been flown by the late Ian Henderson accompanied by his technician, Phil Scott, probably in September or October 1980. It is likely that the photograph appearing in the programme for the Air Force '81 Air Show was taken on this occasion, by an AFZ photographer. On 22 January 1981 Jack Malloch flew again, with a Bell 205 flown by Dave Shirley, with Chris Breedt as his technician. Dave Shirley recalls a request from Air Force photographers to hover, while Jack Malloch approached from the three and nine o'clock positions. No photos can be linked with this flight. There was also a sortie with the Dakota 7312 on 23 October 1981. This was logged as a 1:00 hour flight by Clive Ward and Mark Vernon and was the first of the three sorties the Spitfire flew with the Dakota.[28] Clive Ward recalls:

> I seem to remember doing the very first photo sortie from New Sarum, with Jack flying the Spit. We flew around to the north of Salisbury while Jack attempted to formate on our port side. He probably hadn't done any formation flying since the last big war, and was a little wobbly while he got used to the rudder inputs required with throttle movements, and the resulting changes in torque from the monster engine. I had to edge away on a few occasions when it seemed that the big 5-bladed prop would devour our wing trailing edge as he tucked in a little too close!
>
> We had a young civilian cameraman doing the filming for us. He was perched in the opening left by the removal of the rear door on the Dakota. If I remember correctly, his name was Tim Burditt.[29] After landing, when we had all climbed out of the Dakota, I noticed that Tim was a whiter shade of pale. Enquiring after his health he informed me he was well enough, just scared out of his mind—having only just escaped certain death. He was convinced that the Spit was going to chew our wing off! From his angle of view, from the door, it must indeed have been terrifying as Jack snuggled in behind our wing trailing edge.
>
> Tim recovered and was brave enough to fly on other sorties.

A wonderful photograph features in the pamphlet that came out with the movie *The Pursuit of a Dream,* taken from the port side of an aircraft. The hazy background, depicting a typical early summer day, suggests that it was taken from the Dakota and, importantly, the tail wheel is retracted.

The only other flight/s we could track were those at the Air Force of Zimbabwe Open Day at Air Force '81 on 25 October 1981, two days after the Dakota flight. PK350 was also a static exhibit and was positioned on Runway 14 just where the tar gave way to grass, on the New Sarum side of the main runway. This was very much an air show in the spirit of previous displays at Cranborne and New Sarum in 1951, 1952, 1953 and 1971, respectively, and it attracted a substantial crowd—all the squadrons put on displays that weekend. As it happened this was the only occasion on which the public at large was able to see the Spitfire at close quarters. Sadly the AFZ never arranged a tour of the main centres, in the spirit of the public announcement made way back in April 1980. It was therefore most fitting that it was Jack Malloch who displayed the aircraft on this occasion, a legend being flown by another legend, at this most public venue.

Bill Sykes recalls some of the atmosphere at the Air Force '81 show and how the Spitfire was received:

> From the time Jack taxied out to the time he landed, the many thousands of visitors were transfixed. Most of them had never seen or heard a Spitfire before. Jack 'wheeled and soared and swung', and thrilled the crowd with his low passes, swooping turns and thrilling climbs, while the whistle of the supercharger and the thundering roar of the Griffon engine followed him into the heavens. It was a truly wonderful moment in aviation.[30]

The Spitfire took what was in reality its final public bow in front of the crowds at Air Force '81. Coincidentally, in November 1981 the curtain came down on Dave Hann's time at Affretair. He had decided to leave and move to South Africa, following a path that many had already taken. In his case the move was to join Atlas Aircraft Corporation, later Denel. This was indeed a sad moment for Affretair. Dave had served Jack Malloch exceptionally well and he left behind the Spitfire he had so capably overseen to full restoration. It was now up to Bob Dodds to direct her daily care at a time when Affretair was buffeted by the onset of political interference, struggling to survive in a business environment very different from the sanctions-busting era in which Jack Malloch had developed and ensured his reputation.

Chapter 11
THE PURSUIT OF A DREAM

The Pursuit of a Dream[1] was the suggestion of Mary Ann Sykes—wife of Bill Sykes—in a competition organised throughout the Air Force to find a title for the film. The prize was a framed three foot by two foot colour photograph of the Jack Malloch Spitfire, to be displayed in a mess appropriate to the winner. Bill Sykes had carelessly left the typed list on his dining room table at home and Mary Ann had surreptitiously penned in her proposal. The next day a committee sat in Air HQ and voted unanimously for the last entry on the list—but the winner could not be found. All the entries on file in the admin office were in letter form. The mystery was solved that evening when Mary Ann asked Bill who the winner was. He replied that he didn't know, as there was no name attached to the entry. Mary Ann was over the moon, but as she was not a member of the force and she could not accept the prize—so the picture was donated to the entrant who was closest to the selected title, a member of the Sergeants' Mess at New Sarum. Alyson and Ross Malloch had made it known that it was their father's dream to rebuild a Spitfire, so *Spitfire—The Pursuit of a Dream* was the most appropriate wording.

Bill Sykes had taken over from Alan Cockle in 1979 as the Air Force Public Relations Officer. His father had flown Hurricanes, but Bill's enduring love for the Spitfire was inspired by the memory of his Uncle David Crook who flew them in the Battle of Britain. Bill Sykes had taken a great interest in the PK350 restoration project and, with his innate sense of aviation history, wanted to record it for posterity. So he approached Group Captain Hugh Slatter, the Director of Operations in Air Headquarters. Permission was granted to purchase one reel (ten minutes) of cine film to record the work being done in the hangar, with the ultimate objective of filming the first flight. Thankfully, Hugh Slatter's involvement in the project was encouraged by the results of the first reel, and he continued to supply the camera team with film stock till the end.

Tony Liddel, a commercial cameraman and aviation enthusiast, and friend to Bill Sykes, volunteered to do all the filming for free. Commencing in late 1979 Tony captured the final days of the actual rebuild in the hangar, and the painting of the Spitfire in RAF camouflage. He was also there to film the overlaying of the roundels and the factory registration number, and, most importantly, the letters JMM.

It was coincidental, and extremely fortuitous, that Tony was there on the very day that the coolant hose split during an engine run, spilling all the precious glycol onto the hardstand. The atmosphere of that awful moment was caught on film, with Jack Malloch leaning against the leading edge of the wing and tugging at his floppy hat in frustration.

On the day of the first flight Tony Liddell caught the mood of the engineers and the crowd both before and after the flight. He also filmed the strapping in; the start-up; the Spitfire taxiing out for the first time; her high speed run down Runway 24; her take-off on Runway 06; and finally, those two memorable low-level high-speed flypasts.

Not being able to be in all places at one time, and keen to reenact the day from all its different angles, Bill Sykes set about gathering footage to reconstruct the entire first flight, using the Malloch-Fairey audio recording as a chronological guide. This determined the strategy used to include numerous flights over the following months, utilising the Bell 205, the Dakota, and the Vampire. Steve Kesby dedicated at least three of his Spitfire sorties to this singular objective.

It's worth noting that Bill Sykes' pressing objective was to get just the right footage for the Spitfire film—quite simply the right cumulus cloud backdrop. He was under no other pressure from Air HQ. However, there was a creeping reality that the politics of the country was changing—it was a far cry from the pre-1980 Rhodesian days. As has been previously mentioned in the story, the Air Force had in mind a finite flying-life for the Spitfire once the air to air photography had been completed. Recalling that the Spitfire was the property of the Ministry of Defence, Air HQ was presumably intent on pre-empting any awkward political decisions that might well be thrust upon it. However, Bill Sykes himself was not aware of these matters and whether Jack Malloch knew or not, we don't know.

The final three flights of PK350 were with the Vampire, the first two sorties being flown on 25 and 26 February 1982. The writer flew the Vampire on both these occasions, positioning at Salisbury early on 25 February to have the specially modified drop tank fitted at Airwork. In the words of Bill Sykes:

> A de Havilland Vampire T11, a two-seat jet trainer with the Zimbabwe Air Force was used to film the Spitfire. To accomplish this a 16mm camera was fitted in the port external fuel tank of the Vamp. This 'drop' tank had been converted by cutting off the front 50 centimetres of the tank and installing a Perspex shield to protect the lens, angling the shield slightly to allow moisture from the clouds to

dissipate. The camera was activated by the pilot pressing the 'bomb button' on the left-hand control column of the Vampire.

Because the camera was housed in the fuel tank, some ten feet away from the pilot in the cockpit, a means of aiming the camera was required. To film the target aircraft, the Vampire gun sight was used to indicate the centre of the frame of the film. In order to position the Spitfire in a particular part of the frame, marks had to be made within the Vampire cockpit to indicate the corners of the frame. Masking tape was placed from, say, the oxygen regulator to the port Direct Vision (D/V) panel, to the starboard gun sight, to the rocket selector switches—a perfect rectangle when viewed from the pilot's seat.

Unfortunately the first two sorties produced no useful footage. Bill explains the problem:

the film in the camera had broken at the start and the product of the two aircraft flying around for a total of four hours was an absolute zero.

The first of these sorties turned out to be a bit of a trial run, the main problem being communication—in this situation a relatively junior Air Force officer was required to give commands to a highly-respected and successful airline Captain, who was the force behind the rebuilding of the Spitfire that he was now flying. This problem was ironed out before the second sortie when Jack, in his inimitable manner, explained that he was quite prepared to obey any commands that were given him from behind. As a result, the second session went much better and he did all the right things—'turn port', 'pull up', 'turn tighter', 'relax', 'fly through the top of that cloud'—all to no avail: the camera once again had ground to a halt soon after take-off.

The scene that we would dearly have loved to capture on film occurred halfway through that second sortie; Jack did fly through the top of that cloud and the huge Spitfire propeller sent the cloud into a white spiral vortex, the sight of which will forever be etched on our memories.

On completion of the second sortie it was decided that Jack should lead the formation back to Salisbury. Jack, as ever, never missed an opportunity to enjoy the moment to its maximum.

Bill Sykes recalls the flight home:

We came into close formation on his starboard side and waited for him to lead us back to the airfield for landing. He appeared to take an inordinate length of time, almost a minute, flying straight and level, to get his act together. Eventually he called Harare Tower for rejoining instructions. (This action/inaction did not appear important at the time, but the matter came up at the subsequent Board of Inquiry.)

What happened next was entirely unexpected. Jack, who saw Harare airport under his port wing about 6,000 feet below, put the Spitfire into a 90 degree bank turn (which made formation-keeping difficult), rolled out and then pushed the nose down (which made formation nigh impossible). He pointed his 11-foot propeller at the threshold of Runway 06, pulled out of the dive at 3g, (see the Glossary of Terms for meaning of 'g') doing about 400 knots, and aimed his aircraft down the taxi-track.

The thought that he might now do a simple flypast and break into the circuit was quickly dispelled as he forced the Spit lower and lower until we, as his 'Number Two' became somewhat alarmed. I looked up for a split second only to see a wide taxi-track with a white centreline immediately under our nose. We pulled up five feet for safety, on the principle that if Jack was going to hit his propeller on the ground then at least we would have a chance of avoiding most of his shrapnel.

The subsequent break into the airfield circuit can be described only as spectacular.

A senior member from Airwork UK was watching the beat-up and took a photograph of the two aircraft in formation, coming past ATA and descending onto the taxi-track at high speed. He approached me in the hangar afterwards, looking a little ashen. 'I have never seen any aircraft go so low on a flypast—I really thought the Spitfire was going to hit his prop on the tarmac. Please, don't ever do that again—I nearly had a heart attack.' The Airwork representative was justifiably frightened—a Royal Air Force VC10 was parked on the international apron and the aircraft's distinctive T-tail was well above the Spitfire and Vampire as they thundered past.

The next Vampire flight was carried out with Flight Lieutenant Geoff Oborne, a Weapons Instructor on No. 2 Squadron, as captain. This flight was to replicate the forward view that Steve would have seen from the Spitfire cockpit when he flew the low-level beat-ups and aerobatics display among the Domboshawa hills. It was also an ideal opportunity to film the opening sequence of the documentary, with cumulus clouds as a backdrop for the titles.

Geoff Oborne flew the Vampire up to Salisbury on 4 March:

> I sat in the Vampire whilst Bill did the filming. We didn't actually film the
> Spitfire, as Bill wanted only some shots of flying around puffy cumulus clouds
> and low flying amongst the granite *kopjes*. We flew for 50 minutes into and
> around the clouds whilst the camera rolled. He wanted to use these sequences
> in the film as if the camera was positioned in the Spitfire.[2]

And so to the final flight on 26 March, 1982 …

Air Lieutenant Nev Weir, then doing his weapons training with Geoff Oborne,
was authorised to bring the Vampire to Salisbury for what was expected to be the
final flight to complete the air-to-air footage for the film.[3]

Nev Weir describes that fateful flight:

> On the morning of 26 March I was tasked to position at Airwork, in Salisbury,
> to do the filming of the Spitfire. That afternoon I flew up and taxied across to
> Airwork so that the camera pod could be fitted. I met with Bill Sykes and Jack
> Malloch for a briefing on the detail to be flown.
>
> It was a fairly short brief as both of them had been actively involved in the
> documentary so far, and I was there merely as the captain of the Vampire. It
> was great to meet Jack after all that he had been involved in, to get the Spitfire
> into the air. The brief was to do a fly-by of the airport, and then fly out to the
> northeast to do air-to-air filming.
>
> It was a beautiful summer's afternoon, light winds, a few billowing cumulus
> clouds, with a cloud base around 7,000 feet agl. We taxied out together, and, with
> the wide runway, lined up as a pair. Jack rolled first and shot off into the distance
> with his far superior acceleration to the Vampire. We did eventually catch up, did
> the flypast and then climbed out to the northeast.
>
> For me it was the most wonderful experience to see the Spitfire in flight,
> against the blue sky, flashing past clouds, and at such close quarters. All this
> flying was at about 10,000 feet agl. Bill did most of the flying and after half an
> hour or so it came to the point that we (in the Vampire) had to return to base,
> due to fuel considerations.
>
> We told Jack that we had finished the reel and had to return. He levelled his
> wings and remained on a steady wings level course. I asked Salisbury Main for a
> course to steer to base, which was roughly 180 degrees to the direction we were
> heading. At that point we were slightly behind and to the left of him.

Twenty seconds later Jack started a right turn. At that moment we were flying next to a very large cloud—an isolated, towering cumulonimbus. There was more than sufficient room to do the 180 right turn. Bill flew into line astern of the Spitfire, about 150 metres behind. At this point Bill was flying and I was looking out. After about 150 degrees of turn, Jack rolled his wings level, started a gentle descent and flew straight into the side of the cumulus. We followed.

What happened next seemed an eternity but was probably, in reality, only 30–40 seconds of bone-jarring turbulence. My first concern was avoiding Jack, so we turned off ten degrees. Seconds later we hit the core of the cloud: extreme turbulence, rain and hail, so hard that there was water showering onto us through the canopy seal. My second thought, after hoping not to hit the Spitfire, was what if the engine was going to flame out. Fortunately none of this happened. Suddenly we were into bright sunlight and smooth air. Immediately we looked for Jack, expecting to see him in front or to one side, but no sign of him. We had to return to base due to lack of fuel and could not loiter in the area to look for him. We called numerous times. Salisbury radar informed us that they had the Vampire and the storm on radar, but nothing else. Air force operations were alerted and I believe that helicopters may have been launched, but it was dark soon and not much could be done that day.

Bill and I flew back, fearing the worst but hoping that Jack had safely exited that situation. After landing we taxied up to where the guys on the ground had been filming. Bill made his seat safe and got out of the Vampire (engine running) and I taxied back to the apron at New Sarum. After I had shut down the engines the technicians told me to come and look at the aircraft: the nose looked as though someone had taken a ball-pane hammer and hit the upper part all over, it was completely bashed in—large chunks of paint had come off the nose, the engine intakes, and the wing leading edges. I was quite taken aback by it all.

Bill Sykes brings to mind the events of that day and the incredible spectacle which very few will ever get to witness—the inside of a violent thunderstorm:

There was great tension amongst the pilots and ground crew on 26 March, not only because the camera was suspect but because there might not be another opportunity to fly in cloud for another eight months ... or if either the Vampire or the Spitfire went unserviceable and could not get airborne ...

We went to Jack's office for the pre-flight brief. Jack looked tired but no more so than on many other occasions when dealing with politics and freight. He often said that when he was tired it was a rejuvenating experience to take the Spit for a quick flip and forget, temporarily, the problems of the world.

On the first three filming sorties, I had flown with a QFI or a PAI and I sat in the left-hand seat where the camera/bomb button was situated. This was entirely satisfactory as the frame was designed to be viewed from that seat. On the fourth sortie, however, the captain of the Vampire was not a qualified instructor, and because he was required to occupy the left seat, I had to fly from the right. This meant flying the aircraft with my right hand while reaching across and pressing the camera button with the left, not something that comes naturally. One had to adjust, too, to the offset frame.

As it turned out, everything went smoothly.

Both aircraft were safely airborne at about 15h45 and headed off to the north-east of the city, towards Goromonzi, climbing out gently to an altitude of 15,000 feet through the bluish haze and the puffs of cumulus, towards a cumulonimbus thunderhead.

Everything was perfect.

We flew in and out of the clouds near the edge of a thunderstorm which was shedding its contents over Goromonzi—clouds that had kindly offered us this filming opportunity so late in the rainy season, and which formed the perfect backdrop for the Spitfire. We managed to capture the most breathtaking scenes, a feature of flying in the late afternoons in Zimbabwe in the rainy season.

After about twenty minutes, being well-satisfied with the footage we had taken, I called an end to the sortie. 'Thanks Boss,' I said, 'we can go home now.' [Boss is a term of endearment and respect which is used widely in many spheres of life in Zimbabwe.]

Jack rolled out of the turn and flew straight and level in a north-easterly direction with the cloud on his starboard side. He remained on that heading for nearly a minute, during which time we, in the Vampire, began to get concerned, not for his sake, but because we were heading away from base and we were on 'Bingo' fuel state. This meant that if we did not turn for home immediately, we would not have enough fuel to do an overshoot (for another circuit and approach) if the eventuality arose. (For every one minute that one flies away from base, one requires more than two minutes of fuel to get back, and a jet uses a substantial amount of fuel.)

After what seemed an age Jack turned starboard for home. In turning to the right he at first surprised us, as we were expecting him to turn to port, away from the cumulonimbus storm cloud. But our fears were soon allayed when he completed the turn well clear of the cloud. (When one is flying next to a huge 'cu-nim' that extends to over 40,000ft in height, it looks much closer than it really is.)

All we had to do was to fly round the north-western edge of the cloud and descend gently towards the airport. Jack flew for a while slowly traversing the periphery and we followed, flying 150 metres behind.

We began to relax.

Then, without any warning, Jack suddenly banked 45 degrees to port, turned towards the cloud, rolled out with wings level and pushed the nose down in a 15-degree dive.

In the Vampire we exclaimed to each other: 'What's he doing now?' as he was obviously heading into the storm. Our instinct, of course, was to continue on our heading, but Air Force training overrides such notions, and one tends to follow one's leader. (To lose one's leader is considered very ignominious, even in a desperate situation.)

The enormity of what was to come was not immediately apparent as the edges of a storm cloud are nice and fluffy and fun to fly through. But within seconds the white cloud turned to grey, then to a greeny-blue. We were fast approaching the edges of the storm cell.

Then things changed dramatically—it suddenly got much darker.

We lost sight of Jack and began to experience heavy turbulence. We caught sight of the Spitfire momentarily, just as we flew into the most unbelievable spectacle which only a pilot can witness—a vast subterranean-like cavern of deep blues, greens and greys.

The Spitfire disappeared into the darkness of the storm cell.

At this point we knew we were in real trouble—there was no turning back. When one considers the dangers of wartime flying (WW2) and the chances of one's survival on extended operations, being shot at continually, losing comrades daily, it seemed uncanny that a situation should arise on so serene an afternoon, and in a peaceful country, that could endanger the life of a pilot. Jack had been shot down over Italy in 1944, baled out with a flak-damaged parachute, broken a leg on landing...nothing, it would seem, could come close to such a dangerous and life-threatening situation.

There was no call over the radio from Jack and we made no transmissions—under such circumstances pilots have their time cut out just trying to maintain the aircraft in a flying attitude; the last thing they do is talk. Neither did I make any effort to press the camera button to record the incident; the button was on the other control column and anyway I knew the film was finished.

We were still 150 metres behind the Spitfire and it took no more than a second to reach the position where Jack had entered the storm cell. Then, in as short a time as it takes to say the words, we hit the darkness, the rain, and then the hail. We were doing about 300 knots and the noise was deafening. We throttled back to Turbulence Speed and initiated the Standard Operating Procedure (SOP), which avoids collision in poor visibility by turning ten degrees port and climbing 500 feet. This we attained in no time at all, as the updraft on the edge of the storm propelled us vertically, and even with power off and airbrakes out, we were going up at a rate of over 4,000 feet per minute.

Then, as suddenly as one is swept uncontrollably upwards, the violent downdraft in the centre of the storm takes effect—full power on, airbrakes in, maintain the attitude on the Artificial Horizon. A glance at the Vertical Speed Indicator (VSI) showed that we were now descending at over 4,000 feet per minute, with the altimeter winding down at an alarming rate. Struggling to keep wings level and expecting the engine to fail at any second due to the amount of ice it was ingesting, we waited for the inevitable—the updraft on the other side of the storm. Once again it was power off, airbrakes out, try to maintain the attitude, watch the VSI hit the stops again at 4,000 feet per minute rate of ascent ...

If an aircraft enters a storm cell it is prudent to punch through the storm as opposed to turning back. It takes three times as long to turn back as it does to go through a cloud, and the pilot has to fly in a banked turn all the way as opposed to holding a fixed heading with wings level. The Spitfire with its low wing loading (a large wing area relative to its weight), would have been thrown around very violently, more so than the Vampire, in the severe turbulence, and the aircraft would have been extremely difficult to control in the up- and downdrafts. When confronted with these conditions a pilot must, of necessity, fly an attitude by holding a heading and keeping the wings level.

The altimeter in the cockpit of the Spitfire is positioned down on the left side of the instrument panel and is not easy to see. It is assumed that Jack was watching the Artificial Horizon intently (flying an attitude) and was, perhaps, not paying the required attention to the altimeter.

Then as quickly as it had started, it all happened in reverse—the hail and the rain stopped and we literally popped out of the storm into a clear and calm blue sky. It is a most uncanny sensation, going from the violence of a hailstorm one

Left: On a cool, fresh morning loaded with anticipation, Bob Dodds helps guide PK350 from the ATA hangar on the day of the first flight, 29 March 1980. *The Herald/Paddy Gray*

Left: PK350 is pushed onto the ATA ramp for her first flight. Her inboard cannons are missing their streamlined fairings due to a last-minute hitch, the only flight on which they were absent. *The Herald/Paddy Gray*

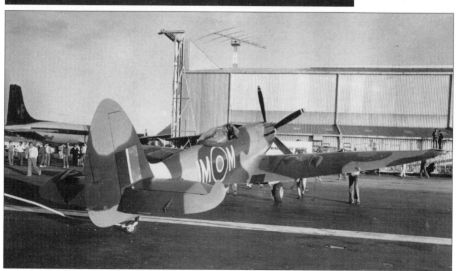

PK350 being positioned on the ramp outside the ATA hangar. *The Herald/Paddy Gray*

… parked …
The Herald/Paddy Gray

… refuelled …
The Herald/Paddy Gray

… and pre-flighted … *The Herald/ Paddy Gray*

... oxygen topped up, VHF comms okay ... *The Herald/Paddy Gray*

... the external power unit standing by ... *The Herald/ Paddy Gray*

... and ready to go. *The Herald/ Paddy Gray*

A final pose for the photographer. *The Herald/Paddy Gray*

Above: An historic line-up—past and present commanders of the Air Force along with ex-SRAF/RRAF Spitfire pilots. From left: Group Captain Charles Paxton, Air Vice Marshal Chris Dams, Group Captain Johnny Deall, Captain Dave Harvey, Squadron Leader Ian Shand, Air Marshal Frank Mussell, Captain Jack Malloch, Air Marshal Archie Wilson, Air Marshal Mick McLaren, Flying Officer Des Anderson and Group Captains Ozzie Penton and John Mussell. *The Herald/Paddy Gray*

Jack Malloch with Bob Dodds, carrying out his pre-flight inspection. *The Herald/Paddy Gray*

Parachute on, and with concealed trepidation Jack Malloch climbs into the cockpit. *The Herald/ Paddy Gray*

… with the ever-present Bob Dodds to help him strap in. *The Herald/ Paddy Gray*

Paddy Gray runs to the starboard wing to get a final close-up of Jack. *The Herald/ Paddy Gray*

Last-minute conference between Jack, Bob and John Fairey. *The Herald/Paddy Gray*

Ready for taxi. Morgan Maitland-Smith (left) and Carlos Martins remove the chocks. *The Herald/Paddy Gray*

The RR Griffon powers PK350 on her way to runway 06. *The Herald/Paddy Gray*

Jack Malloch yields for an Air Rhodesia Viscount ZS-JPU, RH 839 on its way to Bulawayo, Rhodesia's second city. *The Herald/Paddy Gray*

Shortly before the high-speed taxi. An exceptional photograph which shows the Spitfire at its best—a perfect outline on the horizon set against a crisp morning sky. *The Herald/Paddy Gray*

High-speed taxi on R/W 24 prior to take-off on R/W 06 at Salisbury Airport on PK350's first flight. *The Herald/Paddy Gray*

The first of two high-speed passes at 270kts (310mph) at a safe 100ft above the taxi track. *The Herald/Paddy Gray*

Spellbound by the marvellous spectacle. A poignant moment captured by Paddy Gray on the Spitfire's second pass at 290kts (335mph) and 20ft. What young boy would not pursue a career in aviation after such an introduction? *The Herald/Paddy Gray*

Above: Safely down, Jack Malloch taxies to the ATA ramp.
The Herald/ Paddy Gray

Centre: Back on stand and the welcome home has started. Jack's engineering stalwarts, Bob Dodds (on the starboard wing) and Dave Hann (on the port), are relieved at the safe return of PK350, whilst the ever-present Morgan Maitland-Smith scampers away, having chocked the Spitfire.
The Herald/ Paddy Gray

Well done! Bob Dodds helps remove Jack's parachute.
The Herald/Paddy Gray

Smiles all around—Jack and Bob begin to soak up the fully deserved adulation from the public. *The Herald/Paddy Gray*

Jack is button-holed by the media—the first of many such interviews. *The Herald/Paddy Gray*

A moment of reflection for Jack. Carlos Martins looks on whilst doing his after-flight. *The Herald/Paddy Gray*

Jack Malloch giving a Spitfire 'tour' soon after the first flight. Good clear details of the tail-plane and the control trims. *The Herald/Paddy Gray*

Jack Malloch buzzes the Russian delegation arriving for the Zimbabwean independence celebrations on 15 April 1980. *The Herald, 16 April 1980*

Jack Malloch in 1980.
Greg Malloch

'Malloch at it again!' on 18 April 1980, this time at
the invitation of Lord Soames on the occasion of
his departure with Prince Charles, the Prince of
Wales, the Queen's representative at Zimbabwe's
independence ceremony. *The Herald, 18 April 1980*

The Spitfire, escorted by two Hunters, overflies Thornhill.
AFZ Photographic Section, Thornhill/Jeff Hagemann

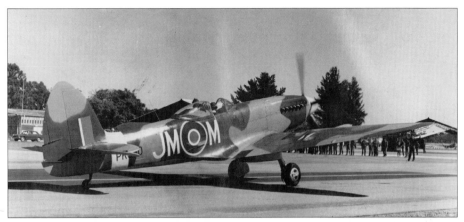

Jack Malloch taxies in at Thornhill. *AFZ Photographic Section, Thornhill/Jeff Hagemann*

… and parks in front of Flying Wing Headquarters.
AFZ Photographic Section, Thornhill/Jeff Hagemann

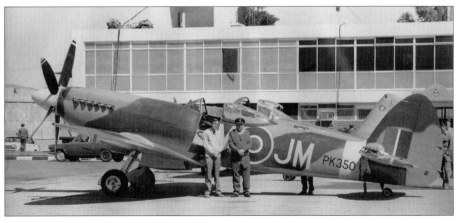

Full circle—Spike Owens welcomes the Spitfire to Thornhill some six years after he initiated the restoration project. A proud moment indeed.
AFZ Photographic Section, Thornhill/Jeff Hagemann

The view from the 'Connie' clubhouse at Charles Prince. The Spitfire seems to revel in the attention given it by the crowd. *Brian Carson*

PK350 flies low along the runway, in salute, before setting course for home. Tail wheel is still fixed down. *Brian Carson*

A fine study of PK350's cockpit during the Charles Prince visit. *Brian Carson*

Above: An iconic image of Jack Malloch in PK350, with the canopy open, taken from the right-hand-side door of the Bell 205, probably in September 1980. *AFZ Photographic Section, New Sarum*

Left: Jack Malloch receiving the Pat Judson Trophy, flanked on his right by Geoff Pullan, Vice-President, Zimbabwe Division of the RAeS, and on his left by Mr A.G. Newton, Engineering Director, Rolls-Royce. *The Herald*

Steve Kesby after his first solo in PK350/SR64, on 23 November 1981. *Steve Kesby*

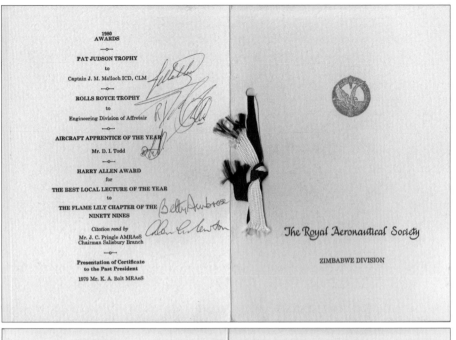

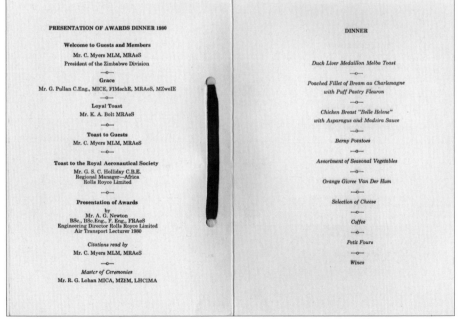

PRESENTATION OF AWARDS DINNER 1980

Welcome to Guests and Members
Mr. C. Myers MLM, MRAeS
President of the Zimbabwe Division
—o—
Grace
Mr. G. Pullan C.Eng., MICE, FIMechE, MRAeS, MZweIE
—o—
Loyal Toast
Mr. K. A. Bolt MRAeS
—o—
Toast to Guests
Mr. C. Myers MLM, MRAeS
—o—
Toast to the Royal Aeronautical Society
Mr. G. S. C. Holliday C.B.E.
Regional Manager—Africa
Rolls Royce Limited
—o—
Presentation of Awards
by
Mr. A. G. Newton
BSc., BSc.Eng., F. Eng., FRAeS
Engineering Director Rolls Royce Limited
Air Transport Lecturer 1980

Citations read by
Mr. C. Myers MLM, MRAeS
—o—
Master of Ceremonies
Mr. R. G. Lohan MICA, MZIM, LHCIMA

DINNER

Duck Liver Medaillon Melba Toast
—o—
Poached Fillet of Bream au Charlemagne
with Puff Pastry Fleuron
—o—
Chicken Breast "Belle Helene"
with Asparagus and Madeira Sauce
—o—
Berny Potatoes
—o—
Assortment of Seasonal Vegetables
—o—
Orange Givree Van Der Hum
—o—
Selection of Cheese
—o—
Coffee
—o—
Petit Fours
—o—
Wines

The RAeS Zimbabwe Division programme, on the occasion of its recognition of the contribution to aviation by Jack Malloch and his engineers, for their restoration of PK350, on 20 November 1980. *Dave Hann*

Above: Steve Kesby after his first solo on 23 November 1981. His partially concealed grin says it all. *Steve Kesby*

Below: The large crater at the accident site, clearly indicating a high-speed impact. Ken Burmeister is on the left. *AFZ Photographic Section, New Sarum/ Guy Cunningham/Steve Nobes*

Some evidence of the rough ride and damage experienced by the Vampire whilst pursuing the Spitfire, just prior to the loss of Jack Malloch and the Spitfire. *AFZ Photographic Section, New Sarum/Guy Cunningham/Steve Nobes*

An excellent aerial perspective of the impact crater. This confirms Charlie Cordy-Hedge's recollection of how difficult it was to see the crater from the air. *AFZ Photographic Section, New Sarum/Guy Cunningham/Steve Nobes*

Centre: The remains of the Griffon Rolls-Royce engine in the impact crater.
AFZ Photographic Section, New Sarum/Guy Cunningham/Steve Nobes

Below: The Griffon engine—with only eight of the original twelve cylinders—rests on the hangar floor with a few other recognisable pieces of the wreckage, after recovery by Chuck Osborne and his team from ASF New Sarum.
AFZ Photographic Section, New Sarum/Guy Cunningham/Steve Nobes

moment to the absolute calm of a hazy afternoon the next. We looked down to our starboard side to where the Spitfire should have been, but there was just an empty sky. We knew immediately that something was wrong. And then we made the call to Salisbury Tower ...

It was too late to launch a search and rescue. This was initiated at first light the next morning and included at least one Lynx from 4 Sqn flown by Charlie Cordy-Hedge and Alouette IIIs flown by Bud Cockroft and Fidor Scholvinck.[4]

Charlie Cordy-Hedge recalls:

4 Squadron had become a Flight based in Sarum when the event occurred. I seem to recall that we were at a function in the New Sarum Officers Mess after work, when the Vamp came home with news of the Spit event. It was late afternoon and too late to send out an airborne search and rescue but we—Helo and Lynx 'drivers' (pilots)—were all primed for a first light take off if there was no news overnight. Again numbers evade me but a bunch of us headed off early the following morning and basically found nothing. Chopper pilots resorted to landing and asking locals if they had seen or heard anything and many hours later—altogether nearly eight hours were flown that day— someone did provide info which sent the helos in the direction of the crash site. When it was located, we used the Lynx from overhead as a relay.[5]

It was mid-morning before the inevitable outcome was made known—an African tribesman[6] in the Goromonzi area had reported the accident to his local police station. This was devastating news. Jack Malloch, who had seen and endured so much in the preceding four decades, had succumbed to a violent impact in a mealie field.

Bill Sykes picks up the story:

It was only when an African man from the communal land appeared at the Juru Police Station at around 10 o'clock in the morning that things fell into place. He had walked for nearly three hours that morning to report the incident. He had actually heard the noise of the crash the afternoon before, but he had been sheltering from the storm and had thought that the noise was that of a lightning strike. It was only when he left his abode the following morning that he saw the devastation. His crops had been flattened and there was wreckage lying over a large area. A Spitfire, with its huge five-bladed propeller, under power from a

2,000 hp engine, hitting the ground at an estimated speed of 300–350 knots, literally explodes. Jack would have died instantly.

The Air Force appointed a Board of Inquiry (BoI) the same day, according to Squadron Leader Dave Haynes,[7] who was OCTW at Thornhill. He was appointed to assist Group Captain Steve Kesby, the Chairman of the Board, and was one of four members including two civilians,[8] probably from the Department of Civil Aviation (DCA), whose identities have been forgotten.

Dave Heyns recalled that it took most of the following day to locate the crash site, with the help of an Alouette helicopter, after which the Air Force made arrangements to recover Jack Malloch's body and the wreckage. Evidently the BoI was on board the Alouette.

Bud Cockcroft[9] was again involved on 29 March, two years to the day after the Spitfire's first flight, this time on the Bell 205 ferrying the BoI and Air Force photographers[10] to the crash site. It fell to Warrant Officer Chuck Osborne,[11] Officer Commanding Aircraft Servicing Flight, New Sarum, to recover the wreckage on instruction from the BoI. Chuck drove out on the Enterprise Road northeast of Salisbury and turned left at Juru Growth Point. This was followed by an hour's drive on a dirt road ending up with some 'bundu-bashing'.

Chuck Osborne states:

> I was in charge of the recovery team that was sent out from New Sarum to retrieve the wreckage. I say 'recovery' but there wasn't much to bring back. Unfortunately I wasn't involved in the navigation to the site, but it was about 50 kilometres east-north-east of Harare, in a remote Communal Land. The impact point was a large crater with a debris field spreading out from there. The furthest piece of wreckage, a two-foot piece of laminated main spar, was found about 400 metres from the crater. We were asked by the BoI to locate the 20mm canons to give an accurate angle of impact, but after much fruitless digging in the soft, wet ground the Board told us to stop. Evidence around the crater suggested a nose-down angle of about 16 degrees, with wings level and engine under power. When the Board released the wreckage they instructed us to collect everything, throw it into the crater and fill it in, which was done, except that the engine was loaded onto the recovery vehicle for further investigation later. The engine was now a V8 instead of a V12, as the front 4 cylinders had gone AWOL …

The Herald had been accustomed to reporting the movements of the Spitfire and Jack Malloch, and for some time after the crash its Death Notices column overflowed with tributes from all over the world. Jack was a classical hero—his reputation and legendary status was that of a clean-cut man who remained humble to the day he died, despite his achievement-filled life.

It fell to the Reverend Frank Mussell, a Methodist minister and father of John and Frank Mussell, to deliver the eulogy[12] at Jack's funeral on 2 April 1982 at Warren Hills:

> The sudden death of a noted man very often has the effect of highlighting his life, his character and also his achievements. The tragic death of Captain Jack Malloch has brought into bold relief the kind of man he was, and the many remarkable things he has done in his lifetime.
>
> I have often wondered what was the secret of Jack's devotion to his work, his doing extraordinary things, the reason for his compassion, his ready sharing of other people's problems and the risking of his life on mercy flights. It was simply this—he was a deeply religious man, one who had a strong faith in God, and as a result had great faith in himself. He was also a man of prayer. Before he went on any ordinary or hazardous mission he and his wife Zoe would kneel in prayer and ask for God's protection and guidance. As the result of his religious faith he was a man of honesty and integrity. He had a cleanness of speech; he hated blasphemy.

The tragedy was a bitter blow both to Jack Malloch's family and to Affretair. On 28 February Jack had endured a major blow when the CL-44 caught fire in the hangar and was destroyed, fortunately with no casualties or collateral damage, in particular to the Spitfire, which had been parked close by. However, that didn't stop him from planning a major move. According to Mike Kruger,[13] his nephew, and an Affretair pilot himself, Jack was about to open an operation with two DC-8 63s in South Africa. This move had high-level backing. In fact Mike, who had seen the Spitfire fly over the Henry Chapman golf course on that fateful day, wondered that evening if Jack himself had flown the Spitfire to a safe haven in South Africa. With Jack's demise the South African operation never came to fruition. Instead, Affretair's destiny[14] was from hereon to be determined by local national politics rather than by the man who had driven the company with such a sure hand for all the previous years.

Three months later the film *Spitfire—The Pursuit of a Dream* premiered at the Kine

400 theatre; it was a fitting tribute to Jack Malloch and the restoration of PK350. The final product was a 16mm, 40 minute documentary which included much of the footage that had been filmed on the day of the last flight, without which the final sequence would have lost much of its poignancy and emotion. So popular was the film that a further three nights were fully booked—one for the Royal Aeronautical Society and two for the Cancer Association.

The professional film makers who gave of their time and expertise, many at a cost to themselves, must all be applauded for their individual contributions: Tony Liddell (16mm photography) for his continual attention to the project and being at the right place at the right time; Jef Fairfield for setting up his cameras for the Tower scene; the staff of Central Film Laboratories (CFL) for the production; Grettl Hughes whose editorial talent was second to none; and Victor Mackeson who travelled from South Africa to do the narration, and whose voice, familiar to thousands of people during the Rhodesian days, suited the commentary admirably.

Other participants included the families and friends of those concerned with production; they gave generously of their time to help with anything and everything, from being ushers at the four premieres to recording the sound of the Spitfire at the Air Show at New Sarum; and, of course, Bill Sykes, for keeping everything together.

The production of the film cost a mere 6,000 Rhodesian dollars, or USD 12,000 (in those days our dollar was close to a British pound). All that had to be paid for was the editing, the production of the film by CFL, and a nominal fee of $100 to Victor Mackeson. Had the Air Force been charged for the flying hours of the Spitfire and all the other aircraft involved, the costs would have been astronomical.

The Royal Aeronautical Society, Zimbabwe Division, in association with Legal and General Assurance of Zimbabwe, had been very supportive of this venture. It contributed to the publication of a colour booklet in memory of Jack and the project.

The ten-page booklet—many of which have been retained by people for more than three decades—was produced by the Air Force and included four colour photographs of the Spitfire, along with many facts, quotes and poems. The tribute to Jack Malloch reads:

> Aircraft enthusiasts throughout the world restore aeroplanes whenever the opportunity arises. Few have the good fortune or the means, and fewer still are able to restore an aircraft to museum standard without the backing of large sums of money.

It is a rare occasion when a unique aircraft can be restored to flying condition. Many of the vintage aircraft seen at air shows today are limited to certain manoeuvres only. 'Our Spitfire' was restored not only to flying condition, but it was the only Spitfire in the world that had no restrictions on it for aerobatic manoeuvres.

With the untimely loss of Captain Malloch and the Spitfire, it is a privilege to possess a permanent record of the culmination of the dream that came true— the magnificent obsession—the restoration and eventual flight of a beautiful, historic aircraft, which was brought about through foresight and dedication.

It is also a tribute to the man himself—his character, his tenacity under adversity, his love for mankind and the respect that was given to him by all who knew him.

Whereas Ian Smith had been unable to attend and witness the first flight of PK350 in the hands of his old war time comrade from 237 Sqn, he made sure he attended the second night of the Spitfire film. Bill Sykes recalls:

> The new Minister of Defence had also been invited, but his invitation was for the third evening. I was showing Mr Smith to his seat when our Air Force usherette stopped me and explained that Mr Smith's seat had been taken by the Minister. Ian Smith, in his usual fashion, was not concerned, and agreed to wait and see if there was a spare seat for him. The show was due to commence in five minutes, so the two of us sat down on the steps in the aisle and chatted until the film started, at which stage it became apparent that one person had not arrived and therefore a seat was available for 'The 'Boss'. The people surrounding him were only too pleased to have him sit amongst them.[15]

In the meantime the BoI carried out its investigations. According to Steve Kesby it was not a full military inquiry:

> The Air Force gave us access to all relevant information, but it was essentially a civil aircraft so it was conducted as a civil inquiry, written as an Air Force board.

This was not previously known and explains why it hasn't been possible to access the BoI through the Air Force of Zimbabwe. Other efforts to locate the BoI in the National Archives and the Civil Aviation Authority have also proved fruitless. So it is that all that is recorded here is from memory. The Board's findings were:

The Spitfire impacted the ground in a slight dive, with the wings level. The engine was under power—i.e. not throttled back. The flaps and undercarriage were still raised in the flying, cruise, position.

Why did the aircraft crash?

An aircraft accident occurs as a result of one, or a combination, of the following:

- Human error (pilot, engineer, air traffic control)
- Mechanical failure (engine, airframe, instrument, avionics)
- Weather (thunderstorm, fog, wind, ice, etc.)

In any Inquiry, each one of these factors would be investigated as thoroughly as is possible. There were of course obvious limitations to this Inquiry as there were no survivors and no witnesses.

There was no available medical evidence to substantiate either a failure in the oxygen system or a heart attack, but neither of these can be ruled out. The weather itself did not cause the accident, as the aircraft was under control at the final impact. One could not eliminate the possibility of a mechanical fault, but both the crash site and the wreckage indicated that the engine and airframe appeared to be working correctly.

The Board of Inquiry also decided that the reason Jack had spent up to a minute flying straight and level towards the end of the last two sorties was to set him up for the rejoin. This would have entailed loosening his safety harness, leaning forward to realign the P9-type compass, resetting the Direction Indicator to read the compass heading, re-erecting the Artificial Horizon (as this gyroscopic instrument would have toppled during aerobatic manoeuvres), and then tightening his straps again.

The BoI concluded:

> Although the findings of an Air Force Board of Inquiry are confidential, the above summary does not impinge on this confidentiality. Many factors have been considered in this accident. It is very difficult to reach a conclusive answer, and in the final analysis it must remain another of aviation's mysteries.[16]

Tragically, inconceivably, Captain Jack Malloch and his beloved Spitfire had perished in mystifying circumstances. This legend of a man, who had worked tirelessly for his beloved Rhodesia, who had achieved so much, touched so many lives along the way, had gone to meet his Maker doing what he loved best—flying—piloting one aircraft in particular. Jack's Spitfire had come to mean so much to him and had become a legend in her own right—PK350, SR64, JMM.

As a rebuild she had flown a total of approximately 39 hours[17] and to this day is the *only* example of the Ultimate Spitfires—the F Mk 21s, Mk 22s and Mk 24s—to have been restored to full flying condition with no restrictions.

Epilogue

JACK'S LEGACY: A CELEBRATION
OF PERFECTION

Jack Malloch's legacy is simply huge. Regrettably, a lot of that legacy is to be found outside the country and mostly overseas now, in the early years of the 21st century. Why? Because Zimbabwe has been through a very turbulent time and many people perceive it as a failed state. Today Zimbabwe is a far cry from the vibrant country that existed in the early 1980's, the resilient Rhodesia in which Jack established his reputation. The aviation sector remains depressed, as is the whole economy, a sad reflection of a far greater malaise within the country than any disorder arising from external sources, such as the worldwide economic crisis. People have emigrated in droves and started new lives in countries that can appreciate and utilise the skills they carry with them.

Nevertheless, if you know where to look you can still find evidence of Jack's legacy, and it's important to start here, in Zimbabwe. Jack Malloch's hangar is still in place at the Harare International Airport, dominating the skyline of that part of the airport, an enduring memorial to better times and pleasant memories. Affretair continued as an airline until the mid-90s but was afflicted by massive political interference which caused its inevitable demise. To this day the few freighters that frequent Harare's airport are handled right where the Spitfire started up for its first flight.

Additional evidence of Jack Malloch's activities can be found elsewhere in Zimbabwe. Spitfire SR65 occupies pride of place in the Military Museum in Gweru. She was ferried to Southern Rhodesia by Jack in March 1951. Regarded by the National Museums and Monuments of Zimbabwe as a most cherished asset,[1] it is one of four Spitfire F Mk 22s[2] left in the world. It rests under cover as the centrepiece in two large adjoining 'hangars' together with examples of all the past aircraft operated by the Air Force. Jack Malloch probably flew the most number of hours on SR65— 34 hours and 20 sorties[3]—and it was the last Spitfire he flew as an SRAF Auxiliary on 17 August 1951. Finally, a replica of the trophy awarded to Jack's engineers in 1981 can be seen in a cabinet at the Mashonaland Flying Club at Charles Prince airport outside Harare.

Poignantly, the more vibrant elements of Jack's legacy nowadays are found outside Zimbabwe. First, Jack Malloch's three children—Alyson, Ross and Greg—all of whom now reside in Cape Town, South Africa. Originally, all three were involved in the world of aviation. Ross and Greg were flight engineers with MK Airlines and have since left aviation. Alyson nurtured young aviators into the commercial aviation sector for many years but is no longer actively involved. Proof of her success is recorded in this book by Paul Maher. As a young boy Paul's love of aeroplanes led him to write a letter of congratulations to Jack, following the Spitfire's first flight. In return, Jack demonstrated his appreciation by flying over Paul's boyhood home in Harare, reinforcing Paul's fascination with flying, forever.

Secondly, numerous pilots who worked for Jack Malloch have since risen to the top of their profession in prominent airlines all over the world—some of whom now fly the Airbus 380. Also, many of Jack's engineers, such as Carlos Martins, went on to do great things and better themselves in other countries. But it was one of his own kith and kin, Mike Kruger, his nephew, the son of his sister Blythe, who was to take up the torch that Jack had carried so well.

Having left the Air Force in the early 1980s, Mike Kruger joined his uncle as a pilot on the DC-8 where he demonstrated his strengths as a forceful and determined leader. He became disillusioned with the increasing political interference and left Affretair in 1989, hoping to start his own airline. Showing great foresight, he partnered with a local Zimbabwean businessman, Robert Rose. Together they started a DC-8 freight airline called MK Airlines, based in the Sussex countryside not far from London's Gatwick airport. MK quickly became a substantial operator of both DC-8 and Boeing 747 freighters, operating in much the same manner as his famous uncle's charter airline had done in the 1970s. Demonstrating great enterprise and determination, MK was operating 15 freighters by the early 2000s and competing with some big name players, e.g. Cargolux. Unfortunately MK failed in 2010 after 20 years of operation, a casualty of the global financial crisis. Many of MK's crew have moved on and settled with other airlines, much like the pilots who had served in Affretair, with Jack Malloch.

As Reverend Frank Mussell stated in his eulogy, Jack Malloch touched many lives. Today, 31 years later, the spirit and steadfastness of this God-fearing man continues to touch people, giving us reason to celebrate the life of this great aviation legend.

Finally, it's time to return to the centrepiece of this story, Spitfire PK350/SR64. Stewardship of Spitfire JMM by Jack McVicar Malloch was surely the icing on the cake for him. While deliberating a title for this Epilogue, I considered using *A Celebration of Perfection*. The whole restoration project was an amazing coming together of timing, circumstance and an Air Force that allowed a civilian to manage a military asset—because that civilian was Jack Malloch. Essentially, the success of the Spitfire rebuild was because of Jack's sense of timing.

If this project had been started at Independence it is likely that it would have dragged on and on, as engineers left the Air Force and Affretair for greener pastures outside Zimbabwe. It is also likely it would have become politicised as an elitist project interfering with a national asset. If the project had been undertaken earlier, there may not have been the same enthusiasm and commitment.

It is evident that the real lobbying only began to gather its early momentum in the mid-1970s. Jack himself may have wanted always to restore a Spitfire, but the real catalyst for the enterprise was Spike Owens.

Jack's intervention rescued the project from a probable slow loss of enthusiasm in an Air Force taxed by a demanding war. It was Jack who ensured that the Spitfire was restored, because of the assets and a network that he had gathered and developed over the years—and because it was his dream.

Jack Malloch was blessed with an amazing sense of business enterprise: he was willing to journey where few others would tread; his initiative was tempered by a quiet but strong sense of self-confidence; he was deeply committed to fairness—all of which gave him his extraordinary charisma. Perhaps his warrior spirit never left him. Jack's sense of timing was perfect when it came to the Spitfire project. All the pieces were in place for him to accept the undertaking—the absolute trust and support of the Air Force, his team of loyal and highly skilled engineers and an airline network that enabled him to source key components such as the canopy and propeller.

Chris Dams and Keith Kemsley knew the Spitfires intimately by the time the aircraft stopped flying in 1954, weary and well used. Chris and Keith were overwhelmed by the finish of Jack's Spitfire after her reconstruction. She was as good as new—photographs of her still convey to us today that mint condition.

On 29 March 1980, PK350 *aka* SR64, in her fully restored state, was a supreme engineering achievement facilitated by an exceptional man, a man who probably regarded himself as simply a pilot at heart, a man who had loved machines ever since he could drive a tractor. Jack Malloch's resuscitation of PK350 was and is *a celebration of perfection*. On that day Man and Machine came together in harmony and a renewed partnership, one that has given us much to celebrate and upon which to reflect.

Postscript
A FINAL VISIT

On 17 January 2012, four ex-AFZ officers set off on a very special journey. Bill Sykes recalls the build-up and the journey itself:

It had long been a wish of mine to revisit the Spitfire crash site, but there was no one who knew exactly where it was, so it was put on hold. It was only when Nick Meikle started writing the story of JMM that interest was revived, in that he, never having been there, wished to see the area. I had spent some hours there on the day following the accident, surveying the scene of devastation with Steve Kesby, but I wanted to go back. With a grid reference to be gleaned from the Board of Inquiry, coupled with today's technology and a GPS, we should not have a problem finding the crash site…

So off we went to Air Force HQ to get authority to draw the BoI from the Archives. The senior staff at Air HQ were only too willing to assist, but, of course, 'protocol' had to be observed…When we had heard nothing after a month, we returned. They had 'not been able' to trace the reference number or date as to when the file had been sent to the Archives. So we gave up. Then a friend of mine who was moving house told me she was a relative of the Malloch family and had some newspaper cuttings from March 1982 which she was going to scrap. Amongst them was an article titled *Spitfire wreckage strewn over 400m*, in which it stated that the Spitfire '…crashed into a maize field near the Chidau school, on the banks of the Nyagui River in the Chikwakwa communal land, about 60km north-east of Salisbury.' Bingo! Soon after this, during a chance meeting with Ken Burmeister, hope was rekindled when Ken casually remarked that he knew where the site was. He said he had been there with Group Captain Peter Ngulu the day after the accident…had travelled there by road transport and, due to the deluge the day before, had to abandon the vehicle and complete the last five kilometres on foot.

'It's a pity that Peter is not around to be able to negotiate with the chief of the area and converse with the locals,' I said.

'Oh no,' exclaimed Ken, 'Peter farms at Beatrice—I'll give him a call.'

Peter, of course, was only too happy to be included in the search, and a good thing too, as he was the lynchpin of our navigation—we would never have found the place without him. It took us two-and-a-half hours to reach the site and we stopped at the local Juru Police Station on the way, to announce our intentions and obtain authority to proceed further. They were very accommodating, probably because Peter disclosed that he was a Brigadier General (which he was, on retirement from the late General Mujuru's office. He is also the longest serving Trustee of the National Museums, and contributes to the excellent state of the Gweru aircraft display.) As a result, there was much rigid standing to attention, clicking of heels and saluting, and a great willingness to accompany us to the site. So off we set with two young and very pleasant guys from the Central Intelligence Organisation (CIO) and a woman Patrol Officer. The road out to the site was in surprisingly good condition, apart from the odd drift, but the last three kilometres in Nick's twin-cab had to be negotiated very carefully along rocky footpaths. Eventually we were forced to stop two kilometres short of the site for fear of holing the sump. We then proceeded to the maize field on foot. It was also fortunate that the first person of whom Peter asked directions happened to be the very person who was herding cattle in the adjoining field at the time of the crash. His name was Joseph Manjonjo, and he is the grandson of the man who walked the many hours to Juru Police Station to report the crash. Joseph's father, Emmanuel, now the headman, was there too—a delightful man with an unusually firm handshake, and who made us feel so welcome. There was no evidence on the ground that anything untoward had occurred those thirty years ago, but we were astonished to find a piece of parachute on the surface. We then combed the area and found many more bits that had not been collected when the wreckage had been uplifted to New Sarum: bits of filters; a piece of windscreen glass; the makers plate from the battery, and so on. We took a full shopping bag home for onward identification by the Spitfire Project Manager, Dave Hann.

On a personal note, I was not so much interested in seeing the actual crash site as to try to piece together the events concerning the last minutes of the flight ... Immediately the Vampire popped out of the hailstorm into the clear, calm air, there appeared beneath us a huge granite 'whaleback' *kopje* with its western side almost vertical, visible on the edge of the storm. We flew over it at right angles, and the area beyond it was open country with no other outcrops. Upon looking at the area on Google Earth and the 1:50,000 map, we discovered two similar whaleback rocks—Nyahungwe and Domborembudzi. These confirmed the direction of flight of the Vampire which coincided with that of the impact line of the Spitfire, both on a westerly heading. My assumption had always been that Jack had crashed a few kilometres back from these granite massifs. Apparently, not so...the Spitfire went in about four kilometres to the north of Nyahungwe, almost abeam of the Vampire. Both aircraft flew through the centre of the storm, so it must have been vast in its extent, a fact that can be confirmed by both pilots of the Vampire—the length of time we spent in the cloud was interminable.

And so, some of the ghosts have at last been laid to rest. It was a moving experience for us all. Nick phoned Dave Hann while standing on the crash site. Dave had requested that a prayer be said to close the chapter, and this we did, with Nick saying all the right words. We then wended our way back through the bush to the vehicle, completely satisfied…remembering that the 30th anniversary of the accident is on 26 March, 2012. To close the book, the Malloch family—Alyson, Ross and Greg—intend visiting the site in the near future.

We intended placing a memorial cross at the site but circumstances, for now, have prevented this. However, a 20-foot Acacia tree stands at grid reference 17:34.126S 031:33.605E. Nature has placed its own memorial precisely where Jack Malloch and PK350 fell from a stormy sky on 26 March 1982. Since that fateful date, this spot, in a most tranquil rural setting, has remained untouched.

NOTES

Chapter 1

1. Viscount ZS JPU (c/n 240) was on lease to Air Zimbabwe Rhodesia from Aviation Hire & Travel Pty Ltd and was registered in South Africa. She was a V.754D series aircraft and had first flown in 1957. She had belonged to Air Rhodesia from 1968–1975 and was registered as VP WAR before being sold to Aviation Hire & Travel Pty Ltd. Air Zimbabwe bought her again in 1981 and she was reregistered as VP WAR. She was withdrawn from service in November 1983 and scrapped in 1986, with 39,985 hours and 29,606 landings on her airframe. The date of her scrapping coincided with the change of registrations to the 'Z' identifier for Zimbabwe in late 1983. Thus she never held the registration of Z WAR.

2. Email from Peter Miller, 11 January 2013. RH 839 was scheduled for 07h30 local time (0530Z or UTC) departure for Bulawayo–Johannesburg–Bulawayo–Salisbury that day.

Chapter 2

1. *Sigh for a Merlin* by Alex Henshaw, p. 176.

2. *Spitfire: A Test Pilot's Story* by Jeffrey Quill, p. 294.

3. According to Leo McKinstry in his book *Spitfire—Portrait of a Legend,* page 352, from the middle of the war the numbering system lost "all logical cohesion" because of the "different stages of development, specification and orders" of the Spitfire marks. Thus the Mk IX came out before the Mk VIII, the PR XI before the PR X, etc. In addition from 1942 the Air Ministry began steadily to replace the Roman numerals with Arabic numerals, such that the Mk IV became the Mk 20 adding to the confusion. After WW2, in 1948, Arabic numerals only were used. Thus the Mk XXII became the Mk 22.

4. The Coupe d'Aviation Maritime Jacques Schneider (commonly called the Schneider Trophy, or prize or cup) was a prize competition for seaplanes. Announced by Jacques Schneider, a financier, balloonist and aircraft enthusiast, in 1911, it offered a prize of roughly £1,000. The race was held eleven times between 1913 and 1931. It was meant to encourage technical advances in civil aviation but became a contest for pure speed with laps over a triangular course (initially 280km, later 350km). The races were very popular and some attracted crowds of over 200,000 spectators. If an aero club won three races in five years, they would retain the cup and the winning

pilot would receive 75,000 francs. The previous winning country hosted each race. The Federation Aeronautique Internationale and the Aero Club in the hosting country supervised the races. Each club could enter up to three competitors with an equal number of alternates. Britain won it for posterity in 1933. Since 1977 the trophy has been on display at the Science Museum in London. (Wikipedia.)

5. *Sigh for a Merlin* by Alex Henshaw, p. 37

6. According to Leo McKinstry in *Spitfire—Portrait of a Legend,* page 244, John Alcorn's authoritative research revealed that Spitfires were 1.25 times more effective than the Hurricanes. Nineteen Spitfire units gained 521 victories for an average of 30 victories per unit. Hurricane units gained 655 victories for an average of 22 victories per unit. The average victory-to-loss on Spitfire units was 1.8 compared with 1.34 on Hurricane units.

7. Aileron reversal is a phenomenon usually associated with high speed and the onset of compressibility and wings that have low torsional strength—simply they are not stiff enough. For instance when the aileron is deflected up-wards to make the wing go down, there is a twisting effect on the wing brought about by the upward movement of the aileron. This increases the angle of attack of the wing and causes the wing to go up rather than down, (down being the desired movement), thus a control or aileron reversal is the result.

8. 'Rhubarb' raids were low-level attacks by RAF fighters on targets of opportunity in northern France, whereas 'Circus' raids were bombing raids into northern France with large fighter escorts.

9. *Spitfire: A Test Pilot's Story* by Jeffrey Quill, p. 203.

10. *Spitfire: A Test Pilot's Story* by Jeffrey Quill, pp. 211 & 238.

11. *Spitfire: A Test Pilot's Story* by Jeffrey Quill, p. 229

12. In simple terms a supercharger is an air compressor used on internal combustion engines to reduce the effect of decreasing air density with an increase in altitude—at 30,000 feet the air pressure is one third of that at sea level. A supercharger consists of an impellor driven by the engine inside a casing, which compresses the air/fuel mix before its introduction to and combustion in the piston combustion chamber. The measure of compression is expressed as 'boost'. On British engines it was expressed as pounds per square inch or psi.

13. The Spitfire Mk VI, which featured a pressurised cockpit, was specifically designed to combat the high level Junkers Ju-86P intruders. The threat never materialised. The Spitfire HF IX was designed to counter the same anticipated threat.

14. The Mk XVIII and PR XIX are also referred to as the F Mk 18 and PR 19 in some sources. See Note 1 above.

15. George Pickering who had assisted Jeffrey Quill on the early Spitfire test flying, luckily survived. Tragically, whilst recuperating he was killed while driving a Bren-gun carrier.

16. *The Spitfire Story* by Alfred Price, p. 232

17. Article titled *Spitfire, Supermarine Type 356—Mks 21 and 22* by Harry Robinson.

18. Internet site *spitfires.ukf.net* by Andrew Pentland. Two hundred and eighty-eight Mk 22s were ordered. The last 20 were converted to Mk 24s, leaving a balance of 268.

19. The Supermarine Spiteful was an unsuccessful attempt by Supermarine to achieve a better performing piston-engine fighter with a laminar flow type wing. The wing profile was not dissimilar to that of the Mustang, also a laminar flow wing. The Spiteful prototype was essentially a Spitfire Mk XIV fuselage and tail fitted to the new wing. As a result the prototype demonstrated the same directional control problems as the Mk 21 and early Mk 22s, in addition to low speed handling problems. The latter problems incurred an unfavourable assessment by the RAF's Aeroplane & Armament Experimental Establishment at Boscombe Down. A larger broad-chord tail-plane was then fitted to the second prototype in late 1945, according to Alfred Price, and earned it the identity of 'the Spiteful type tail-plane'. This tail was then fitted to the Mk 22. With the arrival of the jet age the Spiteful never saw operational service. In any case the laminar flow wing produced no performance advantage over the Mk 22 wing and demonstrated once again how good the Spitfire wing was; a strong vindication for the original design and the work of Joe Smith and his engineers.

20. The SRAF Mk 22s were retrofitted with rocket rails in mid-1953.

Chapter 3

1. It was Daniel Scott-Davies, the former curator of the Alex Henshaw collection at the RAF Museum, who identified Wing Commander Peter Ayerst as the most likely person to have flown PK350. This because he test-flew most of the Mk 22 Spitfires at Castle Bromwich. Email from Daniel Scott-Davies, 1 October 2010.

2. *Sigh for a Merlin* by Alex Henshaw, p. 186.

3. Telephone conversation with Peter Ayerst, 15 October 2010.

4. Reference to p. 248 in Alfred Price's *Spitfire, A Complete Fighting History* (1991

edition) shows PK431 with a smaller Mk XIV type tail. This suggests that at this stage the Mk 22s were still being produced with the smaller tails. PK350, being an earlier production aircraft, is likely also to have had this smaller tail, being modified later—possibly in June 1946 at Eastleigh.

5. Email from Peter Arnold, 14 May 2012. Perusal of the Mk 22 records shows a pattern of aircraft returning to Eastleigh for modifications. It is possible they returned to have the Spiteful tail plane fitted.

6. Letter in the possession of the author.

7. Email from Peter Arnold, 15 May 2012. In the 1970s Peter Arnold managed to copy all the movements of PK350 from Supermarine's aircraft movement card at South Marston. Peter Arnold is the co-author of *Spitfire Survivors Then and Now*.

Chapter 4

1. The Southern Rhodesian Army's contribution was 6,170 according to the *Appendix of The War History of Southern Rhodesia 1939–1945 Volume 2* by J.F. Macdonald.

2. Operation Order No. 2/51 from the personal archive of Bill Sykes.

3. Dave Barbour was the son of H.M. Barbour who founded the famous department store of the same name in Stanley Avenue, Salisbury. Dave served in the Volunteer Reserve in the RhAF in the late 1970s as a Dakota pilot on 3 Squadron during the Rhodesian war. With his sharp wit and engaging conversation he is well remembered for his time at the Forward Airfields—established as operational bases for the Fire Forces and light strike units during the Rhodesian bush war.

4. Johnny Deall bore the rank of WO1 simply because that was the only way the SRAF could induct him at that stage. It may appear odd to the reader that he was deputy leader of the First Spitfire Ferry although he held a lower rank than numerous others in the formation. However, it was his experience and reputation that counted on a task such as this. NCO pilots were common in the RAF in WW2 and this was still the case in these early post-war years in the SRAF. This system fell away with the formation of the RRAF in 1953, after which all pilots held commissioned ranks. Johnny Deall became a Captain after the Spitfire Ferry and was appointed the 'A' Flight Commander on 1 Squadron. He retired as a Group Captain.

5. Dickie Bradshaw's Logbook; email from Dick and Chris Bradshaw, 1 May 2010.

6. Boost is a measure of the output of the supercharger fitted to the Griffon engine and was measured in pounds per square inch (psi) on British designed engines. Standard air pressure at sea level is 14.7 psi. A typical power setting of 6 psi would

represent an air pressure of 20.7 psi. The Griffon had a limit of 18 psi, which would be the equivalent of 32.7 psi. In the US the measure used is inches of mercury.

7. The Griffon engine was started by the Coffman cartridge. The Coffman device used a large blank cartridge containing cordite which, when fired, pushed a piston forward. A screw thread driven by the piston engaged with the engine, turning it over. (Wikipedia.)

8. A pitot tube is a tube affixed to an aircraft which is used to measure the speed of an aircraft. On the Spitfire it was fitted under the port (left) wing.

9. It has not been possible to get an exact definition of what 'inter-feeding'was on the Spitfire during the ferries. John Campbell, a participant on the second ferry, could not recall the phenomenon as an operational issue at all. It would seem this might refer to the aircraft fuel system 'hiding' fuel from the indicating system, as the amount of fuel which the affected aircraft required on refueling was no different to the others.

10. At that time Belvedere Airport was the main international civil airport on the outskirts of Salisbury. It had a longer runway than Cranborne and was used also by the Spitfires until the SRAF moved to Kentucky in 1952.

11. Owen Love was a cousin to brothers Royce and John Love. (In the 1960s and 1970s John Love was a well-known racing driver from Bulawayo, Rhodesia.) Owen was buried in a grave next to his cousin, Royce, at Church Yard in the village of Ste Marguerite des Loges in Normandy. Royce Love was shot down and killed on 17 August 1944 while flying Typhoons on 266 Squadron during the battle for the Falaise Gap.

12. In fact, according to Dave Newnham in his article on the RATG on the Rhodesia & the RAF Blog, the RATG training base at Thornhill was not closed until 31 March 1954. Consequently it is not clear to what closure Dave Barbour was referring. By this stage Thornhill had two units, No. 4 ANS and No. 5 FTS, operating on the base. Thornhill was one of two active RATG training bases with the HQ element at Kumalo, in Bulawayo. The RATG was in its fourth and final incarnation (i.e. the nineteen-fifties phase) in response to the need train aircrew for the Korean War.

13. *Rhodesia Herald* 23 March 1951.

14. According to the signatures in the F700 of SR65 the names of some of the other Spitfire technicians *appear* to be Q. Anderson, J. Hattingh, Watson, K. Gibson, Rowe, Stewart, and Gordon.

15. Keith Kemsley identified the High Altitude Blue colour scheme on the SRAF

Spitfires during research by Phil Wright for a book on the SRAF/RRAF/RhAF aircraft colour schemes. Phil Wright—who is ex-British South African Police—has produced the wonderful drawings included in this book of PK350/SR64 in her various colour schemes.

16. Typed record of PK350's hours from personal notes and records kept by Spike Owens.

17. The F700 belonging to SR65 was most fortunately retrieved by the late Basil 'Brush' Miles, Flying Wing Adjutant at Thornhill for many years. He passed it on to Chuck Osborne, Officer Commanding Aircraft Servicing Flight at New Sarum, who later recovered the wreckage of PK350. A copy has kindly been made available to the writer. The last entry was on 8 July 1954, when Lieutenant Sandy Mutch flew SR65 after a propeller change (loose blades being the original un-serviceability), when she had 220:20 hours. However, as shown by pilots' logbooks, SR65 continued to fly. In fact SR65 flew her last flight on 18 December 1954 in the hands of Chris Hudson. Somehow the last volume (8) of SR65's F700 was never correctly ruled off with the hours being carried forward to what should have been a new volume (9).

18. Jimmy Gordon-Brander, ex-RAF and SRAF Spitfire technician, was the crane operator who placed SR64 onto the plinth. This was confirmed during a telephone conversation with his son, Paul Gordon-Brander, on 17 January 2013. According to his son, Jimmy suspected that one day someone might want to restore her, so he ensured that the aircraft was mounted in a manner that would not damage it structurally (as was the case with SR65 at Thornhill).

Chapter 5

1. Telephone conversation with Paul Gordon-Brander, 17 January 2013.

2. Email from Stu Robertson, 29 July 2010.

3. Telephone conversation with Tony Howard, 5 January 2013. Tony Howard, an airframe technician at ASF, Thornhill in 1977 and who worked on the Spitfire, recalled that Spike Owens was by then warrant officer in charge at ASF, Thornhill. However, all other evidence suggests that Spike was still at 6 Sqn. What is clear is that all the initial reassembly to assess the airframe's state and completeness and later dis-assembly was carried out at 6 Sqn. It was then moved to ASF, no doubt under Spike's watchful eye, before it was moved to Jack Malloch's hangar in Salisbury. Mike Hamence, Officer Commanding ASF, has indicated that Spike Owens was still at 6 Sqn at this stage, which fits with the recall of Bob Garrett and Stu Robertson.

4. Email from Jackie Stone, 26 June 2010. Jackie Stone is Spike Owens' daughter from his first marriage.

5. The signature of Spike Owens, as a senior NCO approving the aircraft as 'Fit to Fly', appears frequently in the F700 of SR65.

6. Number 4 Squadron, based at Thornhill. Its roles included light ground attack, reconnaissance and communications. It utilised the Cessna 337 aircraft, known as the 'Lynx'.

7. Number 6 Squadron, based at Thornhill. This was the training squadron for the RhAF, responsible for carrying out basic and advanced pilot training on the Siai Machetti SF260 and Aermacchi MB326 'Impala'.

8. Email from Frank Mussell, 5 November 2009.

9. Interview with Air Vice-Marshal Chris Dams, 26 January 2011.

Chapter 6

1. Email from Alyson Dawson (*née* Malloch), 10 October 2010.

2. Telephone conversation Andy Wood, 4 December 2010.

3. Telephone conversation with Piet Bezuidenhout, 20 January 2013.

4. Telephone conversation Ian Hunt, 20 May 2013.

5. Letter in possession of Margery Musgrave, widow of Bill Musgrave. The letter's existence was brought to the attention of Bill Sykes through a mutual friend, Colin Saunders.

6. Email from Margery Musgrave to Colin Saunders, 24 June 2013.

7. Email from George Paterson, 20 May 2012. DC-8 A4O-PA became Z-WMJ under the Zimbabwe register and was named 'Captain Jack Malloch'.

8. Emails from Colin Miller, 28 September, 4 and 7 October 2010.

9. Email from George Paterson, 1 May 2012.

10. Email from George Paterson, 20 May 2012.

11. Email from George Paterson, 20 May 2012.

12. Interview with Tony Norton (First Officer at ATA), 15 October 2012.

13. Email from Alyson Dawson (née Malloch), 10 October 2010.

14. The *Sunday Mail*, 6 Dec 1964. "Jack Malloch—a man who refused to lose." By Keith Simpson.

15. The *Sunday Mail*, 6 Dec 1964. "Jack Malloch—a man who refused to lose." By Keith Simpson.

16. Jack Malloch's Logbook.

17. Jack Malloch and Ian Smith served together on 237 Sqn for a short period only, between May and late June 1944, when Ian Smith was shot down.

18. The *Sunday Mail*, 6 Dec 1964. "Jack Malloch—a man who refused to lose." By Keith Simpson.

19. Jack Malloch's Logbook.

20. The *Sunday Mail*, 6 Dec 1964. "Jack Malloch—a man who refused to lose." By Keith Simpson.

21. Jack Malloch's Logbook.

22. Jack Malloch's Logbook.

23. The *Sunday Mail*, 6 Dec 1964. "Jack Malloch—a man who refused to lose." By Keith Simpson.

24. Telephone conversation with Andy Wood, 4 December 2010.

25. Email from Alyson Dawson (née Malloch), 1o October 2010.

26. Interview with Mick McLaren, 13 November 2009.

27. Email from Colin Miller, 28 September 2010.

28. Email from George Paterson, 26 May 2012.

29. Email from Colin Miller, 7 October 2010.

Chapter 7

1. 'Smersh' was a common word at the time used to describe secret activities. It was derived directly from same word which referred to a counter-intelligence arm of the KGB in the former Soviet Union.

2. Email from Colin Miller, 28 September 2010.

3. Email from Colin Miller, 29 October 2010.

4. Interview with Dave Hann, 5 November 2009, and numerous email exchanges.

5. Email from Jim Townsend, 5 November 2009; email from George Paterson, 20 May 2012.

6. Email from Jim Townsend, 17 December 2012.

7. Email from Jim Townsend, 5 November 2009.

8. Email from Jim Townsend, 22 May 2012.

9. Interview with Dave Hann, 12 November 2009.

10. Telephone call with Ian Hunt, 20 May 2013. Ian was the Traffic Manager at ATA & Affretair. He recalls during planning meetings in the late 1970s dealing with Bob Dodds and regarded him as Engineering Manager.

11. Telephone conversation with Andy Wood, 4 December 2010.

12. Interview with Dave Hann, 05 November 2009.

13. Email from Jim Townsend, 20 December 2012.

14. Interview with Dave Hann, 5 November 2009.

15. Interview with Dave Hann, 5 November 2009.

16. Interview George Paterson, 16 August 2013.

17. This list of names was compiled according to the collective memories of numerous people connected with Jack Malloch and the restoration project.

Chapter 8

1. Interview with Mick McLaren, 13 November 2009.

2. Most of this chapter is sourced from the video *Spitfire—The Pursuit of a Dream* and Dave Hann's personal notes and records and four interviews with him. Also, Dave had a record of the rebuild on a website, *SA-Aviation,* under the title of *Re-Birth of a Spitfire.* In addition to the interviews with Dave, numerous email exchanges served to clarify the facts of this chapter.

3. Telephone conversation with Ian Hunt, ex-Traffice Manager at ATA, 20 May 2013.

4. Interview with Chris Faber, 12 May 2010.

5. Email from Keith Kemsley, 13 December 2009 and interview, 25 January 2011.

6. Interview with Tony Smit, 26 January 2011. Johan Locke was an additional name not previously known. The other names were on a photo received from Dave Hann.

7. Email from Jim Townsend, 5 November 2009.

8. Email from Stefan Bichlmeyr, 7 May 2011.

9. Telephone conversation with Andy Wood, 4 December 2010.

10. Telephone conversation with Barry York, 20 January 2013. Barry was OCMU at New Sarum during the rebuild of the Spitfire and later OCTW. He confirmed that the RhAF bay serviced numerous components for the Spitfire, including instruments, the gun sight, the cannons, hydraulic and pneumatic systems and undercarriage. He confirmed also that the original instrument panel was used and because of the commonality with Vampire and Provost aircraft, spares were not difficult to source; the original P9 compass was replaced with a spare compass, the same compass used on the Provost and Dakota. In addition, some adaptations were made e.g. the oxygen system bottles were Vampire bottles. The only instruments likely to have been sourced overseas were the oil pressure and radiator temperature gauges.

11. Email from Bob Lane, 21 September 2011. Bob Lane, an apprentice electrician, confirmed he worked on the aircraft.

12. Chris Faber and Viv Bellamy.

13. There is often confusion about the lettering on the side of the aircraft which most see as JM–M, Jack's initials. From the port side the lettering reads M–JM. JM indicates the RAF squadron identity code (which happens to be No. 20 OTU), while the M is the individual squadron aircraft. The squadron commander's aircraft would therefore be identified as A–JM.

Chapter 9

1. Again, most of the information presented in this chapter was gathered from the video *Spitfire—The Pursuit of a Dream* or personal records kept by Dave Hann.

2. Interview with Bill Sykes, May 2010. Most of the photographs taken of the first flight were taken by Paddy Gray of the *The Herald* newspaper.

3. Steve Baldwin's Logbook; emails from Steve Baldwin, 31 May 2011 and 1 February 2012. Steve recalled that his enthusiastic passengers had been involved with the project and thus may have been 6 Squadron technicians. Lynx number was 3417.

4. Email from Pete Besant, 5 May 2010.

5. Email from Leon Keyter, 30 June 2010. Sadly Leon Keyter passed away later in 2010 after a long illness.

6. Jack Malloch's Logbook.

7. Photograph by Paddy Gray.

8. See note in Chapter 1.

9. Spitfire F Mk 22 Pilot's Notes.

10. Email from Leon Keyter, 30 June 2010.

11. Email from Leon Keyter, 30 June 2010.

12. Interview with Dave Hann, 05 November 2009.

13. Telephone conversation with Andy Wood, 4 December 2010.

14. Email/Facebook message from Nicky Pearce, 22 December 2012. She commented that she also completed flight-crew logbooks for other ATA pilots, citing them as being lazy!

15. Email from Dave Dodds, 7 July 2011. Dave took these photos independently and they appeared later in *Scope* magazine.

16. By sheer coincidence it was discovered that Richard Sandercock, a First Officer on the DC-8 at Affretair at the time, took photos of the Spitfire returning from the fly past. These are included in the story. The author was working with Richard at the time of the revelation.

17. Paul Maher worked for MK Airlines, effectively the successor to Affretair. MK Airlines was started in 1990 by Mike Kruger, Jack Malloch's nephew, by his sister Blythe and Captain Ted Kruger.

18. Alf Wild's Logbook; email from Alf Wild, 30 May 2011; and colour photographs. The Hunter numbers were 1258 (Wild) and 1286 (Oakley).

19. Emails from Chris Faber, 30 May 2011 and 19 September 2011. Chris Faber's Dove started out in 1948 as a Shell VIP aircraft in the UK. It was sold to McAlpine Aviation in SA and then purchased and modified by the Fairey Air Survey Company in Rhodesia, hence the unique observation window. Later, Chris bought the aircraft and parked it at ATA, with Jack Malloch's blessing. Soon after the Thornhill visit the aircraft was sold to an Irish businessman. Sadly the Dove suffered a wheels up landing shortly thereafter, in Ireland, where it remains in storage.

20. Steve Baldwin's Logbook.

21. According to the author's records, the late Ian Henderson was then serving on 8 Squadron. Accompanied by Phil Scott, an engineer with 8 Squadron, he flew a sortie with Jack Malloch in 1980. However his logbook has no record of such a flight. The author also recalls accompanying Ian Henderson, but again no logbook record was found. The photograph listed as taken by Phil Scott is very similar to the official AFZ photo taken by an unknown AFZ photographer.

22. Email from Alyson Dawson (*née* Malloch), April 2013. According to Alyson's logbook she flew Bob Dodds to Charles Prince on 31 August 1980 to attend to the Spitfire on the occasion of the Charles Prince visit.

23. Email from Sean Carson, 6 January 2011.

24. Email from Colin Miller, 4 October 2010.

25. Peter Knobel passed away in 2012.

26. Email from Frank Mussell, 5 November 2009.

27. Email from Frank Mussell, 5 November 2009.

28. Email from Keith Kemsley, 13 December 2009.

29. Email from Keith Kemsley, 13 December 2009.

30. Email from Keith Kemsley, 13 December 2009.

31. The programme of the function, a copy of which is included in this story. *The Herald* also reported the story on 24 November 1980.

32. Interview with Keith Kemsley, 25 January 2011.

33. Emails from Debbie Addison (*née* Carmody), 27 September 2010, 26 January 2011.

Chapter 10

1. Email from Keith Kemsley, 13 December 2009; Logbook and emails from Peter Knobel, 7 January 2010 and 30 May 2011.

2. Steve Kesby's Logbook.

3. Jack Malloch's Logbook.

4. Dickie Bradshaw's Logbook.

5. *A Pride of Eagles. A Definitive History of the Rhodesian Air Force 1920–1980* by Beryl Salt; interview with Keith Kemsley, 25 January 2011.

6. Mick McLaren's Logbook; interview with Mick McLaren, 17 November 2009.

7. Keith Kemsley's Logbook; interview with Keith Kemsley, 25 January 2011.

8. John Mussell's Logbook; emails from John Mussell, 6 September 2011 and 29 November 2011.

9. Frank Mussell's Logbook; email from Frank Mussell, 5 November 2009.

10. Email from Roy Morris, 23 June 2011.

11. Email from Rex Taylor, 6 May 2011.

12. Wally Hinrichs's Logbook.

13. Email from Chris Dams, 1 November 2011.

14. Email from Chris Dams, 1 November 2011.

15. Email from Chris Hudson, 23 June 2011.

16. Emails from Mike Saunders, 10 November 2009 and 13 June 2011.

17. Interview with John Campbell, 16 January 2012.

18. Dennis Spence later joined SAA and has enjoyed a successful career in the self-same airline. He has also played a big part in the air show circuit in SA. Interestingly, on 5 March 2004 he captained SAA's 747-244 ZS-SAN 'Lebombo' into Rand Airport on her final flight before the aircraft became a static display at the SAA Museum. This flight was very reminiscent of Jack Malloch's flight of the Constellation VP-WAW into Charles Prince.

19. Email from Peter Knobel, 13 June 2011.

20. Email from Peter Knobel, 13 June 2011.

21. Peter Knobel's Logbook; Clive Ward's Logbook; email from Peter Knobel, 30 May 2011.

22. Email from Steve Kesby, 14 December 2010.

23. Email from Steve Kesby, 15 December 2010.

24. Clive Ward's Logbook; email from Clive Ward, 15 December 2010.

25. Bud Cockcroft's Logbook; email from Bud Cockcroft, 1 June 2011.

26. Steve Kesby's Logbooks.

27. Email from Dave Hann, 8 June 2011.

28. Clive Ward's Logbook; email from Clive Ward, 15 December 2010.

29. Email from Steve Nobes, 16 January 2013. Steve identified one of the photographers as Guy Cunningham.

30. Email from Steve Nobes, 15 January 2013. The colour photos of PK350 at Air Force '81 featured in this story were taken by Steve Harvey who, at the time, was Officer Commanding Photo Section at New Sarum.

Chapter 11

1. Much of the content of this chapter is drawn from personal notes kept by Bill Sykes and during numerous interviews with him.

2. Geoff Oborne's Logbook; email from Geoff Oborne, 14 May 2011.

3. Nev Weir's Logbook; email from Nev Weir, 15 June 2011.

4. Bud Cockcroft's Logbook; email from Bud Cockcroft, 1 June 2011.

5. Email Charlie Cordy-Hedge, 17 June 2013 and logbook.

6. The African gentleman was identified years later as Mr Manjonjo by his grandson, Joseph. See Postscript.

7. Email from Dave Haynes, 25 July 2011

8. Steve Kesby also thought that the two civilian members were possibly Bob Dodds and Dave Hann. This was not the case according to Dave Hann, who by that time had left Zimbabwe.

9. Email from Bud Cockcroft, 1 June 2011.

10. Email from Steve Nobes, 16 January 2013. Steve Nobes and Guy Cunningham were the Air Force photographers, there being so much to photograph.

11. Email from Chuck Osborne, 16 July 2011. Chuck Osborne also recalled there being two civilian members on the BoI.

12. Personal records kept by Bill Sykes.

13. Email Mike Kruger, 25 October 2009.

14. According to Wikipaedia, Affretair was liquidated in 2000 with a $500 million debt.

15. Personal records kept by Bill Sykes. He also recalled how he managed to get Jack Malloch's name incorrect. It was Jack's widow, Zoe, who pointed it out to him. He had genuinely thought it to be 'James' McVicar Malloch as opposed to John.

16. Email from Steve Kesby, 15 July 2011.

17. See Appendix G—PK350's hours as a restored aircraft. It is a reasonable assessment only where actual flying hours of a number of flights were not available due lack of access to the F700.

Epilogue

1. Meeting with Brigadier Peter Ngulu (Rtd), 17 January 2012. Peter is a Trustee with National Museums & Monuments of Zimbabwe.

2. PK431 is in Perth, Australia, displayed in the RAAF Association Aviation Heritage Museum; PK624 and PK 664 are in storage in the UK.

3. Jack Malloch's Logbook.

Appendix E

1. Email from Guy Revell, 6 June 2011. Guy Revell is the Assistant Curator, Department of Research & Information Services, Royal Air Force Museum, London.

2. Telephone conversation with Wing Commander Peter Ayerst, October 2010.

BIBLIOGRAPHY

Books and Publications

Darling, Kev: *Warbird Tech Series, Volume 32, Griffon-powered Spitfires.* Speciality Press (31 Jan 2002). ISBN-10: 1580070450. ISBN-13: 978-1580070454.

Glancey, Jonathan: *Spitfire: The Illustrated Biography.* Atlantic Books, New Edition (1 Oct 2008). ISBN-10: 1843547996. ISBN-13: 978-1843547990.

Henshaw, Alex: *Sigh for a Merlin. Testing the Spitfire.* Crecy Publishing Limited; Second Revised Edition (30 Sep 1999). ISBN-10: 0947554831. ISBN-13: 978-0947554835.

MacDonald, John F.: *The War History of Southern Rhodesia 1939–1945 Volume 2* (1976) Books of Rhodesia Publishing Company (Pvt) Ltd., Volume 11 of the Rhodesiana Reprint Library—Silver Series; a Facsimile Reprint of the original published by the Government of Southern Rhodesia in 1950. ISBN: 0 86920 140 9.

McKinstry, Leo: *Spitfire—Portrait of a Legend.* John Murray. First Edition in Paperback (29 May 2008). ISBN-10: 0719568757. ISBN-13: 978-0719568756.

Morgan, Eric B. and Edward Shacklady: *Spitfire. The History.* Key Books Ltd; Second Revised Edition (5 Oct 2000). ISBN-10: 0946219486. ISBN-13: 978-0946219483.

Nesbitt, Roy, Dudley Cowderoy with Andy Thomas: *Britain's Rebel Air Force: The War from the Air in Rhodesia, 1965–1980.* Grub Street; illustrated edition (30 Sep 1998). ISBN-10: 1902304055. ISBN-13: 978-1902304052.

Price, Dr Alfred: *Spitfire at War 3.* Ian Allan Publishing; First Edition (27 July 1990). ISBN-10: 0711019339. ISBN-13: 978-0711019331.

Price, Alfred: *The Spitfire Story.* J. H. Haynes & Co Ltd; Revised edition (1 July 2010). ISBN-10: 184425819X. ISBN-13: 978-1844258192

Quill, Jeffrey: *A Test Pilot's Story.* Crecy Publishing; New edition (1 Oct 1996). ISBN-10: 0947554726. ISBN-13: 978-0947554729.

Riley, Gordon, and Graham Trant. *Spitfire Survivors Round the World.* Aston Publications Ltd. (Oct 1986). ISBN-10: 0946627061. ISBN-13: 978-0946627066.

Salt, Beryl: *Pride of Eagles. A Definitive History of the Rhodesian Air Force, 1920–1980.* Covos Day Books, South Africa (Mar 2001). ISBN-10: 0620237597. ISBN-13: 978-0620237598.

Southern Rhodesian Air Force. AP2816: *Pilot's Notes for Spitfire 22 & 24 Griffon 61.*

Thurman, Robin. *Half a Century in Uniform The life story of Group Captain O.D. Penton OLM AFC. Rhodesian Air Force Volunteer Reserve (Retired).* Robin Thurman, 2007. ISBN: 9781409208471.

Personal Papers and Flying Logbooks

Ayerst, Peter: RAF Logbook.

Baldwin, Steve: RhAF Logbook

Barbour, David: *Personal Memories of the SRAF.*

Bradshaw, Dickie: RAF Logbook.

Campbell, John: SRAAF Logbook.

Cockroft, Bud: AFZ Logbook.

Cordy-Hedge, Charlie: AFZ Logbook.

Dams, Chris: RRAF Logbook.

Henshaw, Alex: UK Logbook.

Hinrichs, Wally: RRAF Logbook.

Hudson, Chris: RRAF Logbook.

Kemsley, Keith: SRAF/RRAF Logbook.

Kesby, Steve: AFZ Logbook.

Knobel, Peter: AFZ Logbook.

Malloch, Jack: RAF, SRAAF and Rhodesian Logbooks.

McLaren, Mick: SRAAF and RRAF Logbooks.

Meikle, Nick: AFZ Logbook.

Miller, Peter: Rhodesian DCA Logbook.

Morris, Roy: RRAF Logbook.

Moss, John P.: *Spit Epic.*

Mussell, Frank: RRAF Logbook.

Mussell, John: RRAF Logbook.

Oborne, Geoff: AFZ Logbook.

Penton, Ossie: RRAF Logbook.

Saunders, Mike: RRAF Logbook.

Shirley, Dave: AFZ Logbook.

Taylor, Rex: RRAF Logbook.

Ward, Clive: AFZ Logbook.

Weir, Nev: AFZ Logbook.

Wild, Alf: AFZ Logbook.

Magazine and Newspaper Articles

Flight, 4 October 1945: 'Last of a Famous Line'.

Flight, 31 January 1946: 'A Spitfire Score'.

Flight, 26 December 1946: 'Spitfire and Seafire. Their Development Described by Supermarine Chief Designer'.

Flight International, 2 February 1985: 'Sanctions Busters'.

Scale Models, October 1978: 'Spitfire. Supermarine Types 356–Mks 21 and 22, Harry Robinson'.

The *Rhodesia Herald* newspaper, 1951–1980: numerous articles

The Herald newspaper, 1980–1982: numerous articles.

Internet Links

Airworthy Spitfires: http://www.spitfiresociety.com

Jack Malloch: *Tango Romeo. The Life and Times of Jack Malloch*

Owen Love: http://www.rhodesiana.com/archives/documents/Rhodesian_Air_Crew_Memorial.pdf

RATG: http://rhodesiaandtheraf.blogspot.com.au/2010_09_01_archive.html

SA–Aviation Forum: *Re-Birth of a Spitfire* by David Hann.

Spitfire Performance and Testing: http://www.spitfireperformance.com/spittest.html

Spitfire Production and Numbers: http://www.spitfires.ukf.net

Spitfire Restorations: http://spitfireforums.com/

Vickers Viscount aircraft: http://Vickersviscount.net

Video Footage

Spitfire—The Pursuit of a Dream, Group Captain Bill Sykes.

The Final Flight of the Spitfire Mk 22, Group Captain Bill Sykes.

Appendix A

VICKERS SUPERMARINE SPITFIRE F MK 21
CUTAWAY DRAWING

KEY

1. Starboard elevator construction
2. Elevator tab
3. Tail navigation light
4. Rudder trim tab
5. Fabric covered rudder construction
6. Sternpost
7. Rudder balance weight
8. Fin main spar
9. Tailfin construction
10. Tail ballast weights
11. Fin secondary spar
12. Rudder trim jack
13. Tailplane trim jack
14. Tailplane construction
15. Tailwheel doors
16. Mudguard
17. Tailwheel retraction jack
18. Tailplane control rods
19. Tailwheel
20. Fuselage double bulkhead
21. Port elevator
22. Port tailplane
23. Fin root fillet fairing
24. Tail assembly joint frame
25. Oxygen cylinder
26. Six-cartridge signal flare launcher
27. Tailplane control cables
28. Access door
29. Fuselage ballast weights
30. Battery
31. IFF transponder
32. Radio access door
33. Whip aerial for VHF
34. Harness release
35. VHF Transmitter-Receiver
36. Radio rack
37. Fuselage frame and stringer construction
38. Wing root trailing edge fillet
39. Control cable runs
40. Fuselage main longeron
41. Port side access door
42. Canopy aft glazing
43. Sliding canopy rail
44. Voltage regulator
45. Fuselage double frame
46. Seat support framework
47. Back armour
48. Pilot's seat
49. Sutton harness
50. Head armour
51. Sliding cockpit canopy cover
52. Pilot's rear view mirror
53. Windscreen framing
54. Laminated glass windscreen
55. Reflector gunsight
56. Port side entry hatch
57. Instrument panel
58. Control column
59. Compass mounting
60. Undercarriage control lever
61. Seat adjusting handle
62. Seat pan armour plate
63. Wing root rib
64. Radiator shutter jack
65. Coolant radiator, oil cooler on port side
66. Gun heating duct
67. Wing rear spar
68. Flap hydraulic jack
69. Flap shroud ribs
70. Tubular flap spar
71. Starboard split trailing edge flap
72. Aileron control bellcrank
73. Aileron hinge
74. Aileron tab
75. Aluminium skinned aileron construction
76. Wing tip fairing
77. Starboard navigation light
78. Wing tip construction
79. Aileron outer hinge rib
80. Wing rib construction
81. Main spar
82. Leading edge nose ribs
83. Ammunition boxes, 150 rounds per gun
84. Main wheel fairing door
85. Ammunition feed drums
86. Blister fairings
87. Ammunition belt feed
88. Hispano, 20-mm cannon barrels

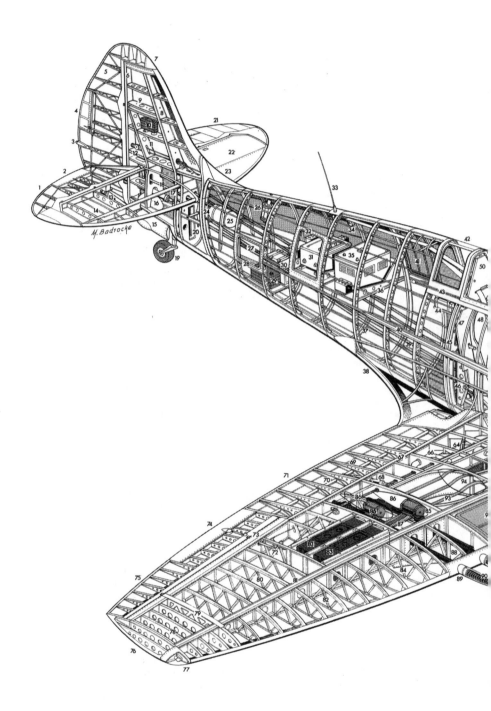

M. Badrocke

Spitfire F Mk 21 cutaway drawing *by kind permission of Mike Bradrocke*

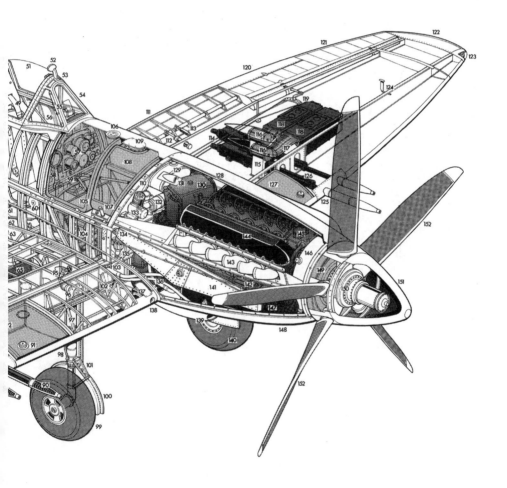

89. Cannon barrel support fairing
90. Recoil springs
91. Fuel filler cap
92. Leading edge fuel tank, 17-Gal
93. Main undercarriage wheel well
94. Main wheel blister fairing
95. Undercarriage retraction link
96. Undercarriage leg pivot
97. Shock absorber leg strut
98. Hydraulic brake pipe
99. Starboard main wheel
100. Main wheel leg fairing door
101. Undercarriage torque scissors
102. Fuel pipe runs
103. Main spar stub attachment
104. Lower main fuel tank, 48-Gal
105. Upper main fuel tank, 36-Gal
106. Fuel filler cap
107. Oil tank vent
108. Oil tank, 9-Gal
109. Oil tank access door
110. Engine compartment fireproof bulkhead
111. Port split trailing edge flap
112. Flap hydraulic jack
113. Flap synchronising jack
114. Port twin 20-mm Hispano cannon
115. Spent cartridge case ejector chute
116. Ammunition feed drums
117. Ammunition belt feeds
118. Ammunition boxes, 150 rounds per gun
119. Aileron control bellcrank
120. Aileron tab
121. Port aileron

122. Wing tip fairing
123. Port navigation light
124. Pitot tube
125. Cannon barrel fairings
126. Cannon barrels
127. Port leading edge fuel tank, 17-Gal
128. Upper engine cowling
129. Hydraulic fluid tank
130. Intercooler
131. Compressor intake
132. Generator
133. Heywood compressor
134. Engine bearer attachment
135. Hydraulic pump
136. Coolant pipes
137. Gun camera
138. Camera port
139. Carburettor intake
140. Port main wheel
141. Engine bearer
142. Cartridge starter
143. Exhaust stubs
144. 2035-hp. Rolls-Royce Griffon 61 engine
145. Engine magnetos
146. Coolant header tank
147. Front engine mounting
148. Lower engine cowling
149. Spinner backplate
150. Propeller hub pitch change mechanism
151. Spinner
152. 11-ft diameter Rotol five-bladed, constant speed propeller

Appendix B

VICKERS SUPERMARINE SPITFIRE F MK 22 SPECIFICATIONS

Engine:	Rolls-Royce Griffon 61, 37 litre 12 Cylinder, liquid cooled (distilled water and glycol mix) in a 'Vee' configuration Maximum power: 2,035 hp at 7,000 ft at 2,750 RPM at +18 psi boost Take-off power: 1,520 hp at sea level
Propeller:	11 ft diameter Rotol five-bladed, constant speed wooden propeller
Dimensions:	Wingspan: 36 ft 11 in. Length: 32 ft 11 in. Height: 13 ft 0 in. Wing Area: 244 sq ft
Weight:	Empty: 7,160 lbs Loaded: 9,900 lbs Maximum: 11,290 lbs
Wing Loading:	40.6 lbs/sq ft at 9,900 lbs
Fuel Capacity:	Normal: 120 gallons Typical Ferry: 210 gallons (with a 90 gallon drop tank) Maximum: 290 gallons (with a 170 gallon drop tank)
Speeds:	Maximum level: 387 kt (449 mph) at 26,000 ft Maximum in a dive: 450 kt (520 mph) Aileron Reversal: 709 kt (823 mph) Take off at 9,900 lbs: 90 kt Climb: 150 kt to 25,000 ft, then reduce by 2 kt/1,000 ft Range Cruise: 170-180 kt (200-210 mph) Clean stall: 75 kt at typical service weight Dirty stall: 65 kt at typical service weight Final approach speed at 9,300 ft: 90 kt
Climb:	Initial rate: 4,800 ft/min Time to 40,000 ft – 20 mins
Range:	390 miles on internal fuel 734 miles with 90 gallon drop tank
Armament:	4 x 20 mm Mk 2 Hispano Suiza Cannons 3 x 500 lb iron bombs 6 x 60 lb rockets

Appendix C

SRAF/RRAF SPITFIRE PILOTS

Ex RAF/SAAF	No. 1 SRAAF Course (Wings 27 September 1951)	
Charles Baillie	Dennis Bagnall	Bruce McKenzie
Jock Barber	Colin Graves	Peter Potter
Dave Barbour	Owen Love	Bill Smith
Ben Bellingan		
Bob Blair		
Dickie Bradshaw		
Neville Brooks	No. 2 SRAAF Course (Wings 21 August 1952)	
John Campbell	Des Anderson	Don Macaskil
Ted Cunnison	Ken Edwards	Mick McLaren
Johnny Deall		
Dickie Dickenson ★	No. 1 SSU (Wings 21 August 1952)	
Alan Douglas	Nigel Bridges	Brian Horney
George Forder	John Cameron	Keith Kemsley
Hardwicke Holderness	Bob d'Hotman	John Mussell
Basil Hone	Dave Harvey	Basil Myburgh
John Hough	Arthur Hodgson	Peter Piggott
Ted Jacklin		John Rogers
John Konschel		
Jack Malloch	No. 2 SSU (Wings 27 February 1953)	
Don McGibbon	Bernard du Plessis	Roy Morris
John Moss	Wally Hinrichs	Frank Mussell
Sandy Mutch ★	Charlie Jamieson	Vic Paxton
Alan O'Hara	Vince King	Barry Stevens
Peter Pascoe	Ray Maritz	Rex Taylor
Charles Paxton		
Ossie Penton	No. 3 SSU (Wings 19 August 1953)	
'Noompie' Phillips	John Allen	Dick Purnell
Dave Richards	Dare Broughton	Barry Raffle
Mike Schumman	Chris Dams	Tommy Robinson
Ray Wood	Solly Ferreira	Mike Saunders
	Chris Hudson	

★ Dickie Dickenson and Sandy Mutch were both from the RAF and came to Rhodesia to assist with weapons training on the Spitfire. Sandy Mutch joined the RRAF and Dickie Dickenson returned to the RAF.

Appendix D

SRAF SPITFIRES

RAF No.	Test Pilot	In service RAF	RAF Units	Ferry Pilot	In Service SRAF	SRAF No.	Eventual Fate
PK 326	Henshaw[1]	Jul '45	33 & 137 MU ME, 73 Sqn		19.12.51	SR80	
330		5.7.45	33, 137, 6 MU	Schuman	25.3.51		
344	Ayerst[2]	3.8.45	33 & 6 MU	Love	4.12.51		Crashed near Paris 7.12.51
350	Ayerst[2]	3.8.45	33 MU, 73 Sqn 'G', 6 MU	Bradshaw	25.3.51	SR64	Crashed 26.3.82
355		3.8.45	39 & 6 MU	Malloch	25.3.51	SR65	Extant Gweru
370	Henshaw[1]	10.8.45	39 MU		19.12.51		
401		5.8.45	33 MU	Cunnison	19.12.51	SR86	
408		3.9.45	33 MU, A&AEE at B Dn, 6 MU	Barber	25.3.51		
432		25.9.45	33 MU		19.12.51		
482		31.8.45	33 MU	Richards	7.12.51		Crashed Entebbe 16.12.51
494		6.9.45	39 MU		19.12.51		
506		12.9.45	39 MU, 504 Sqn RAD-W, 6 MU	Paxton	25.3.51		
514		17.9.45	33 & 6 MU	Bellingan	25.3.51	SR59	
548		27.9.45	33, 137 MU ME		19.12.51		
572		10.10.45	33 MU, 73 Sqn		19.12.51		
575		10.10.45	33 & 6 MU	Blair	25.3.51	SR62	Syrian AF
576	Ayerst[2]	18.10.45	33, 137 MU ME & 6 MU	Penton	25.3.51		
594		15.10.45	39 MU, 73 Sqn 'J'		19.12.51		
625	Ayerst[2]	19.12.45	33 & 6 MU	Deall	25.3.51		
649	Ayerst[2]	20.12.45	33 MU	Campbell	19.12.51	SR84	Crashed 4.12.53
663		1.1.46	33 MU, 600 Sqn RAG-J, 6 MU	Hone	25.3.51		
672		27.12.45	29 & 6 MU	Jacklin	25.3.51	SR68	Syrian AF

Note 1: In the absence of a name, the test pilot was most likely Ellis or Rosser.
Note 2: Still flying in July 1954: SR60, 62, 64, 65, 68, 81, 82, 85, 87.
Note 3: SR88 written off 14 June 1954 following reduction gear failure.
Note 4: Seven airframes to Syria AF: SR60, 62, 68, 81, 82, 85, 87.
Note 5: Nine airframes scrapped during service period March 1951–July 1954: SR58, 59, 61, 63, 66, 67, 80, 83, 86.

Appendix E

ATA AND AFFRETAIR ENGINEERS, 1977–1980

Jim Townsend—Engineering Manager. He also oversaw a company called Societe Robart based in Paris sourcing spares for ATA, the RhAF and the Spitfire project.

Al Binding—Deputy/Acting Engineering Manager and Technical Adviser.

Bob Dodds—Quality Control Manager and later in 1980, Engineering Manager.

Dave Hann—Hangar foreman after Tommy Minks, Chief Structural Engineer and Spitfire Project Manager; later, in 1980, Chief Engineer.

Tommy Minks—ex-Hangar foreman, Facility and MT overseer, including the freight shed.

Inspectors:
Bill Rheeder (Chief Inspector), Fred Burke, Basil Connelly, Ernie De Govia (Chief Electrical Inspector), Tommy Fraser, Gus Goodwin, Dennis Hogben, Barry Owen, Lou Passow, Peter Wright.

Technical Records:
Rex Ovington, Doug Smith.
Tool Store:
Ted Vine.

Stores:
Andy Wawn.

Electrical & Instrument Section (incl. radio):
Phil Mason (Section Chief), Ian Buckle, John Davidson, Grant Domoney, 'Dup' Du Plessis, Jimmy Gibson, Mike Holmes, Mick Kemsley, Tim King, John Knight, Robert Lister, Bob Manser, Fynn Marcussen, Johnny Norman, Mark Summersgill.

Specialists:
Len George (NDT), George Graham (Stressed Skin), Dennis Hewitson (Machinist and toolmaker), Terry Hopkins (Skin), George Merritt (Stresses skin and NDT), John Nicholson (Machinist), Des Pearce, (Sheet metal worker & welder), Steve Whitehorn (speciality unknown), Harry Wolhuter (General Machinist), Name Unkown (Draughtsman).

Engine and Airframe Fitters:
Barry Badenhorst, Louis Bezuidenhout, Trevor Blofield, Mike Brown, Rob Brown, John Clegg (Tyre Bay and Hydraulics), Bill Dixon, John Dodd, Glen Evans, Marty Halbert, Ticky Hawthorn, Mike Hill, Andy McNeil, Frank Morgan, Dave Murtag, Reg Neville, Victor Pereira, Rory Perhat, John Pinta, John Potts, Paul Ranby, Colin Read, Chris Richards, John Scutt, Ken Smith, Bert ver Kerk, Bob White.

Fuel Bowser & ground start units:
Parky Morgan.

Schipol Engineers:
Nick Bylemeer and two others, names unknown.

Apprentices:
Piet Bezuidenhout, Loius Brega, Russel Clements, Ben Dark, Carlos Da Silva, Daryl Deloe, Jack Dent, Dave Ditcham, Ian Fraser, Mark Furnell, Charlie Hall, Bob Lane, Eric Langeveldt,

Morgan Maitland-Smith, Carlos Martins, Pete Massimiani, Rob Myers, Dave Potgieter, George Prentice, Doug Robinson, Tony Smith, Ian Stewart, Andy Wood, Dave Wood, Andy Winter.

The Spitfire Team:
(As engraved on the A1 Piston from the original RR Griffon Engine by Carlos Martins)
Bob Dodds, Dave Hann, Piet Bezuidenhout, Trevor Blofield, Bob Brown, Ben Dark, John Dodds, Jim Gibson, George Graham, Mike Holmes, Dave Lamb, Morgan Maitland-Smith, Ross Malloch, Carlos Martins, Pete Massimiani, Rob Myers, Victor Pereira, Andy Wood, Dave Wood.

Air Force Liaison for Spitfire Project:
At Salisbury Airport: WO1 Jimmy Gordon-Brander
At Air Force HQ: Flt Lt Bertie May (Armaments) and Another (name unknown).

Appendix F

NOTABLE FLIGHTS OF SPITFIRE PK350
1945–1982

Wg Cdr Peter Ayerst DFC (Ret) — Production Test Flight on 25 July 1945

Capt Jack Malloch — Only Flight in PK350 as a Service Aircraft on 22 February 1951

Lt Dickie Bradshaw — Final Leg of Delivery Ferry on 22 March 1951 (Probably the pilot with the most hours on PK350)

Lt Chris Dams — Final Flight as a RRAF Service Aircraft on 18 December 1954

Capt Jack Malloch — First Flight as a Restored Aircraft on 29 March 1980 (Logbook entry by Nikki Pearce *née* Elphinstone)

Gp Capt Steve Kesby — Last Recorded Flight on 25 February 1982 before PK350's final demise on 26 March 1982.

Appendix G
FLYING HOURS FOR SPITFIRE MK22 PK350/ SR64 AS A RESTORED AIRCRAFT

Date	Pilot	Time	Total	Logbook Detail	Remarks
29.3.80	Malloch	0:35	0:35	Air Test	
12.4.80	Malloch	0:55	1:30	Rudder Trim	
15.4.80	Malloch	0:30	2:00	Rudder Trim	Buzzes Russian Delegation
18.4.80	Malloch	0:40	2:40	Rudder Trim	Flypast – Prince Charles/Lord Soames
23.4.80	Malloch	0:50	3:30	Rudder Trim	
24.4.80	Malloch	0:15	3:45	Mixture & Pitch	
24.4.80	Malloch	0:25	4:10	Mixture & Pitch	
3.5.80	Malloch	0:40	4:50	No detail	Flypast – Maher
14.5.80	Malloch	0:15	5:05	No detail	
22.5.80	Malloch	1:15	6:20	Sby-Thornhill	Thornhill Visit
22.5.80	Malloch	1:10	7:30	Sby-Thornhill	Thornhill Visit
18.6.80	Malloch	0:25	7:55	No detail	
15.8.80	Malloch	0:20	8:15	No detail	
22.8.80	Malloch	1:03	9:18	No detail	Possible photo sortie with Bell 205
17.9.80	Malloch	0:55	10:13	No detail	Possible photo sortie with Bell 205
19.9.80	Malloch	0:35	10:48	No detail	Charles Prince Airport Visit
20.9.80	Malloch	0:15	11:03	No detail	Charles Prince Airport Visit
25.9.80	Malloch	0:15	11:18	No detail	
30.9.80	Knobel	0:30	11:48	Aero's/Flypast	
3.10.80	Knobel	0:30	12:18	Local Flying	
4.10.80	Malloch	1:05	13:23	No detail	Possible photo sortie with Bell 205
5.10.80	Knobel	0:15	13:38	Aero's Display	Salisbury Sports Club
12.10.80	Malloch	0:30	14:08	No detail	
17.10.80	Malloch	0:15	14:23	No detail	

Date	Pilot	Time	Total	Logbook Detail	Remarks
18.10.80	Malloch	0:05	14:28	No detail	
22.10.80	Malloch	0:15	14:43	No detail	
7.11.80	Malloch	0:40	15:23	No detail	
10.11.80	Knobel	0:40	16:03	Aerobatics	
22.1.81#	Malloch	0:45	16:48	Photo/Bell 205	Bell 205 flown by Shirley & Breedt
Note 1#	Malloch	05:00	21:48	No detail	30 mins per month Dec 1980 to Sep 1981
23.10.81#	Malloch	0:45	22:33	Photo/Dakota	Dakota flown by Ward & Vernon
25.10.81#	Malloch	0:20	22:53	Display	Air Force '81 Air Show
23.11.81	Kesby	1:05	23:58	General Flying	
10.12.81	Kesby	1:30	25:28	Photo/Dakota	Dakota flown by Ward & Buxton
3.1.82	Kesby	1:20	26:48	General Flying	
15.01.82	Kesby	1:40	28:28	Photo	Domboshawa & Sykes
20.1.82	Kesby	1:15	29:43	General Flying	Bell 205 flown by Cockroft
29.1.82	Kesby	1:05	30:48	General Flying	
3.2.82	Knobel	1:30	32:18	Photo/Dakota	Dakota flown by Ward & Ingledew
6.2.82	Kesby	1:10	33:28	General Flying	
12.2.82	Kesby	1:10	34:38	Display	New Sarum
25.2.82	Kesby	1:20	35:58	General Flying	
25.2.82#	Malloch	1:00	36:58	Photo/Vampire	Vampire flown by Meikle & Sykes
26.2.82#	Malloch	1:00	37:58	Photo/Vampire	Vampire flown by Meikle & Sykes
26.3.82#	Malloch	0:45	38:43	Photo/Vampire	Vampire flown by Weir & Sykes

Note 1: There are no logbook records for Jack Malloch for the period 8 November 1980 to March 1982.

Hours are based on other logbook sources or a reasonable estimate of flight time.

INDEX

Nick Meikle was born and brought up in Rhodesia (Zimbabwe) where he has spent most of his life. Prior to pursuing his passion of flying, he attained a university degree, majoring in history. His very satisfying career in aviation has spanned sixteen years in the air forces of Rhodesia, Zimbabwe and South Africa, as well a similar amount in the airline industry flying heavy jet freighters around the world. Today, he enjoys the more sedate pace of guiding young airline pilots into the basics of their profession at a flight training school in Adelaide, Australia. A strong interest in the history of military aviation, particularly the Second World War and Vietnam, has been the platform for this book. Like so many youngsters of his generation who entered the world of aviation, Nick's dreams of flying were nurtured by the stirring stories of the Second World War RAF fighter pilots, especially those Spitfire pilots who helped defeat the Luftwaffe in the Battle of Britain. Short of owning or flying a Spitfire, the next best thing was to write a story about one, bringing together Nick's passions for flying and history.